DATA COMMUNICATIONS DESK BOOK:
A Systems Analysis Approach

DATA COMMUNICATIONS DESK BOOK:
A Systems Analysis Approach

William L. Harper
and
Robert C. Pollard

PRENTICE-HALL, INC.
ENGLEWOOD CLIFFS, NEW JERSEY

Prentice-Hall International, Inc., *London*
Prentice-Hall of Australia, Pty. Ltd., *Sydney*
Prentice-Hall of Canada, Ltd., *Toronto*
Prentice-Hall of India Private Ltd., *New Delhi*
Prentice-Hall of Japan, Inc., *Tokyo*
Prentice-Hall of Southeast Asia Pte. Ltd., *Singapore*
Whitehall Books, Ltd., *Wellington, New Zealand*

Library of Congress Cataloging in Publication Data

Harper, William L.
  Data communications desk book.

  Includes index.
  1. Data transmission systems.   I. Pollard, Robert C.
    II. Title.
TK5105.H37   001.64′404   81-17794
ISBN 0-13-196378-3   AACR2

Printed in the United States of America

About the Authors

William L. Harper is a Computer Systems Specialist for the Air Force. With more than two decades of experience in data communications and computer systems, he is also founder and executive consultant for Data Monitor Systems, a firm specializing in technical services.

His assignments over the years include marketing for Honeywell's Federal Systems Office, Marketing and Field Support Manager for Futuronics Corporation, Systems Analyst for a petroleum firm, and Data Communications Specialist for the Air Force.

Mr. Harper is the author of *Data Processing Documentation: Standards, Procedures and Applications, Second Edition,* published by Prentice-Hall, Inc. He is a frequent contributor of articles for leading trade journals in his field and holds a Bachelor of Science Degree from the University of Maryland.

Robert C. Pollard has more than 25 years experience in the field of electronics, communications, data switching systems and data processing computer systems. He has held system engineering and design positions with the Western Union Corporation, the Control Data Corporation, and as a private consultant in data communication systems.

A system design coordinator for several major data communication systems in the banking industry and federal government, the author has prepared the system functional specifications, design specifications and other related documents for these systems. He also coordinated the system cutover and followup maintenance procedures. Other activities over the years include the presentation of data communication seminars in the United States, Canada, Australia and New Zealand.

How to Get the Most
From This Desk Book

Data Communications Desk Book is a complete program of proven step-by-step practices and procedures you can use to lower cost and improve the efficiency of your system. Many of these methods, ideas, checklists and working aids are being used to improve profit margins for commercial and government systems. Whether your system is small, medium, or large, the tools and techniques in this book can be adopted or modified to fit virtually all business systems.

• For example, suppose your existing system has started experiencing problems. The users of the system are disgruntled and complain about the service. It is clear that the system is not returning profits to the organization as it once did—operation efficiency has diminished. Turn to Chapters One and Two. They tell you how to perform analysis functions and isolate the problem by charting the existing system; how to organize a competent team to analyze the existing system. They tell how problem modeling and analysis are invaluable in formulating sound solutions. Chapters One and Two offer proven methods and work procedures for designing a new system (on paper) so a mental and visual understanding of the data flow and interrelationship of the work functions may be achieved prior to developing the technical specifications. This approach is essential for reliable system cost projection and to avoid cost overruns.

• Once you have your analysis and design study completed and approved for development, the next step is to write the system solicitation—Request for Proposal (RFP)—document for competitive procurement for the required hardware and software. Addendum A at the back of the book is a tutorial guide for preparation of the solicitation RFP document. The Addendum defines the various methods for competitive procurement and shows why the RFP is the best method for vendor selection. The reader is told how to analyze vendor responses for hidden costs and inadequate technical support. For vendors selling ADP equipment, products or services to the government, the Addendum explains how to be more competitive and how to win more contracts and avoid contract cancellation. Checklists are included for the preparation of the vendor response, and how to evaluate the vendor's response.

• In many cases, the vendor tells the user the types, features, and characteristics of equipment (micro/minicomputer, microprocessors, mainframe processors, and peripherals) that the user needs. This is so because, in many cases, the user is not able to determine his needs. This is a costly process. Often, as case histories reveal, the user is oversold with a high-powered system with redundant and unreliable equipment. Chapter Three tells you how to avoid this costly "overkill."

Are you trying to decide the most economical and efficient (they are not the same) computer configuration? Is a front-end/host configuration best? Or is distributed processing best? Chapter Three has your answer. This chapter gives you the tools and step-by-step guidance to evaluate the capability of the CPU functions and match them against your application and intelligently determine your system equipment needs.

• Data communication experienced phenomenal growth in the last half of the 70s, continuing its accelerated growth in the 80s. Data communication technology has made it possible to expand data processing into new areas of data automation. One of these areas is distributed processing—the decentralization of large central processing sites and data bases. Distributed processing is increasingly replacing centralized systems. Distributed processing is not a simple extension of data processing. The difficult part of distributed processing is not the "processing," but "distribution" of data. Distribution means planning and developing data communications distributive processing networks that will support a geographically dispersed family of terminals and computer systems. Chapter Four tells you how you can do this—how to avoid a myriad of problems and pitfalls of going "distributed." Are you undecided about distributed processing? What is the most efficient network structure? Should part of your network use satellite links? Is Value Added Network (VAN) or time sharing more cost effective? Should you use packet switching for data format and transmission? Chapter Four will enlighten you on these questions, warn you of the pitfalls.

• Chapter Five is a simplified guide for throughput analysis. Key areas of system design are presented to aid you in designing a system that will give the required throughput for your applications. You will grasp the essentials of designing for efficient queuing theory, data protection techniques, and data compression methods that will enhance data integrity and provide the desired system throughput. You learn firsthand why certain transmission modes and data base structures are the major drawbacks to an interactive inquiry-response system. The throughput analysis and considerations of Chapter Five will serve as a ready reference when throughput problems arise—costly problems that have to be solved fast.

• A costly and crippling aspect of any business enterprise is the temporary loss of its information-handling capability. Chapter Six provides analysis for system reliability and for immediate restoration without loss of data (or money) when failure occurs. The reader is led through the analysis and design considerations for a fail-safe system by examining the hardware and software requirements and network components required for 100 percent data protection. It also discusses techniques of redundancy configuration that will insure system equipment reliability. You will be able to weigh your own system's reliability needs against the techniques and system configurations presented in this chapter.

• Chapters Seven and Eight are crystal clear guides to line disciplines, code sets, data formats and procedures for error detection and correction schemes. You will study emulation of discipline copying and why this is necessary for transmission efficiency. You will be able to understand the need for line disciplines (protocols) and the problems encountered. This will equip you to design or specify protocols that will provide optimum line efficiency. You will master code sets, methods for error detection and correction. You will be made aware of the fine points of data protection, security, and data validity analysis for data and error management.

• Do you need help in choosing the terminal configuration? Study Chapter Nine for dollar-saving ideas in the selection of terminals. This chapter is a ready reference for terminal evaluation. It offers schemes and checklists to guide you in terminal selection—from noncontrolled to intelligent micro-processor/computer programmable terminals, including remote configuration. Methods discussed in Chapter Nine can save you thousands of dollars in terminal selection when weighed against the plethora of terminals on the market.

• For money-saving ideas and a step-by-step guide to network and network interface, study Chapters Ten and Eleven. You will learn about components, transmission mode and facilities that offer greater digital capacity. You will learn the pros and cons of multiplexer/concentrators and how they may be configured with transmission disciplines to reduce line costs and increase data transmission capacity. To complete your understanding of network configuration, technical control, test equipment, type of facility, and network line conditioning are analyzed. Cost-saving, time-saving checklists are included for the selection of MODEMs and multiplexers.

• Chapter Twelve presents answers in another area where saving can be realized and headaches and problems minimized. You are given step-by-step procedures for training, site planning, installation and converting to new equipment, testing and system acceptance that will preclude degradation of customer service. You are told why software integration testing prior to actual operation testing and why live testing over simulation will save time, money and headaches after system cutover. It explains why the failure to do so is one of the major weaknesses and cost factors in the initial stages of operation.

• The lack of standards for quality documentation is another major profit-draining area. Chapter Thirteen gives you the types of documentation that are needed in the analysis, design and development, and follow-on maintenance phases of the system. It shows you what is needed, where it is needed, and in what format, for different user groups. You are told how the systematic creation of documentation can eliminate manpower spaces, utilize programmers more productively, improve training, reduce program maintenance, and insure that the loss of a programmer has little, if any, impact on the overall system. *This chapter alone is worth the price of the book.* The procedures in Chapter Thirteen have been implemented in commercial and government sectors at significant savings.

• Project management is the process of making plans, setting goals, analyzing results and making decisions. Project control is the cohesive element that determines the success or failure of an ADP project. Reports and the flow of information for decision making are what interface management to all facets of the project. Chapter Fourteen offers suggestions, poses questions, and suggests an information flow process to ensure effective project control.

Put these tested and proven methods, tools and techniques into practice now. See how they provide answers to your firing line duties—answers that will save time, money, slippage, duplication of effort and backtracking. Smooth and cost-efficient implementation and administration of data communication systems hold the golden key to fast-track profits.

William L. Harper

Robert C. Pollard

Acknowledgments

The authors wish to express gratitude and appreciation to several individuals for typing, editing, and proofreading the drafts of this book during the four years of development: Kay Mester, Faye Eades, Donella Dye, and Mayumi Hirata, all associates and friends of author Harper; and Diane Pollard, wife of author Pollard. We will always be indebted to these talented and professional individuals.

Contents

Chapter Four

Distributed Processing Network Structure – 73

Chapter Five

Systems Throughput and Data Flow Analysis – 93

Chapter Six

System Failure and Recovery Analysis – 109

Chapter Seven

Line and Communication Terminal Engineering For a Data Communications System – 137

Chapter Eight

Data Transmission Codes and Error Handling Techniques – 167

Implementation • **185** Applications and Functional Data Format Considerations • **186** Data Protection • **189** Data Validity Checks • **190** Data Security and Privacy • **191**

Chapter Nine

Communications Terminal Requirements Analysis – 195

Terminal Types • **196** Programmability and Independent Processing • **198** Clustering • **199** Microprocessor or Minicomputer Terminal • **199** Portable Terminal • **200** Terminal Operational Considerations • **200** Visual Display Terminal Selection Consideration • **204** Terminal Human Factors • **205** Software Considerations • **206** Terminal Communications Interface Requirements • **207** Maintenance • **208** Diagnostics • **208** Typical Intelligent (Programmable) Terminal Configuration • **209**

Chapter Ten

Network, Modem and Multiplexer Components – 213

MODEMS (Modulator/Demodulator) • **214** Telephone Line Interface • **220** Terminal Interface • **222** Automatic Calling Units (ACU) • **222** MODEM Diagnostic • **226** Selecting a MODEM • **226** Multiplexer Considerations • **229** Multiplexer Diagnostics • **232** Selecting a Multiplexer • **232** Concentrators Performing Multiplexer Functions • **234**

Chapter Eleven

Network Technical Control, Line Consideration and Conditioning – 235

Siplified Technical Control • **236** Complex Technical Control • **236** Analysis and Selection of Technical Control Facilities • **238** Network Management • **239** Test and Monitoring Equipment • **241** Facility (Line) Considerations • **241** Line Routing • **243** Line Conditioning • **245** Conditioner or Equalizer Functions • **245**

Chapter Twelve

Site Planning, Equipment Installation
And System Acceptance – 249

User/Vendor Responsibility • **250** Site Planning • **252** System Layout • **254** Power Distribution • **254** Environmental Requirements • **258** Equipment Installation Planning • **258** System Test and Implementation • **259** System Cutover and Acceptance • **262** Post-Cutover System Maintenance • **263**

CHAPTER ONE

Data Communications Analysis

Data Communications, as it applies in this book, is a means of electrically transmitting information for human or machine (computer) consumption. The information (or data) is (are) made up of electrical pulses and may be representations of alpha or numeric characters, or symbols, or a combination thereof to provide meaning to human or machine. The information for human consumption is usually in a narrative printed format or displayed on a video screen. For machine, it is usually electrical signals and symbols to control or influence (alter) an ongoing machine processing sequence. The information is handled/processed by data processing and communications equipment. Information is electromechanically or electronically processed in a manner suitable for transmission over a communications line or circuit (channel).

The first step in the design of a data communications system or network is the review and study of the old system or functional area to be automated. This chapter gives step-by-step procedures of "how to do" a total analysis for a data communications system. It treats five major categories that are required for an in-depth study: (1) the experience level and make-up of the study team, (2) planning and controlling the analysis efforts, (3) site visit and evaluation of the present system, (4) the study of existing documents and background material, and (5) planning the development of the new system. Chapter One contains comprehensive checklists to guide the analyst in the analysis study and in developing the new system. Machiavelli reminds us in *The Prince* of the difficulty in implementing a new system:

> "It must be remembered that there is nothing more difficult to plan, more doubtful of success, nor more dangerous to manage, than the creation of a new system. For the initiator has the enmity of all who would profit by the preservation of the old institutions and merely lukewarm defenders in those who would gain by the new ones."

APPROACH TO EFFECTIVE PROBLEM ANALYSIS

Problem analysis is a process where the old system is examined, identifying the interrelationship of documents and work functions, and specifying how the new system will be developed. Chapters One, Two, Twelve, and Thirteen give methodologies, techniques and invaluable checklists for accomplishing this task. The problem analysis phase may include a feasibility study.

A feasibility study is an investigative process to determine the practicality, effectiveness and economical benefits of a stated objective or proposed system. Its purpose is to determine if the objective or proposed system design is practical and can be accomplished. The feasibility study can also determine the soundness of applying a new application to an existing system.

A system analysis and design study is a thorough analysis of the procedures, techniques, and methods currently used in the functional system, and determination of the most effective methods to be used in designing a new system. Its purpose is to study older methods, isolate problems, and specify steps to take in accomplishing the new system.

The scope or general area to be covered in the system analysis and design study should include all work functions, related functional areas, and users who are participating in or being served (or will be served) by the system or functional area selected for study. At the outset, a team leader or lead analyst for each team (if more than one team), and a project manager, should be appointed to head the analysis study and design effort. It is important that this be done at the time the system is selected for study. This will permit the team leader(s) (herein after referred to as the lead analyst or analyst) and/or the project manager to be in on the discussions and conferences concerning the system under study. The function of the lead analyst or project manager, who may be one and the same and is treated as such in this book, is discussed under the topic "Selection and Assignment of the Analysis Team Members."

In becoming familiar with the system which may encompass a total system or a number of subsystems or functional areas that interface with the prime system, it is often easy to spot areas outside the immediate scope that could be improved if given the necessary resources—men, funds, and time. If the system is small in scope, both the prime and interface areas may be studied in depth at the same time. When the scope of the total system is complex and large, the system may be broken up in small teams with each team concentrating on an individual functional area or on equipment selection and installation problems. For example: analysis and survey for an on-line data communications network to replace a batch and mail system, linking plant facilities to the corporate offices, may be assigned to one team. Another small team, working in conjunction with the "analysis and survey" team, would study the equipment requirement; and yet another team may examine the site and installation problem. This will limit the study effort range to individual aspects of the total system. Periodically, the lead analyst or project manager should meet with team members and review the overall progress of the analysis efforts. This will insure progress and continuity of the study effort.

During the analysis process of the individual areas, it may be tempting to become involved in other related areas that interact with the area being studied. Don't do this! Stay within the scope of the planned objectives. If these other areas are entered, the validity of the study effort may be jeopardized. There are three overriding factors that dictate this: personnel, time, and money resources. Usually, knowledgeable personnel and money available for the study are scarce and the time factor is short.

Although these may be limiting factors, the overall system scope does give direction, depth, and purpose to the study effort. The known factors such as resources available (men, money and time), area to be studied, and objectives, are invaluable to the study team or the individual analyst. The planning and resource allocation is dependent on the size and complexity of the area to be studied.

SELECTION AND ASSIGNMENT OF THE ANALYSIS TEAM MEMBERS

The area to be studied and its complexity, and time allocation, should dictate the team size, management structure, and degree of experience required for each team member. For system revisions, new applications, or an individual area study, the team should be relatively small—two to five members. Small groups are more homogeneous. A large team tends to "join sides" and pair off into groups that support different ideas, methods, and concepts. (This hinders or interferes with the total team effort).

Personnel selected for the study team should be relieved of other duties until the study is complete. If a member tries to perform his normal duties along with the study effort, both will suffer. The member's primary job will take precedence.

The lead analyst in charge of each team must be given full responsibility and authority for the work assignment of each team member, and the methods and procedures for conducting the study. Although top management, sometimes at the vice presidential level, gives direction and guidelines, this level of management should remain in the background and interfere as little as possible with the study. When top management feels that interference or new direction is necessary, it should make itself heard at conferences and meetings with the lead analyst, never openly in the presence of other team members or user personnel, who are doing the actual work.

A common weakness of a system analysis and design effort is assigning inexperienced individuals with limited knowledge to a study team. If an individual is assigned as a team member because of his position, rank, or seniority, without regard to his experience or knowledge of a given system or functional area, that individual's input may hinder the efforts of other team members.

The lead analyst must have current experience and knowledge of the total system to be studied. He must have organizational ability and demonstrate effective written and oral communication ability. This is important because the lead analyst must "sell" various attributes of the proposed system to management and user personnel. (The selling will come through written reports and briefings which are discussed later).

Individual team members must have extensive and current experience in the various aspects of the system (and knowledge of the functional areas) to be studied. Team members who grew up with the old methods or system and understand them at the operator, supervisor/management and technical discipline levels; who have imaginative and comprehensive concepts of future requirements; and who understand the hardware and software characteristics and limitations, should be screened as team members.

The team members should have dissimilar background experience in the total system being studied. Collectively, a mixture of experience will make it easier for the team to listen, advise, define, organize and identify solutions when dealing with functional areas and user personnel.

MAKEUP AND MANAGEMENT STRUCTURE
AND THE ANALYSIS AND DESIGN TEAM

The size of the project or system will determine the makeup, experience level, management, and reporting procedures to be used in the control of the analysis, design and development of the system. The following checklist contains considerations for personnel selection.

PERSONNEL STRUCTURE CHECKLIST
FOR SYSTEM ANALYSIS AND DESIGN

- Manning Consideration
  - Project manager/lead analyst
  - Team leader or lead analyst
  - Subteam leader/analyst
  - User (functional area) personnel
  - System analysts
  - Programmers
- Span of Control
  - Top ADP management gives direction, controls resources
  - Project manager supervises overall system analysis, study, design effort
  - Team leader or lead analyst normally supervises up to five team members
  - If more than five, use subteam leader/analysts

- Attempt to limit team members to five or less
- Advantages of teams with five or less
  - team leaders close to the work of team members
  - nature of work often complex, creative, with activities usually problem-infested
  - small team is more homogeneous
- Project Manager Duties and Experience
  - Develop the analysis/project plan
  - Supervise the analysis and development efforts
  - Monitor progress of systems analysis and development
  - Ensure proper coordination among the various teams and top management
  - Identify development problems
  - Reallocate resources when required
  - Update the analysis and development plan when necessary
  - Evaluate performance of team members
  - Report to top management
  - Experience working on similar projects/systems
  - Knowledge of the functional area
  - Knowledge of and experience in system analysis and design
  - Current knowledge of the state of the art
  - Management and leadership ability (open-minded, creative, disciplined, flexible, tactful, etc.)
  - Experience in management-scheduling tasks, e.g., PERT, CPM, etc.
- Team Leader/Lead Analyst Duties and Responsibilities
  - Supervise the development of the tasks assigned to his team
  - Identify problems and recommend solutions
  - Coordinate with team members and other team leaders
  - Evaluate the performance of team members
  - Report to the project manager
  - Have experience on a similar project/system
  - Appropriate expertise for the assigned tasks
  - Management and leadership ability
- Functional (User) Personnel
  - Thorough knowledge of their functional area
  - Have some knowledge of ADP
  - Have some experience or knowledge of systems analysis and design
- Systems Analysts
  - Thorough knowledge of and current experience in the state of the art

- Have a background in systems analysis and design and experience in similar projects/systems
- Have some knowledge of the functional area and its current systems
- Programmers
  - Experience in language used for application programs
  - Some knowledge of functional area
  - Diversified experience in computer programming
- Hardware, maintenance of installation personnel
  - Experience with various hardware features and functions
  - Knowledge of cabling, power, equipment functions and troubleshooting techniques
  - Capability to review and analyze equipment features
- Operations
  - Experience in operations of various type systems
  - Capability to develop operational procedures
  - Prepare documentation suitable for continuous revisions

GATHERING AND ANALYZING BACKGROUND MATERIAL

The lead analyst should gather background material relating to the system revision, application or total system being considered for study. This material should include documents, letters, messages, and other general related correspondence concerning the management and use of the existing system, as well as correspondence on the proposed system. It is necessary to obtain sufficient background knowledge in order to discuss various aspects of the old system, as well as the proposed system, with management and users at conferences and meetings prior to the actual analysis and study effort.

The lead analyst is the front man in the study efforts. It will be necessary for him to attend management and user conferences in the initial formation of the general plans and objectives for the new system. The lead analyst should present management's viewpoints, supported by his professional and technical knowledge.

When the analyst attends conferences with sufficient knowledge to absorb, discuss, and at times lead the discussion, coupled with an insight into the proposed system's characteristics and limitations, he will win the confidence of those participating in the conferences. He will also be able to sway them to his viewpoint on certain aspects of the system.

The information obtained at the conferences, written or oral, may be meaningful knowledge for the analyst. He should take careful notes, either in writing or with a tape recorder. This will be important supplemental information to the documentation the analyst has already gathered.

PLANNING AND CONTROLLING THE ANALYSIS EFFORT

Failure to plan the systems analysis phase is one of the major weaknesses of an analysis effort. Without preparatory planning, the results and usefulness of the study may have little value and the study may have to be reaccomplished. The analyst may sometimes find himself repeating the same efforts and covering the same ground. The two primary considerations that have a direct bearing on the success of a study are planning and controlling the study efforts. Appendix A, The System Analyst Checklist, will be an invaluable tool for planning and performing the analysis study of the old system and the design of the new system. Planning requires laying out a course of actions (making an outline) to follow in conducting the study. It requires clarification of objectives, and identification of administrative channels and procedures to guide and control these actions. Some minor details may be overlooked, but if the analyst has done his homework well, these minor changes will not appreciably affect specified objectives or delay the analysis effort.

Controlling is guiding the efforts of the system analysis in accordance with established plans and objectives. The analyst should set his analysis objectives on the present operations philosophy; however, his analysis (and later the design efforts) should not be cemented to the present operations. The analysis and particularly the design efforts, should lend themselves to an open-end (modular) system so new concepts may be added that will allow transition to a more advanced stage of automation without a major disruption in the ongoing system.

Defining plans and objectives requires information from both internal and external sources. Internal sources are the functional area personnel who are operating and supervising the daily operations of the present system. External sources are the users and managers of the subsystem or functional areas that make up the total system. When the scope is defined, the team selected, the functional area(s) identified, and the plans and objectives established, the analysis of the present system and the design of the new system is undertaken.

STANDARDIZATION OF ANALYSIS TECHNIQUES

Standardization of analysis techniques is a critical portion of the system analysis effort. The effort and attention paid to analysis techniques will determine the reliability and viability of the new system. To insure the best possible system, standardization of techniques and approaches to be used in the analysis efforts must be established by the lead analyst in conjunction with appropriate top management and functional managers at the onset of the analysis study.

The lead analyst should study the plans and objectives established at the outset of the analysis study and write standard procedures for the team members to follow while conducting the study. The procedures should stress the following:

- The immediate goals and the methods of accomplishing the study;
- The type of information to be gathered and the likely source of information;
- Documentation methods to be used in recording the investigative work inputs;
- Directives, regulations and policies that govern the operations of the system or functional area under study;
- Uniform reporting, type of procedural flowchart, and data gathering procedures to use;
- Communication and administrative channel to follow;
- Standardization and definition of system terms in order to establish a clear understanding of their meaning;
- Rules to follow when deviating from set procedures and methods adopted for the analysis study.

Unless procedures are standardized and made known to each team member, additional time will be wasted in coordinating, gathering, analyzing and organizing the data in a meaningful way. Completely stated objectives and standardized procedures will permit the lead analyst to adjust his schedule and analysis techniques as necessary. It will also identify where the busy, complex, or bottleneck areas exist. This information is helpful in assigning the right individual to a particular work area.

EVALUATION STUDY OF THE PRESENT SYSTEM

The evaluation study requires that the present system be analyzed in order to find out what data is involved, what processing is done, and what results are obtained or required. This can only be done successfully by observing and analyzing the present system, functions, operations, physical layout, and studying work habits. Chapter Two is devoted to procedures and techniques on how this can be done.

There are two basic approaches to system analysis and design. One approach is that a clear understanding of the present system is required to find out which procedures and methods should be retained or changed. The other approach argues that a study of the existing system is not needed. Proponents of this argument believe that the new system can be designed from statement requirements and general objectives set down by management. It is also argued that exposure of team members to the old system, with its shortcomings, is bad because their thinking may be influenced by the existing methods and procedures.

It is difficult to envision how an improvement in the existing system can be effected, within the period usually set for the completion of a system analysis and design study, without a clear understanding of the existing system. The new system must encompass the old system operation, fulfill additional requirements and perform more efficiently. Therefore, the understanding of the present system is essential for designing the new system. An understanding of the present system is also required to measure input processing, elapse time or throughput, sequence of operations, data volume, output distribution and operating cost.

To argue that nothing can be achieved from studying an old system is to argue that history holds no answers for the future, or that knowledge of the past cannot contribute to a better system. The more current the information is regarding the past, the more useful it is as a tool for guiding the design efforts of the new system.

SITE VISIT

As a preliminary step in the analysis evaluation study phase, a visit to the system and related functional area(s) should be made prior to actual investigative or analysis work. This visit serves three vital purposes: (1) it gives the team members a chance to meet personnel involved in the work, (2) it gives the team members an opportunity to observe the current working environment, and (3) documentation on the existing system can be gathered and studied prior to the actual analysis work.

Upon the initial visit to the area to be studied, the lead analyst should introduce himself and the team members to the management and supervisory personnel and brief them as to the purpose of the study. The first day at the site should be spent getting to know the operating personnel and getting a feel for the working environment. The layout of the functional area(s) should be sketched showing the placement of equipment, furniture, and the flow of data within the functional area (See Figure 1-1.) The layout will show the heavy traffic areas and the congestion of the work functions. This is helpful in grasping a mental picture of the functional area and the processing involved.

In addition to permitting the team to become familiar with the working environment and its people, the preliminary site visit serves another valid purpose. It gives the team members an opportunity to meet likely prospects for later discussions when the actual interviewing, data gathering and analysis begins.

Interviewing Functional Area Personnel

Interviewing supervisors, operators, and clerks who are involved in the day-to-day operations can provide team members with important information that is not contained in documents such as forms, operating procedures, and manuals. The approach and method of conducting the interview (discussion period) will determine the initial cooperation of functional area personnel. The attitude of individual team members is a big factor. If the team member is pompous, the responses for the most part, will be the "yes" and "no" types.

In the discussion process, team members should start with personnel involved in the lowest levels of operation and work their way up through the highest levels of supervision within the system under study. The analyst is initially concerned with the operating details of the work positions of the functional area or system. The operators and clerks are more apt to know these details. As the analyst works his way up, he will have a clear understanding of everyone's viewpoints, processing steps, and what documents are involved.

The purpose of the discussion is to determine the "how, why, when, where and who" elements of a particular work function. During the discussions, the analyst

FIGURE 1-1
Clerical/Semiautomatic Communications and Message
Distribution Center
(Beehive of Activity)

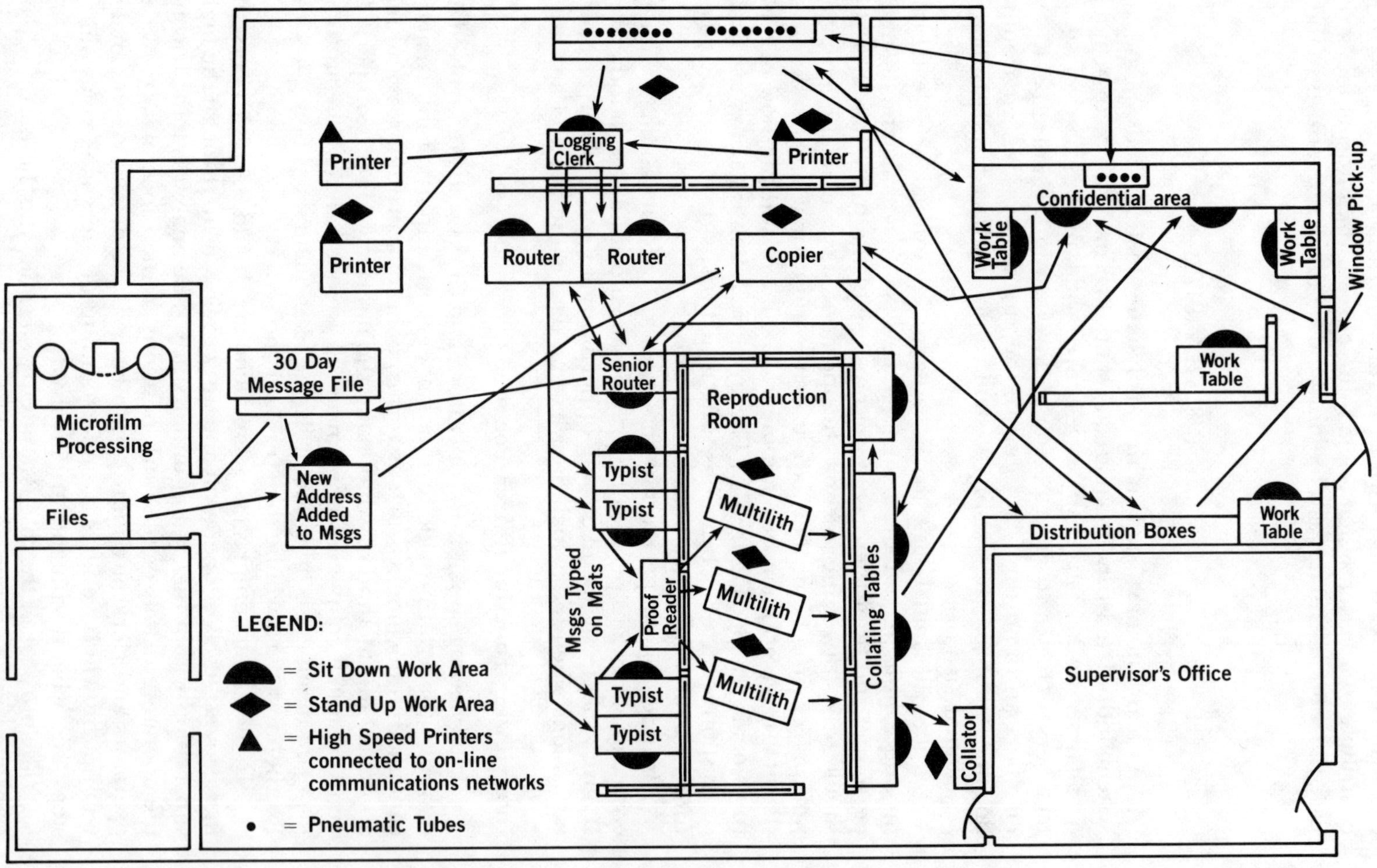

LEGEND:

● = Sit Down Work Area

◆ = Stand Up Work Area

▲ = High Speed Printers connected to on-line communications networks

• = Pneumatic Tubes

must also determine the initiation and flow of each form, report, log, worksheet, and other documents used in a particular work function.

Much can be learned from the individuals at the detail working level. If these individuals are skipped over to talk to the supervisors and managers "behind the desk," much detail may be overlooked. Talk to the person who is doing the work first—then talk to management. The analyst will find that he is able to discuss the present system more knowledgeably with management.

The analyst should not give the impression that he knows a lot. He should be a good listener. He should ask leading and intelligent questions that encourage the other person to talk. He should listen well and take careful notes. Anything that does not sound or appear plausible should be analyzed and questioned either then or later.

Practice simply psychology. The analyst should convey an impression that he has less knowledge in the work area under review than the person being interviewed—and no doubt he does. The analyst should not criticize or engage in an argument with the other person. During the discussion, a friendly atmosphere must prevail. It is up to the analyst to demonstrate the attitude and intelligence that is conducive to a friendly dialogue. It is often necessary to talk to individuals other than those assigned to the work area. Users of a system who receive output or give input to the work area should be interviewed. These users often have valuable information on how to improve the old system. After the discussion, the analyst should rework his notes, and write down his mental notes while they are fresh in his mind.

Reviewing Functional Area Documentation

This is a vital ingredient to the analysis effort. It is crucial to the speed and progress of the study. The amount of attention devoted to this facet of the analysis determines, to a great extent, the success of the total team's effort. An important source of information is the functional area documentation such as local operating procedures, directives, manuals, regulations, briefings, organization charts and write-ups that relate to the functional area. Copies of these documents should be obtained (if possible) and studied by each team member. These documents will give the analyst much insight into the present system that may not be brought out in the interviewing process.

It is suggested that these documents be gathered during the first day of familiarization (site visit) for later study. If these documents are studied before interviewing the functional area and user personnel, the analyst may be tempted to bring up something covered in one of the documents. This may put the person being interviewed on the spot and he may tend to defend a current procedure or method of operation.

The analyst should bear in mind that what is being done may not be according to the "printed" procedures and rules. The printed procedures and rules may be outdated or not followed. After observing the operation and after having talked with the functional area personnel, the analyst will be in a better position to understand the documentation that he has gathered. He will also be more knowledgeable of the present system and work functions, and be able to discuss certain processing steps in depth during later discussions with management and functional area personnel.

FORMS, RECORDS, LOGS AND WORKSHEETS

Most manual, semiautomatic or automatic systems use a variety of forms, records, logs, and worksheets that are unique to that system. During the course of interviewing and visiting the functional areas, team members should collect copies of the documents being used. These documents may be classified as *Source Data Documents, Internal Data Documents,* or *External Data Documents.* The functions of these documents are as follows:

Source Data Documents. This document contains data to be processed; it only feeds data to the system, it does not receive data from the system. It may be initiated by users outside the functional area or by the functional area personnel. This document provides raw data from its source of origination. The data may or may not be partially (clerically) processed prior to entry into the system. An example of a Source Data Document may be payroll data, a file update request, or data for generating an end-of-the-month report.

Internal Data Document. This document is used to feed data to, and receive data from the system. Usually, this document is used for internal day-to-day operations and administrative controls of the system. It contains statistical and control information for historical and accountable purposes. This document is initiated within the functional work area(s) and normally remains in the area. An example of an Internal Data Document is an equipment malfunction log, file update, payroll data, inventory changes, etc.

External Data Document. This document contains information that is generated manually, or automatically by the system. It is usually a statistical or administrative report and is passed on to the user or management for planning and control purposes. This report is initiated by and within the operational work center (automated or manual). The nature of the report determines the recipient. It may remain in or be sent out of the operational work center. In creating the External Data Document, data may be obtained from the Source Data Document and the Internal Data Document.

Regulations, manuals, operating directives, forms, logs, and worksheets are vital to understanding current procedures and work functions. The analyst must get to know these procedures in order to determine new ones. He can only do this by studying the documents and by observing (at close range) the actual work procedures. The analyst can speed up the process and create a work function in his mind by actually doing the work himself. This may not always be possible, but when it is, it would be to the analyst's advantage to do so. If the analyst proposes new procedures while being unaware of the old procedures, he may incorporate procedures into the new system that are inferior to the old ones. The foremost prerequisite of the new system is that it perform with greater capability and more efficiency than the old system.

PLANNING THE SYSTEM DEVELOPMENT CYCLE

Design and development of the new system takes place after the system analysis study has been performed and decisions have been made concerning the objectives, nature, size, and scope of the project. An initial system development plan must be compiled. The plan will be continually changed and refined during systems development. The following outline and Appendix A will aid the project manager and lead analyst in developing the new system.

Systems Development Outline

- General Steps for Plan Development
  - Break down system concept into modules.
  - Identify and define the activities required to develop the modules.
  - Define dependencies between activities.
  - Estimate the time required for each activity.
  - Estimate the resources required (manpower, money, equipment).
  - Document the planning information.
  - Identify milestones for control purposes.
  - Perform project staffing based on the estimates.
- Contingency Planning
  - Identify critical events.
  - Estimate the chance for deviations from the plan and determine the effects.
  - Develop contingency plans to minimize the impact of
    - A critical event.
    - Deviation.
  - Make assumptions that certain things that are planned will not occur as scheduled. NOTE: In developing the system, the planner should identify those assumptions which have a reasonable possibility of not occurring.
  - Define alternative actions to handle
    - A critical event.
    - Deviations.
    - Milestone slippage.
    - Lack of adequate resources.
- Controlling Changes in the Development Plan
  - Changes that are requested must be formally documented and approved by the approving authority.
  - Requested change(s) should be evaluated by the project manager or lead analyst.

- Approved changes will be incorporated into the original development plan.
- System Development Planning Considerations/Decisions Include:
  - In-house or contractor developed,
  - Centralized or decentralized system,
  - Equipment requirements,
  - Design strategy (top-down or bottom-up),
  - Use of specialized software,
  - Method of system turnover,
    - Paralleled (duplicated),
    - Phase-in (some overlapping),
    - Pilot (test one system before installing several).
- Likely Problem Areas in System Development Are:
  - Indecisiveness and bad decisions by top management,
  - Personnel turnover,
  - Badly assigned or incompetent team members,
  - Unstructured environment,
  - Lack of expertise in key areas,
  - Contractor nonperformance.
- Top Management (User and ADP) Review and Approval of Plan
  - The functional manager (user) who has the requirement must review and approve the plan before work starts.
  - The functional design of the system, its success or failure, rests with the user who initiated the requirement.
  - The plan must be documented and signed by top management (user and ADP).
  - Areas of significant review by top management are:
    - Cost projections,
    - Personnel requirement,
    - Time projection for development,
    - Milestones for top management control,
    - Controlling parameters for the plan,
    - Reporting procedures and information requirements,
    - Adequacy of contingency plans.

APPENDIX A
SYSTEM ANALYST CHECKLIST

- What Is the Function or Mission of the Organization Requiring a Computer System?
- Why Is the System Required?

- What Is the Configuration of the Existing System?
  - Type of system hardware/software
  - Number and types of circuits (lines)
  - Number and types of terminals/computers
  - Flow of the data/messages by circuit/terminal/computer
  - Volume of data/messages per peak hour
  - Average size of record or message
  - Single and multiple route factor
  - Is input-output computer delay time (response time) critical
  - Allowable data/message backlog (queuing)
  - History record requirements
  - Retrieval capability
  - Others
- What Are the Problems with the Existing System?
- Must the New System Interface, Incorporate or Replace the Existing System?
- What Types of Service Must Be Supported by the New System?
  - Inquiry/response (computer front end)
  - Conversational/interactive (computer front end)
  - Remote batch entry (computer front end)
  - Time sharing (computer front end)
  - Data collection/record update (computer front end)
  - Message switching
  - Controlled/noncontrolled network
  - Others
- Preliminary Communications System Design Categories (If Any) for the New System
  - Communication terminal requirements
  - Communication facility requirements
  - Communication computer hardware/software requirements
  - Planned expansion requirements
  - Others
- System Problem (Design) Definition–New System
  - Lay out the entire network configuration
  - Determine mainframe and device requirements
  - Determine the flow of data/messages from point to point
  - Determine the average message/data stream size in characters for each circuit, terminal, device and computer application

- Determine the single and multiple address factor for each circuit, terminal and computer application.
- Determine the number of messages, records, or data stream transmissions per peak hour
- Determine forms requirements
- Input-output delay (response time) requirements
- Computer Mainframe Requirements
  - Computer mainframe backup requirements
  - Message, record, file format requirements
  - Message/data history (disk) and file protection (disk) requirements
  - Message/data retrieval requirements; how long should a history copy be retained for retrieval purposes?
  - Magnetic tape and/or disk requirements
  - Is the system requirement a stand-alone data/message communication/ system?
  - Does the system require a front-end?
  - Off-line processing requirements
  - Others
- Communication Terminal Requirements—New System
  - Define the number of terminals by operation and type
    - teletypewriter (TTY)
    - CRT (Display)
    - Card reader/punch
    - Batch terminal
    - Magnetic tape
    - Optical readers
    - Programmable
    - Graphics
    - Audio
    - Other considerations
  - Terminal Characteristics
    - Forms control
    - Paging control (Blocking)
    - Friction feed
    - Sprocket feed
    - Vertical tabulation
    - Horizontal tabulation
    - Single/multiple copy
    - Back spacing
    - Screen size (CRT)
    - Special controls (CRT)
    - Buffer size
    - Ease of operation

–Ease of training
–Others

- Define the Network/Terminal Operation Requirements
  –Controlled
  –Contention
  –Noncontrolled
  –SPX (simplex)
  –HDX (half duplex)
  –FDX (full duplex)
  –Single terminal/controller/station, single circuit
  –Multiple terminals/controller/station, single circuit
  –Multiple controllers, multiple stations on the controllers clusters, single circuit.
  –Asynchronous operation
  –Synchronous operation
  –Code Set(s)
   ANSCII
   Baudot
   BCD
   Binary
   EBCDIC
   Hollerith
   PTTC/EBCD
   Others
  –Data framing requirements
  –Parity checking requirements
   Character
   Block
   Cyclic
   Error correction
   Others
  –Baud rate, words per minute, bits per second, line per minute
  –Direct/buffered circuit interface (facility-terminal)
  –Block by block transmission requirements
  –Multiple messages within a single block transmission
  –Modem-Circuit connection requirements
  –Control code (handshaking) requirements
  –Others
- Transmission Facility (Circuit/Line) Requirements –New System
  - Define the number and type of facilities required, such as:
    –Dial in/dial out
    –Switched voice network
    –Teletypewriter exchange network (dialed)
    –Private circuits
    –Shared circuits
    –Repeater points

—Data processing computer interconnects
—Facility transmission speeds in bits per second (BPS)
- Mainframe (Hardware) Failure/Backup Considerations
  —Reliability
   MTBF (mean time between failure)
   MTTR (mean time to repair)
  —Specifications
  - Front-end
  - Message switching/data protection
  - Maintenance requirements
    —Preventive
    —Corrective
    —Hardware
    —Software
- System Environmental Requirements —New System
  - Power
  - Floor space
  - Floor loading
  - Floor cutouts
  - Air conditioning
  - Humidity
  - Others
- System Scheduling/Delivery/Cost—New System
  - Manufacturing
  - Testing
  - Site preparation
  - Shipping
  - Installation
  - Acceptance tests
  - Cutover
  - Support
  - Cost per item/function
  - Others
- Documentation/Specifications—New System
  - System description RFP or RFQ) for submittal to applicable vendors
  - Proposal—answer to the RFQ or RFP
  - Functional Specification—governs system design and implementation
  - Installation/site preparation specifications
  - System acceptance criteria

- Hardware maintenance specifications
- Operator manuals
- Software descriptive documents
- Miscellaneous–New System
  - System review meetings—schedule
  - Customer liaison during system design/implementation/acceptance testing/cutover
  - Training:
    - Maintenance
    - Operations
    - Programming
  - Establish coordination channels for all systems activities
  - Others

CHAPTER TWO

Avoiding Data Communications Pitfalls By Procedural Flowcharting Analysis of the Old System

Historically, in the design or enhancement of a DP batch system, much of the analysis was concerned with studying the handling and processing of input and output documents. It is hard to envision a DP system today that is not part of a data communications system or network. Word processing has become part of DP and DP facilities are enmeshed in data communications systems, interlinking a number of DP facilities. Whether an information processing system is known as a DP system or a data communications system, the study and analysis of the documents (forms, reports, etc.) that are used in the system should be a vital area of study in the analysis and design of a data communications system.

In this chapter, we present a methodology for examining and flowcharting the work functions and procedural steps involved in processing documents of the existing system or functional area. We also discuss how to analyze source documents and inputs that drive the old system or control individual work functions. Also presented is how to review output documents from individual work functions, which in turn drive or contribute to another work function. The analyst must comprehend these factors in order to design a new system that is cost-effective and more efficient than the old system.

SYSTEM ANALYSIS—AN INVESTIGATIVE PROCESS

The nature of analysis often dictates different approaches because different solutions to the same problem could be correct. Many consider analysis as an art rather than a science. It follows then that an analysis problem could have more than one suitable solution, with one solution more attractive than another, according to constraints, objectives, and operational philosophy.

Since systems analysis is an investigative process, analysis is not easily systematized. General procedures are suggested and discussed in this chapter and in Chapter One to guide the analyst in the investigative discovery-oriented analysis effort.

The analyst is quite often faced with the problem of trying to make sense out of verbal statements and poorly written narratives describing a problem. The analyst's job is to make sense out of this unstructured stuff and communicate a structured solution to the customer or user. This can be effectively and easily done with a well-devised methodology for the investigative analysis work. Answers to the following questions will give the analyst a clear understanding of the present system so that the weaknesses and shortcomings of the old system will be eliminated in the design of the new system.

- What are the data?
- How are the data recorded?
- What documents are used?
- How are the data or documents processed?
- Where does the data or documents come from?
- How are the data used?
- Where does the data go?
- What documents are generated by the system?
- What data are generated by the system?
- Do the documents cross-feed data to each other?
- How are the data transferred from one document to another?
- How frequently are the data processed?
- What is the volume of the data?
- What are the primary data (types) that drive the system?
- What are the primary documents that drive the system?
- What subsystems or functional areas feed data to the system?
- What subsystems or functional areas receive data or documents from the system?
- What amount of data/documents are received?
- What are the restraints of the system?
- What are the policies and guidelines that govern the system operations?

—Are there redundant data?

—Are there duplicated or similar documents being used for the same purpose?

—Can data or documents be eliminated?

—Can documents be merged?

—What are the heavy volume periods?

—Where are the time restraints and bottlenecks: input processing, internal processing, output processing?

Answering these questions and applying the techniques and procedures discussed in this chapter, while studying the existing system, will be invaluable to the analyst in the design of the new system.

ANALYZING AND FLOWCHARTING WORK FUNCTIONS AND DOCUMENTS

It is often difficult to tell when analysis stops and design begins. They are interwoven and overlapping. The analysis starts by examining documents and other documentation that has been gathered, including any notes or write-ups prepared by the team members, as discussed in Chapter One.

The lead analyst and the team members should collectively examine and discuss this documentation. The purpose of this examination serves three principle needs: (1) to expose the study team to the various documents associated with the existing system (or functional area); (2) to relate these documents to the appropriate processing steps of the system; and (3) to identify any subsystem or related work area documents that relate to the total processing requirements and to put them in a category for assessment.

Team members at this stage of the system analysis and design effort should have a clear understanding of the present system. In order to effectively analyze the various work functions, each document relating to a particular function must be analyzed and the processing steps flowcharted. Each form, log, worksheet, and other documents that are used as a Source, Internal, or External Document, must be analyzed in detail and compared against other documents to determine data item duplication, duplication of processing steps and to assess the data processing needs of the new system.

LEVELS OF PROCEDURAL FLOWCHARTING

There are three levels of functional and procedural flowcharting that are important to the analyst: Individual Document Flowcharts, Combination Documents Flowcharts, and the General System Flowcharts. Procedural flowcharting is an invaluable technique that will quickly aid in the understanding of the present system.

Individual Document Flowcharts: are used for documenting the sequential steps as obtained from the various work function document(s) or from interviews. The Individual Document Flowchart is used to trace and depict the flow of a single

FIGURE 2-1
Individual Document Flowchart

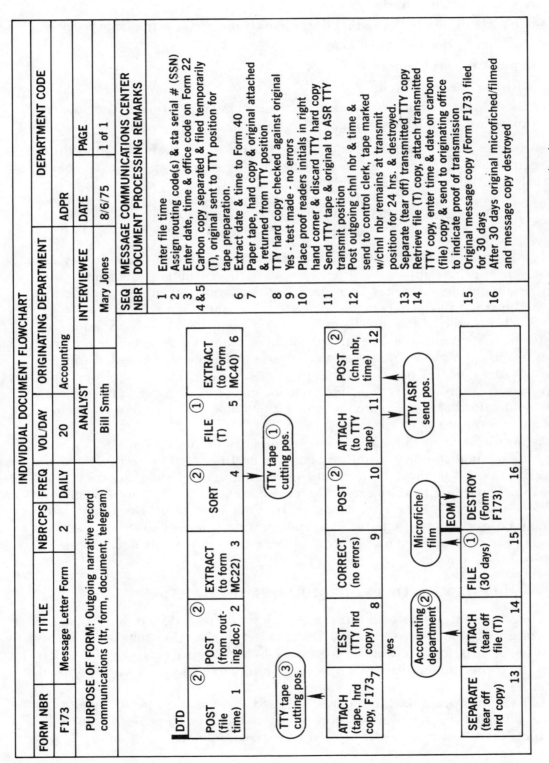

FIGURE 2-1: is a typical daily routine of repetitive outgoing message processing in most clerical message mail centers. During-the-day (DTD) messages are continually being processed until they are transmitted, then filed for a period of time. Later, the message is usually microfiched or filmed, and the message destroyed. In this example, the message is destroyed at the end-of-month (EOM) — 30 days.

document by work function through the system. These charts are used to create the Combination Documents Flowcharts.

Combination Documents Flowcharts: are used for identifying the various documents of the system or functional area and their interrelationship and the recording of information contained on the Individual Documents Flowcharts. A Combination Document Flowchart shows where a document comes from, the number of copies, and what is recorded on or extracted from each document. It also shows the document disposition and how the various documents intermingle with each other. These charts are used for study and analysis and for creating the General System Flowchart(s).

General System Flowcharts: are used to document graphically the processing steps and the interrelationship of the various documents and to identify the various work areas and the input and output media. They give a clear picture of the present status of the system or functional area under study and are used for determining new design concepts.

INDIVIDUAL DOCUMENT FLOWCHARTING

The Individual Document Flowchart traces each processing step and identifies the form (document), its title, originating office, interrelations to the other documents and its disposition over a period of time. The documents used in the system and other interrelated work areas are categorized by the processing steps of the work functions, and are flowcharted. See Figure 2-1.

Manual, semiautomated, and automatic systems use a large number of forms, worksheets, logs and other documents for data processing. The use of function and procedural flowcharts will be an indispensable tool in the analysis and design of a new system or in the upgrading efforts of an existing system. When the analysis process is complete and the design effort starts, functional and procedural flowcharts play a diminishing role in the actual design effort of new systems. Their main role is to gather data, identify inputs and outputs, and to acquaint team members with the processing functions, procedures, and documents that are used in the old system.

The procedural flowchart forces the analyst to see how a job is done and how it relates to other jobs. There are two important values of procedural flowcharting: (1) it clearly and graphically depicts the processing steps of the present system; and (2) it shows the weakness in the old system and indicates different processing steps and requirements for the new system.

RULES FOR CHARTING WORK FUNCTIONS AND DOCUMENTS

There are four basic symbols used in preparing Individual Documents Flowcharts:

= ACTION VERB BLOCK SYMBOL. This symbol is used to record a processing action and to contain a number to denote the sequence processing step.

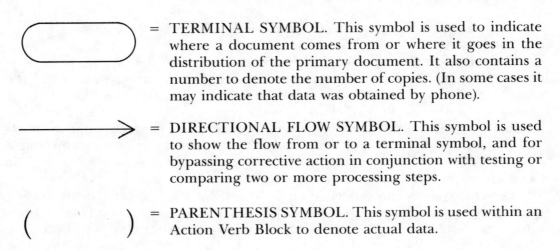

= TERMINAL SYMBOL. This symbol is used to indicate where a document comes from or where it goes in the distribution of the primary document. It also contains a number to denote the number of copies. (In some cases it may indicate that data was obtained by phone).

= DIRECTIONAL FLOW SYMBOL. This symbol is used to show the flow from or to a terminal symbol, and for bypassing corrective action in conjunction with testing or comparing two or more processing steps.

= PARENTHESIS SYMBOL. This symbol is used within an Action Verb Block to denote actual data.

Action Verbs and the Rules for Their Use

There are nine action verbs used in procedural flowcharting. These verbs describe a certain action that is required in filling out and processing a form, log, worksheet, etc., used in the telecommunications message center or related functional areas. The type of action verb is written inside the action verb block on the Individual Document Flowchart and the Combination Documents Flowchart (See Figures 2-1 and 2-2). The action verbs are:

POST: This verb is used when any data is entered on the primary document (the document of the work function being analyzed and flowcharted). The data may be obtained from a secondary document (another functional area document or by phone). The action verb block must identify the document from which the information came. When it is obtained by telephone, it must be entered in the action verb block as indicated in the POST and EXTRACT examples. In the example, the date-time-group (DTG) information on the primary document waş in error. The message center clerk called the releasing office for the correct data. After the correct data was entered on the primary document, the releasing office's department code and DTG was extracted from the primary document to another document to denote an error in message preparation by the releasing office.

EXAMPLE:

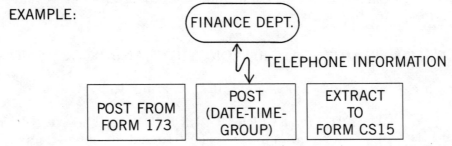

EXTRACT: This verb is used when any data is taken from the primary document and entered on a secondary document. The action verb block must identify the document that the data was extracted to (in some cases, information may be given by telephone).

The communications link symbol ⟋⟍⟶ will be used as the Directional flow symbol when data is given or received by phone.

EXAMPLE

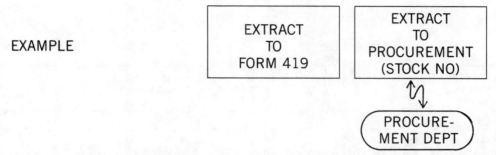

```
┌─────────────┐   ┌──────────────┐
│  EXTRACT    │   │   EXTRACT    │
│    TO       │   │     TO       │
│  FORM 419   │   │ PROCUREMENT  │
│             │   │  (STOCK NO)  │
└─────────────┘   └──────────────┘
                         ↑↓
                  ╭──────────────╮
                  │  PROCURE-    │
                  │  MENT DEPT   │
                  ╰──────────────╯
```

ATTACH: This verb is used when two or more documents are brought together to be filed, or to be processed together throughout the flow.

EXAMPLE

```
┌──────────────┐
│   ATTACH     │
│  FORM 301    │
└──────────────┘
```

TEST: This verb is used when the primary document is checked, edited, or compared for the presence or accuracy of data. Some type of corrective action must follow the test action. Corrective action is taken on a document only if an error is found. If an error is not found, the flow direction symbol is used to bypass the action verb block containing the corrective action. The following are examples of the TEST action verb and the various types of corrective action that can be used.

EXAMPLE 1: When the primary document may be in error and the secondary document is known to be correct:

```
┌──────────────┬──────────────┬──────────────┐
│  TEST =      │    POST      │              │
│  FORM 310    │    FROM      │    POST      │
│  COL A       │   FORM 310   │   (DATE)     │
│  TOTALS      │              │              │
└──────────────┴──────────────┴──────────────┘
        └───────────────────────────┘↑
           ERROR FOUND AND
             CORRECTED
```

EXAMPLE 2: When the primary document is correct and the secondary document may be in error:

```
┌──────────────┬──────────────┬──────────────┐
│  TEST =      │   EXTRACT    │              │
│  FORM 333    │     TO       │    POST      │
│  ORGN CODE   │   FORM 333   │   (DATE)     │
└──────────────┴──────────────┴──────────────┘
        └───────────────────────────┘↑
              CODE CORRECT
```

FIGURE 2-2
Combination Document Flowchart

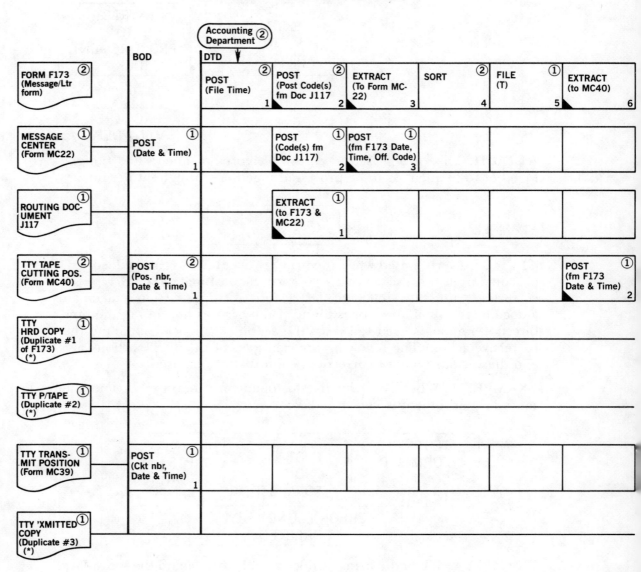

Note: (*) Documents created during the processing and flow of message Form F173.

Accounting Department ②   Microfilm

								EOD	EOM
ATTACH (TTY Hrd Cpy & Paper Tape) 7	TEST (TTY Hrd Cpy) 8	CORRECT (No Errors) 9	POST (Initials in u/rt H/Cor.) ① 10	EXTRACT (to MC39) 11	POST (Chn nbr, Date & Time) ① 12	(Separating Duplicate #3) 13	ATTACH (TTY Hrd Copy) 14	FILE (30 days) 15	DESTROY (Form F173) 16

Yes →

					POST (Chn nbr, Date & Time) ①				

ATTACH (to F173) ① 1	TEST (F173) 2	CORRECT 3	DESTROY (TTY Hrd Copy) 4						

ATTACH (to F173) ① 1			FILE (T) 2					DESTROY 3	

			POST (Date & Time fm F173) 2	EXTRACT (to F173 & MC2) 3	SEPARATE (TTY 'xmitted Copy) 4				

			SEPARATE (fm Trans- mit Position) 1	ATTACH (F173) 2					

EXAMPLE 3: When testing for the completeness of the primary document:

TEST COMPLETE-NESS	POST (TOTAL)	POST (DATE)	POST (CLERK'S SIGNATURE)

ERROR FOUND AND CORRECTED

Note 1: The analyst should TEST first and then POST or EXTRACT.
Note 2: The corrective action may require more than one action verb block, as noted in Example 3.

CORRECT: This verb is used after a TEST action when the corrective action is not indicated or as a result of a test between documents when either document may be in error. The following are two examples demonstrating this:

EXAMPLE 1: When the corrective action is not indicated:

TEST COMPLETE-NESS	(CORRECT ERROR)*	POST FROM FORM 310

CORRECTIVE ACTION TAKEN

EXAMPLE 2: When either document may be in error:

TEST = FORM 418	(CORRECT ERROR)*	POST FROM FORM 310

DOCUMENT CORRECTED

*NOTE: The analyst must investigate to determine corrective action and record the proper action on the primary and the secondary document, if required.

SORT OR SEPARATE: This verb is used when separating copies for distribution, or when arranging the primary document into a sequence, or when separating copies that are handled differently within the functional area. SORT is not used when all copies are being sent out of the functional area. SEPARATE may be used when copies are separated as indicated in Figure 2-1 and Steps 1 and 4 of TTY Transmit Position and TTY Transmitted Copy Documents of Figure 2-2.

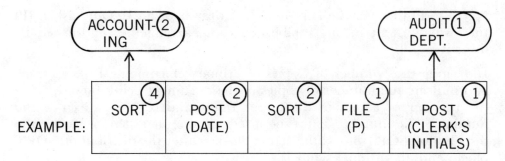

DESTROY: This verb is used when the primary document is destroyed.

EXAMPLE

COMPUTE: This verb is used when any type of arithmetic operation takes place with the data on the primary document. The following are two examples of the use of the COMPUTE verb:

EXAMPLE 1: Computing totals on the primary document:

COMPUTE (TOTAL)

EXAMPLE 2: When computing totals from data on the primary document and entering these totals on both the primary and secondary documents:

COMPUTE (VOUCHER TOTALS)	EXTRACT TO FORM 419

FILE: This verb is used when the primary document is placed in a file. Files are designated as temporary (T), permanent (P), or the actual life of the file, i.e., day, week, quarter, year, etc. When known, use the actual data life of the file.

EXAMPLE:

FILE (T)	FILE (P)	FILE (MONTH & DATE)

NOTE: (T) files may be kept in a desk drawer or an In/Out basket. (P) files will be kept in any established filing arrangement governed by directives.

Indicating the Number of Copies of Primary Document: To keep track and indicate the number of copies of the document being flowed, enter the number of copies in the upper right-hand corner and circle the number. The number must be used in the first action block; the distribution SORT block; the action block(s) after the distribution SORT block; and all terminal symbols.

EXAMPLE:

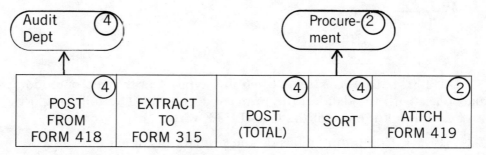

Distributing Primary Document: The TERMINAL symbol is used to indicate the distribution when the original or any copies of the primary document are received or sent out of the functional area.

EXAMPLE:

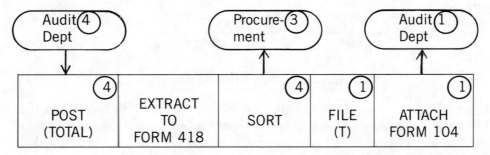

Numbering the Action Verb blocks: Each action block should be numbered sequentially in the lower right-hand corner and left uncircled.

EXAMPLE:

POST (DATE)	COMPUTE (TOTAL)	EXTRACT TO FORM 310	SORT	FILE (P)
1	2	3	4	5

GROUPING WORK FUNCTIONS AND DOCUMENTS INTO TIME PHASES

All processing actions must be grouped according to the time phase in which they occur. Time phases will be arranged chronologically from the earliest to the latest time phase. Note how the phases are used in Figures 2-1 and 2-2. Examples of various time phases are:

- Beginning of Day (BOD)
- During the Day (DTD)
- End of Day (EOD)
- Beginning of Week (BOW)
- End of Week (EOW)
- Beginning of Month (BOM)
- End of Month (EOM)
- Beginning of Quarter (BOQ)
- End of Quarter (EOQ)
- Semiannual (SA)
- End of Six Month (EO6M)
- Beginning of Year (BOY)
- End of One Year (EOY)
- End of Two Years (EO2Y)

COMBINING DOCUMENTS AND CHARTING THEIR INTERACTIONS

Combination Documents flowcharting is the second level in the procedural flowcharting of the functional area under study. Here, the processing steps are flowed in chronological order, and the individual work sections are lined up vertically according to the time phases. See Figure 2-2.

The Combination Documents Flowchart aids the analyst in the following ways:

- It graphically depicts the interaction between primary documents, by work function or section, within the functional area.
- It indicates processing errors of omission or the accuracy and completeness of the primary documents collected.
- It serves as the documentation for developing the General System Flowchart.
- It provides information for writing up specifications for the new system.
- It aids in preparing document grid charts.

Rules for Combination Documents Flowcharting

In addition to the nine action verbs and the four basic symbols discussed earlier, there is an additional symbol used in preparing the Combination Documents Flowchart. The symbol is:

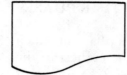 DOCUMENT SYMBOL. This symbol is used to present any input/output function in which the media is a document. This may include:

- Source message document,
- Forms, logs, worksheets, etc.,
- Teletype punch paper tape (the paper tape symbol may be used) as in Figures 2-2 and 2-3,
- Computer printed reports, forms, etc.,
- Adding machine, cash register tape,
- Credit card,
- Bank checks,
- Graphic plotted output,
- Other documents such as catalogues, manuals, work copies, etc., which are used to record or extract data.

RELATIONSHIP BETWEEN DOCUMENTS AND ERRORS OF OMISSION

Interaction between documents occurs when there is a POST, EXTRACT, ATTACH, TEST or SEPARATE involving more than one Individual Document Flowchart. A corresponding interaction takes place when one of the following happens:

- Information is taken (EXTRACTed) from one document and recorded (POSTed) to another document. The corresponding interaction is: EXTRACT to POST. The reverse of this is: POST to EXTRACT.
- One document or certain data on the document is TESTed against another document. The corresponding interaction is: TEST to TEST.
- One document is ATTACHed to another document. The corresponding interaction is: ATTACH to ATTACH.
- A document (multipage, manually or computer printed report) is sorted by separating it into single copy reports. The corresponding interaction is: SEPARATE to SEPARATE.

Errors of Omission happen when an Individual Document Flowchart specifies an interaction with another document but the second document does not have a corresponding interaction verb. Example: If an action verb or an Individual Document Flowchart specifies a POST but the corresponding or second document does not contain an EXTRACT verb, an error of omission has occurred.

PREPARING THE COMBINATION DOCUMENTS FLOWCHART

The Individual Document Flowcharts are the only source used in preparing the Combination Documents Flowchart. The following rules will aid the analyst in this process:

1. Group Individual Document Flowcharts by work function or section.

2. Flow documents left to right.

3. The Individual Document Flowchart with the earliest time phase and/or the most interaction with other documents should be flowed first.

4. If two or more documents begin in the same time phase, flow the document with the most interactions first.

5. Draw the Document Symbol for each document to be flowed down the left side of the chart. Write the document title and number in the symbol. Enter the number of copies of the primary document in the upper right-hand corner of each Document Symbol.

6. Separate the time phases by drawing a line on the chart from top to bottom.

7. When a primary document originates in a work function or section being studied, draw a line to connect the document to its first action block; otherwise, the terminal symbol is used to indicate where the document came from.

8. To aid in quickly identifying the corresponding interactions of various documents, a uniform marking (preferably a small triangle) or color code should be used.

9. When an Individual Document Flowchart does not contain an interaction verb that corresponds to an interaction verb of another Individual Document, an ERROR OF OMISSION has occurred. When this happens, an action block or blocks must be added to the document containing the omission.

10. The inserted block will have the same sequence number as the preceding correct block but suffixed with an alpha character. To quickly identify where the omission occurred, the same marking or color should be used under the bottom of the left-hand corner of the action block.

11. When documents from more than one functional area or section are flowed on the same Combination Documents Flowchart, the work function or section should be separated horizontally with a heavy line the length of the chart.

The first nine rules are illustrated in Figure 2-2.

RULES FOR GENERAL SYSTEM FLOWCHART

Some of the rules discussed for preparing the Individual Document, Combination Documents Flowcharts apply to the General System Flowchart.

- To separate departmental or functional boundaries, a heavy line should be drawn horizontal to the length of the chart, as mentioned in Rule Number 11 above. This is illustrated in Figure 2-4.

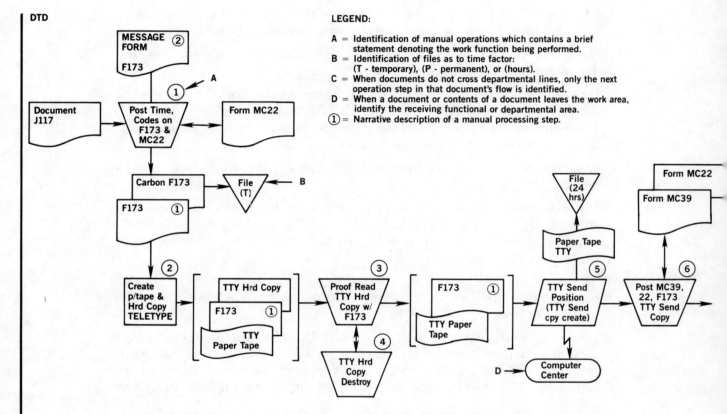

FIGURE 2-3: is a graphic and narrative description of the clerical and electro-mechanical processing functions required in message processing in a typical tele-communications message center. The chart depicts the interactions and relation-ship of all documents and equipment encountered in the normal flow and processing.

Narrative Description of Processing Steps of Figure 2-3

(1) When an outgoing message is received, the file time, routing codes (from Document J) are recorded on Message Form 173. The office symbol of the originator, date-time-group (DTG), and routing codes of the addressee(s) are entered on the Message Register Form MC22. The Message Form 173 is assigned a Station Serial Number (SSN). It is the number that the message is logged in under on the MC22. The carbon or second copy of F173 is filed and the original is sent to the tape cutting position.

(2) A paper tape is produced and the TTY hard copy, paper tape, and F173 are sent to the proofreader.

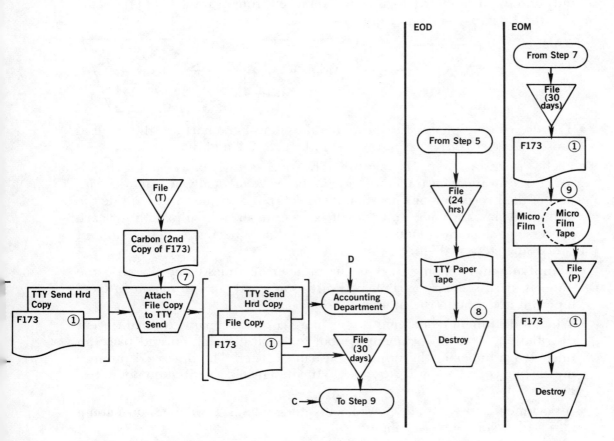

(3)(4) The message is proofed against the original and the TTY hard copy destroyed. The paper tape and F173 are sent to the TTY send position.

(5) The paper tape is transmitted by Teletype (ASR-37) and the paper tape filed for 24 hours. A TTY send hard copy is created and is flowed with the F173.

(6) The transmit log MC39 is posted with the DTG and SSN of the transmitted message and time of transmission. The TTY send hard copy is annotated with the outgoing channel number and time of transmission. The message is then given to the Message Register Clerk. The Clerk records the outgoing channel number and time of transmission on the Message Register log MC22.

(7) The Clerk retrieves the carbon F173 from file (T) and attaches it to the TTY send copy and sends it to the originating office— Accounting Department. The original is filed for 30 days.

(8) The TTY paper tape is destroyed after 24 hours.

(9) The original F173 is retrieved from 30-day file and microfilmed and destroyed.

- The flow should be from left to right, top to bottom, and bottom to top. The only exception is when a document is removed from or returned to the same file; the flow may be from right to left.

EXAMPLE:

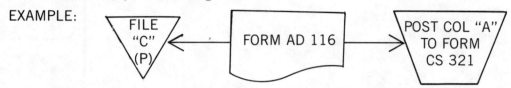

- The use of time phases for the General System Flowchart are the same as those described earlier, as illustrated in Figures 2-2 and 2-3.

- Each processing step, as identified by one of the Processing Symbols (discussed in the next topic) will be numbered sequentially. A brief description of the processing or operation that takes place will be written inside the symbol. A narrative, identified by the step number, will be written for each processing step. See Figures 2-2, 2-4 and the narrative description of processing steps of Figure 2-2.

- Identifying and keeping track of the number of copies being flowed is the same as discussed earlier. (Punched cards, punched tape, or magnetic spool tape will not contain the number of copies).

- When a document containing two or more copies is separated for different distribution, draw a document symbol for each distribution and place an uncircled number in the upper right-hand corner. The uncircled number means that copy 1, copy 2, etc., goes to the designated distribution point. See Figure 2-4.

- A document should not be flowed across time phases. It will be shown going into a file. Note Step 7 of Figure 2-3.

- When a document is shown going into a file in one time phase for later use in another time phase, the file symbol and the document symbol will be redrawn in the new time phase. Note the document flow between the two time phases of Figure 2-3.

- All documents that flow into an operation step must be shown coming out of that step, unless the operation is to DESTROY the document. Note the flow of TTY send hard copy, F173 of Step 6 and TTY send hard copy, file copy, and F173 of Step 7 of Figure 2-3.

PREPARING THE GENERAL SYSTEM FLOWCHART

The General Document Flowchart is a graphic presentation of the processing steps, the documents involved, and the input/output media used in the functional area under study. It is the "big" picture of the old system. It shows every action and processing step involved as illustrated in Figure 2-4.

The General System Flowchart permits the team members to review, study, and make judgments about the present methods of doing business. By now each

FIGURE 2-4

General System Flowchart Showing Document Flow and Distribution

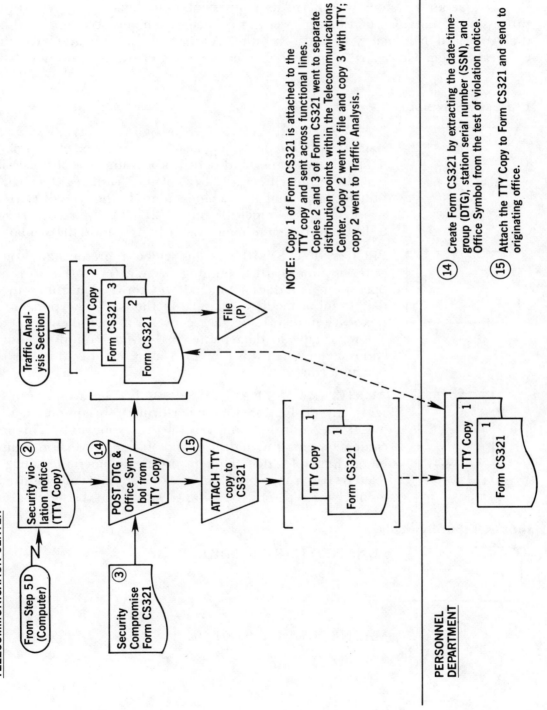

FIGURE 2-4: This illustration depicts a security violation notice being received from a computer. It is processed according to ⑭ and ⑮ and a copy of the TTY violation notice along with the original copy of Form CS321 is sent to the originating office.

analyst is able to get his mind around the total system, and can set about to design the new system.

The General System Flowchart uses many symbols to depict the flow and the processing of data. Certain data processing flow-chart symbols recommended by the American National Standards Instutite (ANSI) are recommended for the General System Flowchart. The symbols used for the General System Flowchart are:

Processing Symbols:

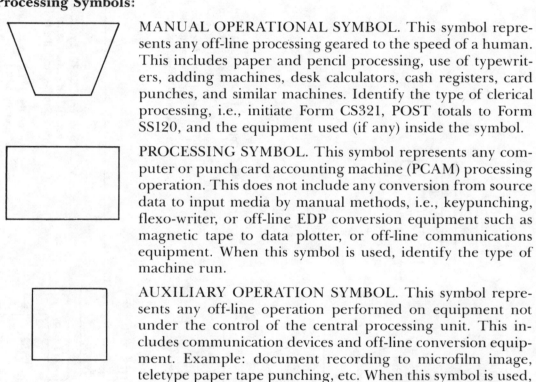

MANUAL OPERATIONAL SYMBOL. This symbol represents any off-line processing geared to the speed of a human. This includes paper and pencil processing, use of typewriters, adding machines, desk calculators, cash registers, card punches, and similar machines. Identify the type of clerical processing, i.e., initiate Form CS321, POST totals to Form SS120, and the equipment used (if any) inside the symbol.

PROCESSING SYMBOL. This symbol represents any computer or punch card accounting machine (PCAM) processing operation. This does not include any conversion from source data to input media by manual methods, i.e., keypunching, flexo-writer, or off-line EDP conversion equipment such as magnetic tape to data plotter, or off-line communications equipment. When this symbol is used, identify the type of machine run.

AUXILIARY OPERATION SYMBOL. This symbol represents any off-line operation performed on equipment not under the control of the central processing unit. This includes communication devices and off-line conversion equipment. Example: document recording to microfilm image, teletype paper tape punching, etc. When this symbol is used, identify the type of processing or equipment being used.

Input/Output Symbols:

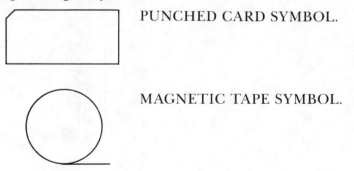

PUNCHED CARD SYMBOL.

MAGNETIC TAPE SYMBOL.

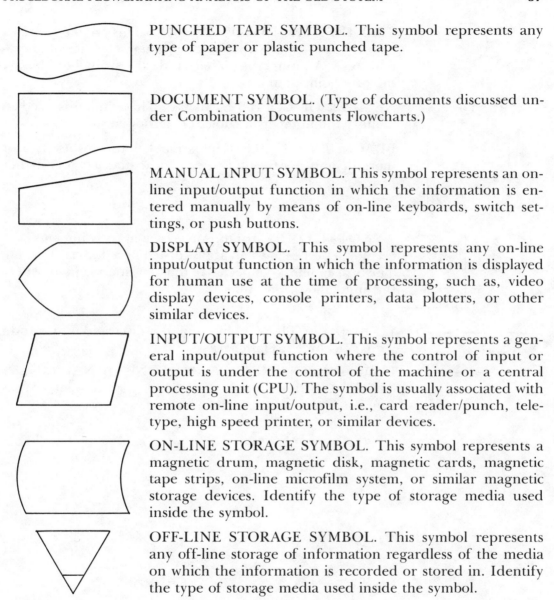

PUNCHED TAPE SYMBOL. This symbol represents any type of paper or plastic punched tape.

DOCUMENT SYMBOL. (Type of documents discussed under Combination Documents Flowcharts.)

MANUAL INPUT SYMBOL. This symbol represents an on-line input/output function in which the information is entered manually by means of on-line keyboards, switch settings, or push buttons.

DISPLAY SYMBOL. This symbol represents any on-line input/output function in which the information is displayed for human use at the time of processing, such as, video display devices, console printers, data plotters, or other similar devices.

INPUT/OUTPUT SYMBOL. This symbol represents a general input/output function where the control of input or output is under the control of the machine or a central processing unit (CPU). The symbol is usually associated with remote on-line input/output, i.e., card reader/punch, teletype, high speed printer, or similar devices.

ON-LINE STORAGE SYMBOL. This symbol represents a magnetic drum, magnetic disk, magnetic cards, magnetic tape strips, on-line microfilm system, or similar magnetic storage devices. Identify the type of storage media used inside the symbol.

OFF-LINE STORAGE SYMBOL. This symbol represents any off-line storage of information regardless of the media on which the information is recorded or stored in. Identify the type of storage media used inside the symbol.

Additional Symbols Used in General System Flowcharts

In addition to the symbols discussed in the Individual Document, the Combination Documents, and the General System Flowcharts, the following symbols are used:

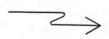

COMMUNICATION LINK SYMBOL. This symbol represents an input/output function in which information is transmitted over a communications line from one location to another.

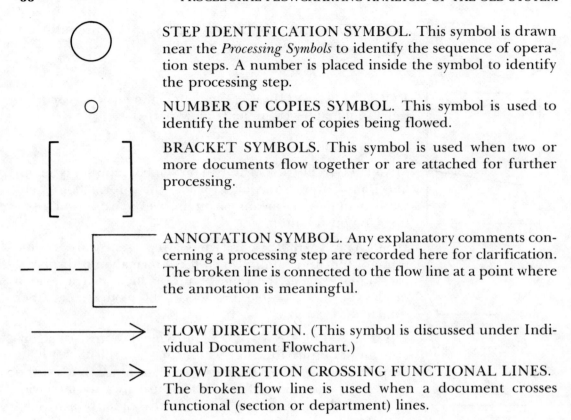

STEP IDENTIFICATION SYMBOL. This symbol is drawn near the *Processing Symbols* to identify the sequence of operation steps. A number is placed inside the symbol to identify the processing step.

NUMBER OF COPIES SYMBOL. This symbol is used to identify the number of copies being flowed.

BRACKET SYMBOLS. This symbol is used when two or more documents flow together or are attached for further processing.

ANNOTATION SYMBOL. Any explanatory comments concerning a processing step are recorded here for clarification. The broken line is connected to the flow line at a point where the annotation is meaningful.

FLOW DIRECTION. (This symbol is discussed under Individual Document Flowchart.)

FLOW DIRECTION CROSSING FUNCTIONAL LINES. The broken flow line is used when a document crosses functional (section or department) lines.

CHAPTER THREE

Data Communications Considerations for the Central Processor and Associated Units

The low cost, capacity, miniaturization, and transportability of computers have made it possible to place central processing units at the very source of data collection and data base users. These processors range in size and capacity from large mainframes to minicomputers to microprocessors to processors on chips, and can be configured in data communications systems or networks to serve a given geographical area or span a whole continent or globe.

The major benefit of these advanced processors and data communications is the ability to capture or control an event where and when it takes place, so that it can make its impact on the system immediately. Data communications allow for events to be instantly transmitted and processed by combining DP technology with data communications technology whereby remote input-output devices can have on-line (instant) access to data bases of the system.

This chapter discusses certain configurations and the benefits of small computers in data communications systems. The central theme of this chapter is the flexibility and adaptability of minicomputers and microprocessors for data communications functions. Small computers are very fast and powerful. They are the driving force in the tremendous growth in data communications.

Small computers are more efficient for data communications functions than large mainframe computers. They are used for a variety of data communications functions, but they are used primarily for front-end processors (FEP), preprocessing functions, line concentrators, as well as the primary processor for certain data communications systems.

SELECTING THE APPROPRIATE DATA COMMUNICATIONS CONFIGURATION

The Central Processing Unit (CPU) peripheral and software requirements should be developed during the problem and system analysis phases of system design. A review of Chapter One will provide an insight into the methods and material to be gathered for determining equipment requirements. The flexibility, capacity of the CPU, hardware characteristics of the CPU, and associated equipment and software can vary to a great degree. Also, the various equipment components can be assembled in many different configurations. This is one reason why the Request for Proposal (RFP) document is prepared and sent to a number of appropriate vendors for responses. The RFP is discussed in Appendix A at the back of the book.

The hardware requirements are directly related to the types of applications that will function within the system. The equipment design and configuration selected should be studied thoroughly to insure all aspects of the data communications requirements will be fulfilled.

STAND-ALONE COMPUTER CONFIGURATION

The stand-alone system is configured with all devices and hardware located within the confines of a single room or building. Figure 3-1 is an illustration of a typical stand-alone configuration.

Data is input and output to local devices and then, in many cases, handled manually outside the system area. Stand-alone systems are normally utilized for such batch or scientific processing activities or functions as accounting, file or record maintenance and updating, inventories, statistics, analysis, mathematical calculations etc. Communication functions are usually a minor part of a stand-alone system.

FRONT-END HOST COMPUTER CONFIGURATION

Large mainframe data processing computers are designed primarily to perform best as data processing machines. Communication functions are usually a secondary consideration in both hardware and software design. A large mainframe computer may serve the system as a network or host computer while utilizing a front-end communication processor as a communication interface. The host computer will treat the front-end as any other high-speed device.

In this configuration the host need not be concerned with varying terminal speeds, code conversions, protocol variations or other data communications functions. Input data is passed to the host in a constant and unvarying fashion

FIGURE 3-1
Stand-Alone Computer (Host)

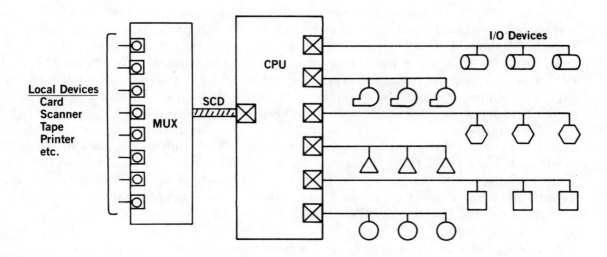

FIGURE 3-1: In this stand-alone host configuration, local devices are utilized and treated in a manner similar to remote terminal devices. The host processor assumes the communications functions. The terminal devices are configured to conform with the host processor's communications protocol.

LEGEND:

SCD = **Signal, Control, Data Signals**

CPU = **Central Processing Unit**

MUX = **Multiplexer**

I/O = **Input/Output**

⊠ = **Device Controller**

▢ = **Line Interface Adapter**

completely buffered from the variable inputs received by the front-end. Outputs from the host are broken down by the front-end and reformatted to conform to the varying requirements of the different terminals, front-end, or other computers receiving data from the front-end. Depending on network design and message or data destination, the front-end processor can also act as a message switching unit. In addition, the front-end could route (switch) data or messages around a host computer that is in trouble, without the local host computer having to intervene in the process.

The front-end processor performs seven major functions that relieve the requirement of the data processor (host computer) to perform communication processing. They are: (1) allowing message (data) buffering and store and forward functions; (2) allowing terminals having different speeds, character codes and line protocols to communicate with each other; (3) allowing error detection/correction and fault isolation; (4) allowing for message (data) editing; (5) making very efficient use of data communications and carrier facilities through on-line monitoring and system diagnostics; (6) allowing for the complete separation of data communications and data processing functions, since all data communication functions are performed by the front-end, and (7) in case of host computer failure, allowing for the processing of critical functions and continuing to function as a message (data) switch thus allowing partial network operation.

The front-end is treated as a high-speed peripheral device by the host computer which uses a device protocol for receiving and transmitting data to the front-end. Figure 3-2 is an illustration of a front-end host configuration. The front-end processor is usually configured with its own peripheral subsystems. Front-end functions will vary, depending on the network or system design concept, but generally, the functions of the front-end are as follows:

- It provides monitoring features for the communications network.
- It detects and takes appropriate action on all communications network error conditions.
- It provides data queuing and storage functions.
- It blocks and deblocks data transmitted to and received from data terminals.
- It sorts data input and output according to application and/or job type.
- It performs some data processing functions for the host computer.
- It eliminates the host line multiplexer hardware.
- It performs data code conversion.
- It performs symbol and data format editing.
- It allows for data priority queuing and processing.
- It handles data compression functions.
- It provides for data security and privacy requirements.
- It provides memory and disk (high speed devices) selective queuing and storage.
- It places lines and terminals in or out of service.
- It provides temporary system overload control for:
  - Excessive queue requirements,
  - Excessive data storage requirements,
  - Protecting for terminals out of service,
  - Excessive data rate—exceeds system capability.
- It provides for parity generation and detection.
- It has concentrator functions.
- It provides various statistical information for:
  - Data error rates per line/terminal,
  - Data transfer per line/terminal,

–Data blocks per line/terminal,
–Overall data transfer rates,
–System overload conditions,
–Line/terminal operational status,
–Security or privacy key word usage,
–Etc.

• It generates and edits formatted forms for the various terminals.

FIGURE 3-2
Front-End Host Configuration

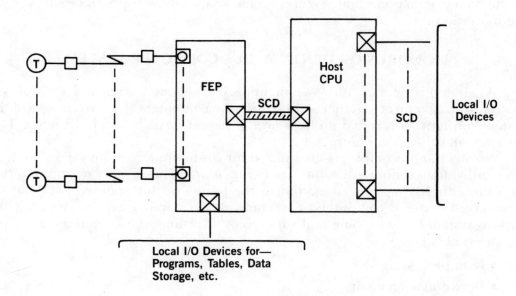

Local I/O Devices for—
Programs, Tables, Data
Storage, etc.

FIGURE 3-2: depicts a straightforward front-end host configuration where all remote processors or terminals access the host CPU through the front-end processor. The front-end processor may have its own local peripheral devices for data storage, and provide look-up tables, and other housekeeping programs.

LEGEND:

CPU = Central Processing Unit

FEP = Front-End Processor

◯ = Line Interface Adapter

▢ = MODEM

⌁ = Communications Line

Ⓣ = Terminal

⊠ = CPU/FEP Device Controller

SCD = Signal, Control, Data
Cables

The front-end allows the host computer access to various types of terminals, and other front-end or host computer systems. It provides error-free preprocessed data, allowing the host computer to strictly perform data processing functions for which it is best suited.

PREPROCESSING SYSTEM

A remote preprocessing system is one where data is edited, formatted and generally prepared for final processing in the main host data processing system. Also, pertinent local files could be stored for local use. This reduces the overhead requirements of the host and places a portion of the data processing requirements at the data origination point. Figure 3-3 illustrates a typical preprocessing system configuration.

MONOBUS OR CENTRAL BUS COMPUTER SYSTEM

A Monobus/Central Bus system utilizes a common data and control bus matrix, which connect together several different computers. The advantages of the system configuration is that it offers overall system flexibility and efficiency. This system is illustrated in Figure 3-4.

Normally, minicomputers are utilized for configuration of this type of system. Each individual computer is connected to the common buses and can communicate with any other computer connected to the buses. In this manner, data may be transferred between computers. Each individual computer may be assigned the various system housekeeping and supervision functions. This could include such functions as:

- Data processing
- Device management
- Files and record maintenance
- Communications front-end
- Analytical and statistical processing
- Monitoring functions
- Other special requirements
- Spare or fallback computer

MICROCOMPUTER OR MINICOMPUTER CONSIDERATION

Minicomputers and microcomputers are at the forefront of data communications and data processing (DP) for small to medium-sized business organizations and for remote plants and operating locations of large organizations. Some combinations of mini- and microcomputer systems offer the capacity and flexibility of big mainframe systems. The impetus behind this is economics—the main reason for improvements in capacity and flexibility of these small computers and microprocessors.

FIGURE 3-3
Preprocessing System Configuration

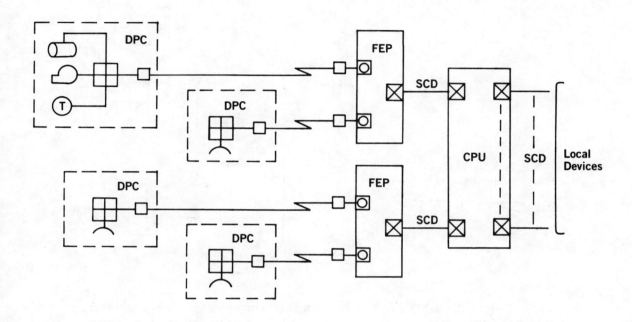

FIGURE 3-3: depicts a preprocessing environment where several remote preprocessing centers have access through a host CPU via a front-end processor.

LEGEND:

SCD = **Signal, Control, Data Cables**

DPC = **Distant Preprocessing Centers**

CPU = **Central Processing Unit**

FEP = **Front-End Processor**

⊠ = **Device Controller**

◯ = **Line Interface Adapter**

▢ = **MODEM**

⌇ = **Communications Line**

⊞ = **Micro/Minicomputer**

⌒ = **Local Devices**

Ⓣ = **Terminal**

FIGURE 3-4
Mono/Central Bus Computer System

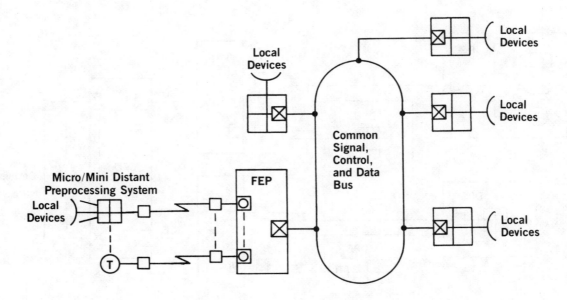

FIGURE 3-4: illustrates a central bus computer configuration where each micro/minicomputer is assigned data processing tasks, device management, or communicatons functions.

LEGEND:

FEP = Front-End Processor

⊠ = Device Controller

◎ = Line Interface Adapter

☐ = MODEM

⌁ = Communications Line

⊞ = Mini or Micro Local or Distant Processor

Ⓣ = Terminal

Micro- and minicomputers are bringing significant changes to the community of data processing and communications. The result of these changes is placing the end-user at the focal point for system development, programming, data entry and data processing operations. Using the tools of mini/microcomputer/processors and the applications of distributed processing techniques, the end-user is in a position to control most of the DP resources.

The classical DP environment is changing. First, the costs of owning or leasing DP equipment are continuously moving downward. It is now economically feasible for each department manager, remote plant or office manager to have his own data processing resources. This trend was started with the minicomputer in the early seventies; the microcomputer will accelerate it in the 80s.

The user, who has the DP requirement, is insistent on controlling the DP operation. This is a logical demand because the user provides the data to the system and receives the output products. Why shouldn't the user control the data entry, product production, and have a big say in the system design, and even programming?

The state of the art is shifting in that direction. For the most part, data entry has shifted to the end-user. With distributed processing and departmental micro/minicomputers, operation and production functions will also shift to the end-user.

Micro- or minicomputers can be configured to provide those features and functions available in the larger computer systems, but at a lower system cost. The art of hardware modularity has been made simple through the microprocessor/computer design concepts. It should be pointed out, however, that software design, languages, and assembly procedures have not kept pace with the hardware design. This situation is gradually changing and improvements are occurring daily, but the users should review the software, languages, and assemblers very carefully.

The micro- or minicomputer can provide the capability to implement various system functions at a reasonable cost. These functions could include such areas as front-ends, distributed processing, word processing, preprocessors, concentrators, device management controllers, intelligent or programmable terminals, multiplexers, data analyzers and other specialized functions.

Figure 3-5 illustrates where micro- or minicomputers could be utilized to provide system operational functions at a reasonable cost, and at the same time allow system modularity and flexibility.

Microprocessor

A microprocessor, as the bit is to a data system, is the smallest element in the family of central processing units. The microprocessor is a semiconductor integrated circuit without any supporting circuits or I/O device connections. When electrical pathways (circuits), I/O device capability, and memory are added to the microprocessor, it becomes a microcomputer capable of performing limited functions similar to those of minicomputer configurations.

The most common word size of microprocessors are: 4-bit, 8-bit, 12-bit, 16-bit and bit slice with the latter being usually microprogrammed to perform primitive operations very fast. Word size refers to the number of bits contained in registers that are used to perform arithmetical and logical operations on data elements. Minicomputers commonly use word sizes up to 32 bits, and in some cases, larger.

The small end of the word size (4 bits) is used primarily for binary coded decimal (BCD) calculators operating on one decimal at a time. The 8-bit through 16-bit word size has a much broader processing range. The 16-bit microprocessor is suitable for handling communications functions because of its flexibility and working range.

FIGURE 3-5
Micro/Minicomputer Configuration

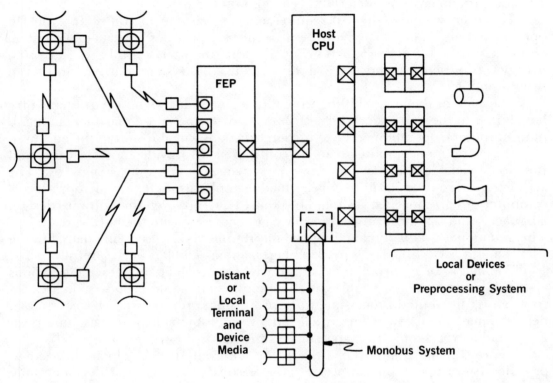

FIGURE 3-5: This figure illustrates a minicomputer configuration structured as a distributed processing network. As may be noted, some of the remote distributed processing systems are interconnected for direct interchange of data. A number of the minicomputer systems may be directly connected to the host processor while others may be connected to the host via a front-end processor or connected to the host via a monobus (ring or loop) system.

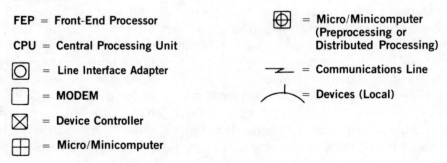

LEGEND:

FEP = Front-End Processor

CPU = Central Processing Unit

○ = Line Interface Adapter

□ = MODEM

⊠ = Device Controller

⊞ = Micro/Minicomputer

⊕ = Micro/Minicomputer (Preprocessing or Distributed Processing)

⚡ = Communications Line

⌣ = Devices (Local)

Microcomputer

The microcomputer is configured along the classical lines of the minicomputer and the large mainframe. It has the three main parts required of a general purpose computer: Memory, CPU and I/O ports to handle subsystems and communication channels. The memory, CPU and I/O ports are physically and logically connected to a set of buses. A bus is an electrical path or channel for passing data, control information and memory addresses. Components of a microcomputer are packaged on one or more printed circuit boards. When microcomputers are integrated within minicomputers, word sizes range from 8 bits to 32 bits.

Microcomputer memory consists mainly of a combination of ROM (Read Only Memory), PROM (Programmable Read Only Memory), and RAM (Random Access Memory). The speed of microcomputer memories is comparable to those of minicomputers. The amount of memory that may be directly addressable is determined by the number of bits assigned to the address field of its instruction and the size of its address bus.

In micro- and minicomputers that use a 16-bit address register, both have the ability to directly address up to 65,536 words of main memory. Memory may consist of core or a combination of semiconductor ROM, PROM, or RAM.

Reliability and maintainability are about equal for the micro- and minicomputers, with the micro having a slight edge because of fewer components and less power requirements. Because of this, isolation of problems is generally easier.

FIRMWARE AND SOFTWARE CONSIDERATIONS

Firmware programming is normally accomplished in the following manner:

- Wire strapping between pins and terminal block connections. This strapping is accomplished within the device. This method of programming is permanent, difficult to change, and limited in functions performed.

- Strapping between jacks using specially designed patching cords and jacks. This method is similar to wire strapping, but more easily changed. Functions are limited.

- Chip programming. Chip micro logic is a method of programming where a chip is electronically etched or printed with the program instructions of the functions that the device is to perform. These chips are either plugged into a socket or rack, or the chips may be permanently installed in the device. This provides a fairly simple method of reprogramming the device. Programmed features are limited in comparison to a software programmed device. Read Only Memory (ROM) could be considered a programmed chip.

- Using a microprocessor as an internal control module within a device. The microprocessor is programmed in much the same manner as the larger computers. The programs are loaded via paper tape, magnetic tape, or disk. The program functions are limited because of the memory capacity, hardware registers, word size, and instruction set restrictions of the micro-processor. The microprocessor may be a chip.

- Software subroutines or microprograms. This software is designed to support frequently operated computer functions, allow new instructions to be implemented, or old instructions to be changed. A section of memory is allocated to permit storage of and access to these subroutines.

This changing or addition of instructions is possible when the main machine instructions utilize the microprograms to cause the mainframe to perform the necessary functions. A change in a microprogram will change the main instruction operation.

When the microprograms are also used to support subroutines, it becomes a simple matter to add, delete, or revise the subroutines. This permits total flexibility of computer operation.

The term "macro" should not be confused with microprograms except that both provide subroutines for programmer purposes. Macros are utilized to ease the programmer's work load, but are very inefficient when machine run time, memory and device space are considered. These macro routines are not as easily changed as are the microprograms when they are in a segmented section of memory.

SOFTWARE-MAINFRAME CONSIDERATIONS

Software packages are designed to perform the required functions as limited or permitted by the hardware. When the many variations in hardware design are analyzed, it follows that software design must vary for all the possible hardware configurations. The main emphasis should be placed on a software system that takes full advantage of the hardware and the hardware has been selected to provide flexibility and modularity.

When mainframe cycle speed, flexibility and system operational speed are prime system considerations, main memory is the logical area to place all software programs and data. This is not always possible since the memory area available is usually exceeded by the system programs and data requirements. When main memory is not sufficient for the storage of programs and data, external storage must be considered. The external storage selected should provide the highest possible cycle speed or data transfer rate. This could be external memory or some magnetically operated device, such as a disk.

DISK OVERLAY

Most computer systems store the application and utility programs on disk units or some other magnetic storage medium. They are called into main memory as required to perform various tasks. These tasks are normally performed in a serial fashion. This type of serial processing is fine for some systems, while in other systems this method is very inefficient.

When the requirement exists for parallel operation of applications, tasks or functions, a disk overlay system should be considered. In a disk overlay system the software system is designed in a modular form with each software module operationally linked to other modules as necessary.

A central memory resident control program controls all software module run times based on scheduled time, interruption or abnormal conditions. The module size would be dictated by the allowable memory space and the number of modules to be placed in memory at any given time. This is necessary since the software modules will be placed in memory overlay areas during the assigned run time of the module.

Each application, task or function would be divided into modules, linked as necessary, to complete the assigned tasks. These modules would be stored on disk units, and called in by the control program. The number of overlay areas in memory assigned for module storage is important because the number of machine operations being performed concurrently would be based on the demands of the programs placed in memory. The prime concern is that of utilizing every microsecond of available machine run time. This can be accomplished by running several programs concurrently.

MODULAR SOFTWARE

A modular designed programming system provides many benefits. This would include the following:

- It provides a means of easily assembling programming packages or systems.
- Complete or minor programming revisions are easily accomplished.
- Memory/disk overlay systems can be implemented.
- Multiprogramming and multiprocessing functions can be accomplished. This allows complete utilization of total machine cycle time.
- Variable application functions are easily performed.

The prime consideration for modular software is a system that will provide: (1) expandability, (2) flexibility, (3) variable application capability, and (4) sound operational capability. This can only be accomplished within a modular hardware and software designed system.

UPGRADING AN EXISTING SYSTEM

Operational computer systems continually go through evolutionary and normal growth changes. The usual changes occur in the devices connected to the mainframe. Additional devices are incorporated into the system or new more efficient devices replace the older devices. As time passes and these minor changes continue to occur, the system reaches a saturation point. When this happens, major hardware and software changes are usually contemplated. This major system enhancement normally will follow one of two directions. One direction would be the addition of mainframe, memory, and device equipment, which would be connected to or integrated into the existing hardware. The second course of action is the installation of a totally new modular system, either replacing the existing system, or to be used in conjunction with the existing system.

Some existing computer systems are easy and relatively inexpensive to expand, while others are very difficult and expensive to expand. If the existing hardware and software are structured in a modular manner, allowing addition of components by hardware cabling and/or software linkage facilities, the system may be easily expanded. On the other hand, if the expansion must be accomplished through hardware redesign or electrical rewiring, and a total reproduction of the software package is necessary, the system may be difficult to expand.

Eventually, a point will be reached where expansion of a nonmodular hardware and software system will prove to be uneconomical and operationally inefficient. This same condition could also result where a small modular system is in use.

The initial cost of total modular hardware/software replacement of the existing obsolete system may exceed the cost of expanding the existing system, but the long-term operational efficiency and future expansion requirements should be considered. Continuous system enhancements, modifications and expansions are a normal happening within most companies. It is during these future changes where the initial system replacement costs will be returned, along with the continuous return through a more efficiently operating system.

Chapter Twelve provides a brief overview of the important areas to consider when installing a totally new system. These same considerations could be applied to system enhancements of an existing system where: (1) significant software changes are made, (2) mainframe equipment will be installed, (3) components or devices are being added or replaced, (4) change out or addition of communications equipment, e.g., multiplexer MODEMS, lines, etc., is being accomplished. In addition, software changes required when additional mainframe and memory are being installed will normally create the most problems. It is this area where the prime emphasis on system configuration should be placed. Software testing to confirm the system operation, following installation of additional equipment, will confirm both the software and hardware operation. To aid in the isolation of failures, the software should provide a means of pinpointing the reason for failures.

Most hardware and/or software manufacturers provide isolation routines to aid in debugging the system. The software should automatically accomplish the isolation, with minor manual analysis required.

System testing before placing the upgraded system on-line ensures that complete acceptance tests are performed to confirm that the system operates according to specifications. It is sometimes possible to operate a portion of the system while testing new additions.

When communication lines and terminals are added to the system through the addition of line multiplexers, testing must be accomplished with the terminals in addition to central software and hardware testing. This terminal testing should be performed in such a manner as to ensure all individual terminal functions operate satisfactorily, and that the system will not fail while operating in a saturated or overloaded condition. This requires all terminals to be operated concurrently, in the same manner, as may occur under live conditions. Regulation of inputs and outputs should be accomplished automatically to avoid system failure.

CHAPTER FOUR

Distributed Processing Network Structure

The challenge of meeting computer networking and distributed processing needs can be achieved by applying data communications technology. Data communications planners are adopting various distributed data processing methodologies for their networks. They are using data bases designed for distributed processing in an effort to give users sufficient control and keep communications costs down.

In the 80s, distributed processing will replace centralized processing systems. Distributed processing is not a simple extension of data processing. The difficult part of distributed processing is not the "processing," but "distribution" of data. Distribution means planning, developing and installing a complex but sophisticated data communications network to support geographically dispersed terminals and computer systems that make up a distributed processing network. Configuring a network structure and implementing line protocols for distributed processing is not a straightforward simple matter.

Distributed processing is not for everyone. Before a decision is made to implement it, four major questions should be carefully considered: (1) Will it significantly speed up and improve the quality of data for management decisions? (2) Will it improve response and user satisfaction? (3) Will it reduce communications cost? and (4) Can ADP management and system problems be lessened by delegating more decision-making to subordinate areas? If these questions can be answered in the affirmative, then it would be profitable for the firm to develop and install a distributed processing network.

Distributed processing offers great opportunities for improving management information systems. However, there are many variables that the planner must contend with. Some of those are the type of equipment for each location, operational support, data communications requirements, network integrity and capability, network ownership or lease, maintenance and system controls. Without careful study, plans and controls, "going distributed" may be overcome by a myriad of problems and pitfalls.

This chapter will discuss some of those problems, and suggest certain concepts of network planning and network configuration that will aid analysts in developing and installing a successful distributed processing network. Part of the network structure may require linking the network to a satellite system. Propagation is a problem in adapting the satellite to ground data communications networks. But this problem is gradually being eliminated. Users may structure part or all of their distributed processing requirements around a common carrier's value added services or network (VAN). A broad variety of VAN services is available from the common carriers and computer service firms. Users wishing to take advantage of these services will have to do careful planning and network rethinking.

MAJOR ADVANTAGE OF DISTRIBUTED PROCESSING

Distributed processing involves two or more computers, each matched to the processing, functional and organizational requirements of the network, which are separated geographically. There are a number of ways that a distributed processing network can be configured in a data communications environment. The most frequently configured networks are: (1) Hierarchical, (2) Star, (3) Ring, and (4) Multistar. They are depicted in Figures 4-1, 4-2, 4-3, and 4-4, respectively. Figure 4-5 depicts a more detailed multistar structure with semidependent remote processors linked to each other with a host to provide monitoring and some controls for the network. The hierarchical network is the most common and the multistar is the most complex.

The major advantages of distributed processing are:

- Reduction in data communications costs,
- Greater user access to the network resources,
- Improved throughput and response time,
- More availability and reliability through available access to alternate nodes of the network.

The network is determined by the data processing requirements, data flow and distribution. In determining the structure, the advantages and disadvantages, and cost of each configuration should be carefully evaluated. When the network structure is determined, the communications requirements (lines, MODEMS, tech control) and their connectivity must be defined.

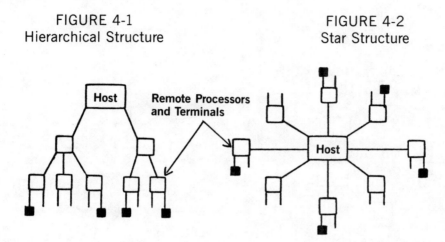

FIGURE 4-1
Hierarchical Structure

FIGURE 4-2
Star Structure

FIGURE 4-1: Remote processors of the Hierarchical Structure are dependent on the host for supervision and network control. If the host fails, the network is down. The advantages are: (1) Software overhead less expensive, (2) Data flow more controllable - data move up and down, (3) Processing more functionally distributed—less complex. The disadvantages are: (1) Contention for host service, (2) No ready backup or alternate service should host fail.

FIGURE 4-2: Remote processors are semidependent on the host processor for supervision and network control for normal operations. One or more remote processors may be designated as network backup when host failure occurs. The advantages of the Star Structure are: (1) Ease of control, (2) Simple data flow, (3) Backup for host. Disadvantages are: (1) Increase in overhead software, (2) Increase in communications protocol/traffic for backup, (3) Duplication of software/processing.

One of the major problems of line and component connectivity is data-code and communications protocol compatibility, and the equipment's electrical interfacing requirements. In a hierarchical structure, with a general purpose mainframe acting as host, and minicomputers as remote processing nodes, code conversion is best handled by a host computer front-end processor (FEP) to perform bidirectional code conversions. The FEP's performance efficiency (its full use) is improved if various line types, with protocol differences, have to be handled. The FEP can perform other communications and network functions in order to take advantage of its full potential. The FEP can serve as backup for the host, or a myriad of other functions (See Chapter Three).

The handling of different protocols is a major problem area that the planners must consider in the network structure. Protocol is the bidirectional electrical interface of the line to a component, a component to the computer. The protocol procedures are involved in framing bits or characters, error control, numbering of messages, transparency control, line control, timing control, start-up control and the resolution of special conflicts and other transmission/communications problems.

FIGURE 4-3
Ring Structure

FIGURE 4-4
Multistar Structure

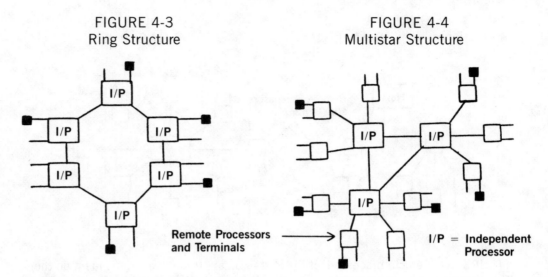

Remote Processors
and Terminals

I/P = Independent
Processor

FIGURE 4-3: In the Ring Structure the remote processors may share similar software but operate independently of each other. They can back up each other in case of failure. The advantages of the Ring Structure are: (1) Alternate switching is available, (2) Load Sharing, (3) Backup and redundancy. The disadvantages are: (1) Software overhead and redundancy, (2) Duplicate configurations, (3) Supervision and control can be difficult.

FIGURE 4-4: The Multistar Structure is the most complex and difficult to configure. It may be defined as a combination of the Star and Ring configuration. The Multistar Structure can provide a high degree of flexibility to a wide range of allocations. The advantages of the Multistar are: (1) Variable and redundant processing, (2) Flexible controls and switching capability, (3) Adaptable and open-ended in application, (4) Independent local processing. Disadvantages are: (1) Complex software supervisory controls, (2) Difficult network management, (3) Expensive communications components and protocols, (4) Contention among processor for communications and switching services, (5) Duplication.

It is best to minimize the protocol and code conversion points of the network to a limited number of nodal points, or to a single nodal processor. This can be accomplished by using a special purpose mini- or microcomputer to make the conversions. Also, if one or two computers in a network do not support the protocol of the majority's protocol, then a single processor would be best suited for protocol and code conversion.

The major problems that exist in distributed processing network design involve access, control, conversion, linkage, and data integrity among the various nodes. One of the major cost factors for a distributed processing network is software development. Appropriate software must be installed and maintained for the different processing needs throughout the network.

Distributed networks are still configured in the classical centralized configuration. Data processing, data base management, and resources are centrally located.

FIGURE 4-5
Distributing Data Processing with Switching Capability

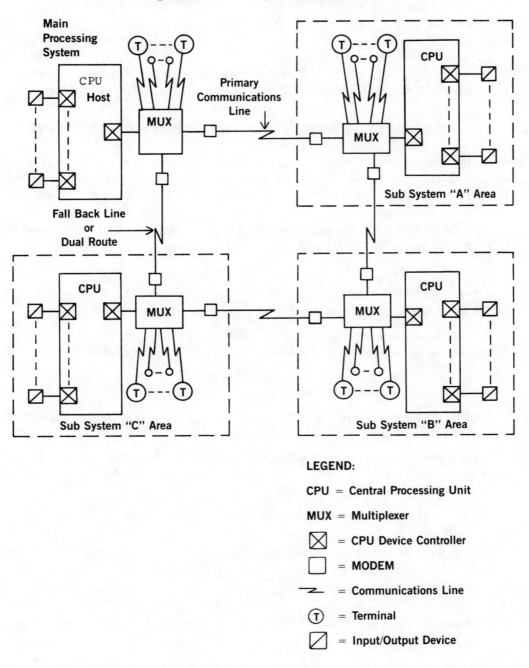

LEGEND:

CPU = Central Processing Unit

MUX = Multiplexer

⊠ = CPU Device Controller

☐ = MODEM

⤳ = Communications Line

Ⓣ = Terminal

⬔ = Input/Output Device

FIGURE 4-5: depicts a more detailed multistar structure, with semi-dependent remote processors linked to the host and each other. The host incorporates network monitoring and system controls. Each distributed processing center maintains the records and the files for the respective geographic location. Communications between subsystems and/or the host system is monitored and controlled by the main system.

The central site is accessed from remote terminals through data communications lines and facilities. In the 70s, centralization was universal practice. Problems with logistics and remote user satisfaction arise when multiple large-scale systems are centrally installed to perform all processing for the network. When a large number of terminals are connected to a central site, data communications problems arise from line problems, decrease in throughput, and contention for data base access.

PRINCIPAL FUNCTIONS OF DISTRIBUTED PROCESSING

Hardware architecture, communications facilities, and software technologies will support sophisticated distributed processing networks. The primary functions of distributed processing are: information processing, data base processing, and communications processing.

Information processing function: The data acquisition and manipulation of information to produce desired results. This includes:

- Assembly and compilation of user's data and application programs.
- Scheduling, executing, and controlling application programs.
- Production of output products in user specified media and format.

Data base processing function: To store large amounts of information for access by the network nodes and its terminal users. This includes:

- Creation and management of data bases.
- Providing access to the data bases.
- Providing data base integrity (accuracy, restart/recovery, and data protection and security).

Data communications processing function: To transmit data (both information and control data) and ensure its protection among nodal locations within the network. This includes:

- Control of communications (protocol) interface between terminal devices and the network.
- Control of communications interface between the node processors, central site or data base processor(s), and other network facilities.
- Control information and data movement between terminals and the central or data base processor(s), and between terminals and node processors, and between the central site or data base processor(s), or any terminals or nodes in the network.

DISTRIBUTED DATA BASES FOR DISTRIBUTED NETWORKS

Dispersing computers and interconnecting them puts processing power where it is most useful. The dispersed computers can access each other's data files and programs, submit reports to corporate headquarters and other sites, perform remote diagnostics, back each other up when failures occur, shift overloads to other sites, and forward computations to the central computer that are too complex for a local site to handle.

Different approaches may be used to distribute individual files or data bases in decentralized data communications networks. A common data base may be (1) accessed by all processors in the network; (2) each processor may be sent a copy of the common data base; or (3) each processor may be sent a subset of the data base for its assigned application. Of the three methods, the most effective way to structure data in a "ring" network is, for most applications, the distribution of data base subsets, so that each node operates only on its own data. This is usually more cost-effective because to have a copy of the centralized data base at each node requires a large amount of computing resources.

Placing distributed processing functions at remote areas is, for the most part, necessitated to offset cost, enhance network control, and to satisfy local ADP applications. The central site has sometimes been completely removed from processing functions that are best performed at remote sites. This is based on two principle facts: different computers are good at different kinds of jobs and communications costs can be more effectively controlled by placing DP resources where the source data and users are.

Distributed processing divides and disperses data processing functions so the network can be more efficiently managed. Data processing solutions can be tailored to the various objectives and problems of configuring and managing the network. At times, strong overall centralized management and control is necessary to ensure compatibility of remote computing facilities, standardization of distributed software and data for network integrity, and to hold cost down. Data communications solutions must be centrally managed to effectively tie together the distributed data processing components as well as to accommodate future growth.

CENTRALIZED VS. DISTRIBUTED DATA BASES

The primary disadvantage of a centralized data base(s) is that increased terminal usage will lead to a conflict because the three functions (information processing, data base, and data communications) compete for access to the data base and processor time. In such a network configuration, user dissatisfaction will eventually force management to disperse the appropriate data base(s) to provide adequate ADP resources to remote functional users.

Centralizing the data processing activities and the data base of the central site is not without its problems; especially in a company with (1) decentralized operations, (2) profit center accountability, and (3) workload distribution responsibilities. In such cases, centralized DP may be wrong for the organizational structure. Some of the problems may be:

- Remote users have little or no control over costs, but DP services are charged to their budget.
- There may be a poor response from the heavily utilized central site.

- Remote users may perceive a lack of rapport and understanding from the centralized DP staff and get a negative feeling from the slow response to their requests for DP support.
- Remote users may prefer their own control over the DP resources they are using.
- The centralized DP staff may be having difficulty managing the network involving several nodes.

A distributed data base is defined as a shared data resource whose components have been appropriately divided to enhance nodal access and control while at the same time providing integrated application support. Some advantages of distributed processing are:

- Lower communications costs,
- Faster response by making available local data bases,
- More flexibility and adaptability of designing data bases for local requirements,
- Improved networks and nodal processing because of the successive backup characteristic of distributed systems,
- Increased user satisfaction for the system's success because users identify more with the local ADP resources,
- Increased sharing of resources and integrity through standardization of data communications interfaces between data base partitions.

Distributing data bases does not imply a lack of central coordination among the data base user's partitions. To effectively integrate or design the partitions, there must be an overall company plan and data base management authority. When data and software must be distributed from a centralized data base to a number of nodes for processing, communications support can be a major cost factor.

There are three major caveats that should guide planners in data base distribution efforts:

- Individual node requests: The vast majority of data base requests that originate at a node should be able to be satisfied by the data base partition at the local node.
- Clustering: Common data items that are usually requested together should be available in the same partition of the local data base.
- Data base integrity: If data are duplicated across data base partitions among the nodes, then updates of those partitions must be considered to satisfy the user's need for data integrity and data base consistency.

These three caveats, for the most part, can be satisfied by locating the data base where the users are. Data base design and user requirements dictate the need for balancing communications costs and the need for data base consistency. Controlling data base duplication and consistency can be a problem with respect to updating.

How do you access or find data items once the data is distributed? Two examples are given. You can build the data item's node location into its access key or logical address; or you can maintain at each node a directory that maps data items to node location. An advantage of a directory look-up method is that locating of data items is directory driven. The finding of data items, to include programs, data entities, etc., is locally directory-managed rather than by a data base management system (DBMS) which must communicate across nodes to find data items. A directory-managed look-up system facilitates the interfacing of dissimilar DBMS. Designing distributed data bases and DBMS can be a complex matter for distributed processing systems. Prior to undertaking such a task for a data communications network, analysts should study several successful and familiar systems, compare requirements and characteristics of data allocation and directory management, query and update operations and data base administration.

COST CONSIDERATIONS FOR DISTRIBUTED DATA BASES

For cost consideration in the design, operation, and maintenance of distributed data bases, the analysts should consider the following major areas of expense for:

- Hardware and network communications cost to support distributed data bases
- Software development and maintaining cost for:
- Data base design for distribution
- Data sharing/allocation
- Update problems
- Communications protocols
- Directory building and management
- Memory management
- Scheduling resources
- Data security and recovery
- Accessing, maintaining and managing the distributed data base
- General housekeeping function
- Storage cost for application software and data for access and data base manipulation

As distributed data bases assume a greater role in distributed processing, their success will depend largely on the user's abilities to integrate them into data communications networks.

SATELLITE DATA COMMUNICATIONS CONCEPTS

Since the first message was transmitted to and from a satellite in 1958 by President Eisenhower, the satellite has progressed from the experimental stage to a highly reliable and economical medium for data communications and distributed processing. Unlike landlines (wire and cable), satellite transmission costs do not increase with distance. This, coupled with other unique features of satellite communications, offers attractive cost-effective services for a diverse group of users. Any form or type of communications, television, radio, telephone, facsimile, telegraph and digital data can be sent to and received from any point on the globe at the speed of light (186,000 miles per second) via satellite. All of these types of communications meet or exceed international standards of quality. Long distance communication by satellite is more effective than ground-to-ground radio because it has better quality and can handle a wider range of microwave radio frequencies.

The demand for satellite services is in the forefront of data communications networks. Satellites are ideal for connecting many sites located in the coverage area of the satellite's communications range. This allows for small, relatively inexpensive earth stations to economically transmit digital data as well as voice. The major advantage of the satellite is that it replaces the line-of-sight (LOS) or ground cable/wire signal repeaters. This usually results in better service at a lower cost. Microwave signals are subject to degradation because of atmospheric conditions for up to a height of approximately 30 miles. After the signal passes through this distance, it will be essentially free of atmospheric interference for the rest of its journey of approximately 22,300 miles.

Satellite circuits permit fewer signal fade outs and "line hits" than do long distance terrestrial (landline) circuits. Since landline circuits are more susceptible to background noise, noise interference increases with distance, while satellite circuits are relatively error-free. In most cases, it is less costly to use satellite circuits for both data and voice transmission.

Data transmission by satellite is almost indistinguishable from that of terrestrial circuits and the same type of MODEM may be used. In some cases compensation can be made for time delays in the interface protocol by selecting the MODEM's tuning-strap options. Aside from this, almost all long-line voice grade data MODEMs up to 9.6KB will operate normally on satellite circuits.

How to Handle Propagation Delays

As was alluded to before, transmission delay is the one major difference between satellite and terrestrial communications. In order for the satellite to remain in one area over the earth, its orbit must be synchronized with that of the earth's revolution. To accomplish this, the satellite must be placed in orbit approximately 22,300 miles over the equator. Because of this far distance, there is a one-way propagation delay of about 300 milliseconds, or approximately 600 milliseconds to get a signal to the satellite and back. The increase in response time has a corresponding decrease in throughput. The delay can be minimized by utilizing IBM's synchronous data link control (SDLC). Some network protocol control procedures are designed to minimize long delays. IBM's SDLC gives both efficient channel utilization and response time fast enough for the use of interactive terminals in a distributed processing network. This signal delay and line turnaround problem is discussed further in Chapter Seven.

On the other hand, other types of protocols that use the automatic repeat request (ARQ), such as IBM's binary synchronous communications (BSC), decrease throughput. With the best of results, an earth station transmitting over a satellite circuit and using BSC must wait approximately 600 milliseconds before it receives an acknowledgment (ACK). Using the ARQ and BSC protocol, a station must have buffers large enough to hold several data blocks which are awaiting ACKs while the station operator continues to transmit messages. Throughput can be increased in the stop-and-wait ARQ protocol mode over satellite channels by modifying software to optimize the block size to accommodate the channel data bit rate and the bit error rate.

Another method of increasing throughput over satellite channels is by using a continuous ARQ technique. This method allows the terminal to continue to transmit data (blocks) without waiting for an ACK after each block. This process allows the transmitting terminal to examine the ACKs while blocks are being transmitted in a continuous stream. When the terminal fails to receive a positive ACK, it determines, through an algorithm, which block was erroneous. Blocks are then binary numbered, and the ACK will contain the number of the ACKed block.

Another method of controlling block acknowledgments is by recovering the errored block in question and retransmitting that block. This may be referred to as the backup or pull-back scheme and is a characteristic of the high-level data link control (HDLC) protocol. The selective repeat ARQ is more efficient because it only retransmits the block in error without any subsequent error-free block on that data stream. This is a very efficient method for transmitting data over high bit-rate circuits which have low bit error rates.

THE FUNCTIONS AND CHARACTERISTICS OF SATELLITE COMMUNICATIONS

Satellite operation can be viewed in much the same manner as microwave radio; both are very efficient methods for transferring information over long distances. Satellites eliminate one of the major problems of microwave transmission—the requirement of terrestrial line-of-sight between microwave relay towers.

There are basically two types of satellite operation in relation to the earth's rotation. One may be referred to as a random or asynchronous satellite and the other a synchronous satellite. The asynchronous satellite is not stationary and orbits the earth. It does not maintain a stationary location over a particular area of the earth, as the synchronous satellite does. This requires relay transceiver earth or ground stations to be located at various points under the satellite orbit. If loss of sight between the satellite and the ground station should occur, data storage capability for nontransmitting and receiving periods would be required.

A synchronous satellite solves the line-of-sight requirement when only a particular area of the earth, i.e., the United States, is the area requiring communications coverage. The satellite is positioned above the earth approximately 22,300 miles, and is set in a synchronous orbit with the earth's rotation while maintaining a set position. This provides for a direct link from east to west coast and other areas in between. Transmitting signals between a satellite and ground stations is by line-of-sight microwave transmission.

In order to transmit and receive messages from a satellite, sending and receiving ground stations must point their antennas directly at the satellite. Figure 4-6 identifies components of the COMSATs INTELSAT IV. Two types of satellite orbit systems are used: asynchronous or random system and synchronous orbit system. In a random orbit system, several satellites are placed in different orbits around the north and south poles, as well as the equator.

A ground station will beam its antenna directly at a given satellite and track it across the sky. As the earth revolves and the satellite drops below the horizon, the line-of-sight is broken and communication between the ground stations and the satellite is terminated. When the satellite drops below the horizon, the ground station may rehome its antenna to another satellite and follow it while it is above the horizon; and when this one disappears, the ground station may switch again to another satellite.

Modern satellite technology now uses synchronous orbits which are by far the most effective system. In this system, satellites are launched in an equatorial orbit to an altitude of approximately 22,300 miles and are positioned over a preselected area of the earth for maximum communication benefit. This orbit synchronizes the motion and fixes the satellite with the rotation of the earth. As the satellite completes one orbit, the earth makes one revolution. From 22,300 miles, one satellite can "window" one third of the earth's surface. Three can blanket the globe. Narrow-beam antennas on the satellite can spotlight a smaller area of the earth for regional two-way communications. This permits more effective use of satellite capacity as communications demands change due to the various time zones.

The characteristics and functions of the antenna are the key to earth/space communications. The satellite antennas can be focused on a preselected area of the earth's surface. The antenna/satellite can communicate with many earth stations that are located within the preselected area. The signals are amplified by the satellite's transponders (repeaters) and retransmitted back to ground stations. Spot-beam antennas are steerable to permit the concentration of signal power on smaller selected areas of the earth to meet heavy traffic requirements of a given area.

To keep the satellite from nodding (nutating) as it spins in space, two nutation dampers are attached to the central antenna mast. To keep its antenna pointing toward the preselected area on the earth while the satellite's main body spins, the entire communications system, including transponders and antennas, is automatically "despun" (or counter-rotated) at precisely the same rate as that of the satellite's main body. The rate of spin may be controlled and resynchronized by ground command. Another method of keeping satellites properly oriented in space and keeping their antennas aimed at the preselected area on earth, is the use of tiny engines on board the satellite. These engines produce a small thrust to steer the satellite as required.

Communications satellites were engineered to serve various ground stations. They provide global communication links to all points on the earth regardless of topography, climatic, or economic conditions of that "window" of the earth— providing there is a receiving antenna. They can serve ground terminals far better than fixed ground relay stations. Ground terminal and large communication

FIGURE 4-6

INTELSAT IV
INTERNATIONAL PARTICIPATION

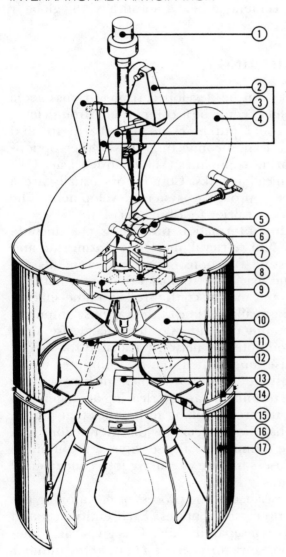

LEGEND:
 1—Telemetry and Command Antennas
 2—Nutation Damper
 3—Earth Coverage—Transmit and Receive
　　Antennas
 4—Spot Beam Communication Antennas
 5—Telemetry Horn
 6—Repeater
 7—Telemetry and Command Equipment
 8—TWT Power Supply Converters
　　For Drivers
 9—Antenna Positioning Electronics
10—Positioning and Orientation Subsystem
11—Battery Controller and Relay
12—Solenoid and Squib Drivers
13—Despin Control Electronics
14—Sun Sensor
15—Battery Pack
16—Structure and Harness
17—Solar Cells

Source: Comsat Information Office,
Communications Satellite Corporation,
950 L'Enfant Plaza South, S.W.,
Washington, D.C.

centers originate and transmit messages to a satellite and receive messages that have originated in other regions of the world. Ground switching and distribution systems complete the ubiquitous communications chain by routing and distributing messages to and from various users.

Satellites, in addition to the other types of information they transport, can handle large amounts of digital data on a domestic or global scale. This is made possible through wide band or broad band channels and the exchange of high-speed data among remote computer centers either domestically or globally connected.

TIME SHARING

The distributed processing networks can be developed from various media available to the user. The system development could be accomplished through lease or purchase arrangements. The user could purchase the total hardware and software required and lease the communication connecting lines. Other options could include consideration of time-sharing companies (Value Added Data Carriers) for both processing and communication links. Cost factors usually are a major factor in determining the proper approach to system development. The various media available should be researched prior to a final decision.

A distributed processing network for information processing may include message/data collection, message storage and retrieval, message transmission and distribution, and a host of other processing functions. These requirements are based upon a user's information needs and may vary from user to user, or network to network. A distributed processing network may be configured as a time-sharing network of computers that permits sharing available time of the various computers or the transmission line of the network among computers or terminals. Also, time sharing makes processing time of the computer or network available for two or more different applications. The response time is such that the computer seems dedicated to each user. This is made possible by software which intersperses the actions of a user, a computer, or a remote terminal in an interleaving arrangement. Interleaving is made possible through multiprogramming techniques that permit the sequencing of actions or events so that they alternate with other actions and events of a user, a computer, or a remote terminal for the services of a computer, device, or communications line. Several users may be executing jobs concurrently under a multiprogramming environment.

For simplicity, time sharing can be described as the process of partitioning the memory of a large CPU into separate processing entities. Each entity acts and performs (as far as the user is concerned) as a separate CPU. This gives each time-sharing user his own portion (CPU) of core storage. There is a limit to the number of remote terminals that can be used in a time-sharing capacity with each user having his own private area of memory. The availability and size of memory and the requirements of the user are the limiting factors.

With modern concepts, many time-sharing computers use a technique that is called virtual memory. Virtual memory may be a combination of software and hardware techniques that extend core memory to a storage device beyond the physical boundary of core memory. This combination of software and hardware uses a device that has a fast data transfer rate. Throughput and response is so fast that the remote user will not notice a delay in his job processing.

The time-sharing system concept is basically that of providing remote access and data processing capability to unrelated system users. Individual user programs are loaded into common data processing computers and then are called up by the assigned user as required.

A national time-sharing system can provide the capability for a number of geographically separated users to access a common data base or program. This is accomplished via communication lines to one common time-share computer, or through the use of several geographically located time-share computers, with data base transfer functions from one computer to another. The final destination could be the user's private in-house computer.

Primarily, time-sharing companies or value added carriers permit access, via a network matrix, to a common computer system file enabling users to share various programs and data.

The services of time-sharing companies may vary in network capability, the number of geographic computer locations, communications capability, and the types of processing services offered, but generally the following services are available:

- They allow access to programs on a national basis. The programs may be provided by the user, the time-sharing company, or a software development firm.

- They allow the operation of multilevel management information systems. Data exchanges could occur between remote computer systems and a central system. The hardware and software utilized could be a combination of user and vendor owned.

- They coordinate and assist in the development and maintenance of programs for various users. These programs may be made available with a large number of users on the network or limited to local computer sites.

- They allow access to data bases, private or public. The accesses may be brief, i.e., a question or answer, or a major report, or may require the use of a large computer for special tasks, including program debug.

- They provide communications capability for both conversational data transfer modes.

VALUE ADDED SERVICE/NETWORKS

Users of communications services are finding themselves confronted with the decision of whether to own the basic communication facilities/components, e.g., MODEM, multiplexer, etc., or whether to let computer service firms or common carriers provide total end-to-end communications services as Value Added Network (VAN) services. A typical user of VAN communication services may choose a vendor primarily to provide total or partial VAN services at a reasonable cost for certain communications hardware cost and other network services in areas where his own system does not reach. Modern VAN services are reliable and economical. Increased competition will reduce costs and improve performance of VAN services. Critical planning is a must when contemplating VAN services because the temptation may be to subscribe to unnecessary services that can lead to an increase in cost without a corresponding increase in performance. VAN services are not for everyone.

The VAN services that are available to data communications users range from total transmission services to sophisticated and complex services to distributed data base inquiry services.

The function and services of VANs may be technically implemented by a user or by a common carrier. When they are provided by a carrier and tariffed by the FCC, they become value added "services" by definition. Five major VAN services may be classified as (1) data/text/inquiry, (2) image service, (3) support services, (4) electronic mail services, and (5) time-sharing services.

Data/test/inquiry services: These services are offered in transmission modes of (1) packet switching, (2) circuit switching, (3) store and forward, and (4) polling. All of these transmission modes have been around for quite some time, and may serve different needs for the same user in a data communications network.

Packet switching was perfected in the late 60s and early 70s and was the first to be offered under the VAN services. Packet switching is very reliable for digital transmission and requires a certain amount of software overhead, but is not fully perfected for voice transmission.

Circuit switching, on the other hand, requires little, if any, computation or software overhead once the circuit is set up. Circuit switching permits higher transmission speed than packet switching and is suitable for voice communications.

Store and forward and polling are suitable for users who do not have a need for immediate response, throughput, or turnaround requirement. The major advantage of these VAN services is they permit a large number of remote users who have message switching, credit checking, airline ticketing/reservations, etc. requirements to take advantage of these low cost VAN services.

Image service: This service enables the digitizing and transmission of graphs, drawings, photographs. It is facsimile compatible and can function in the store and forward mode.

Support services: This service is available to planners who wish to design data communications systems. This service is a growing requirement because:

- Until VAN services were available, users usually dealt with one common carrier (AT&T) for end-to-end communications services, but now may deal with many carriers.

- Services and network structures are becoming more sophisticated and complex as more and more users have requirements for data/text/inquiry, message switching, image service and voice combined into one network.

- With the increasing growth in data communications and with users becoming more and more dependent upon their networks for total communications service, the short periods of network or service failure are intolerable.

- Maintenance service such as fault isolation and diagnosis are extremely important both in user owned or VAN leased systems.

- Network designs and training of operations personnel and communications facilities management, as well as data processing facilities management, are offered by VAN vendors.

Electronic mail service: This service is designed to bypass the mail system. It involves the preparation, transmission, and distribution to the addressees/readers of normal corporate correspondence via electrical and automated means.

Time-sharing service: This service may include remote batch processing to remote on-line interactive time-sharing systems. See previous topic on time sharing.

PACKET SWITCHING CONCEPTS

Packet switching differs from message switching in that in message switching no data is transmitted over the line until the entire message has been received in the message switch. This means that the first message to be completely received is the first one to go out. Messages are not equal in length or size. The first message that may be completely received may not be the first one that was starting to be received by the switch. A short message may start coming in after a long message has started and be completely received before the long message is fully received. In this case, the short message would be transmitted out ahead of the long message even though much of the long message is received and in storage at the switch awaiting the "end of message" receive signal before it may be transmitted from the switch.

Packet switching partially alleviates the delay problem of message switching because long messages are partitioned into packet segments and queued for transmission. This way, transmission begins before the total message has been received and stored at the first packet switching node.

The term packet switching normally implies the movement of fixed length blocks of data from point to point via a switching system matrix. Figure 4-7 illustrates a typical packet switching system matrix utilizing intermediate switching computers. Packet switching could be considered a distributed processing medium shared by unrelated users. The system is normally designed for the movement of large volumes of data. The user provides the data processing system at each user location and is a subscriber of the packet switching interlinking computer network. The user's data is sent to a packet switching computer over a local access line. At the switching computer, the data is organized into packets of from one to a given number of characters, depending on the customer's application. Packets received at the switching computer from many customers are merged into a high-speed data stream and passed to the network line, where each line is connected to two or more switching computers.

Depending on the address of the destination switching computer in the packet header, a packet will be routed to or through one or more network, switching computers until it arrives at the final destination. The destination switching center (SC) will then pass the packet to the addressee by another local access line.

FIGURE 4-7
Packet Switching Network

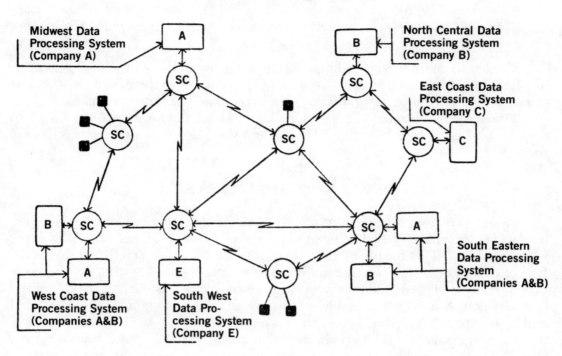

LEGEND: SC = Switching Computers
        A, B, C, ■ = System Users
                     = Communications Line Structure

FIGURE 4-7: depicts a packet switching network configured on a geographical scale which permits unrelated users to share the resources of the network.

Merging individual customer packets into packet streams means lower hardware communications cost and high utilization of the lines and switching equipment, while carrying larger traffic volumes. This results in lower cost for the network users.

During transmission, within the packet switch system, the data are divided into blocks framed by control and header characters and error controls bits. In this manner, the transferred data are protected against distortion and possible loss. Each data block being transferred is retained at each switching computer until a positive acknowledgment is received from the next two switching computers receiving the data block. In addition, each switching computer has an alternate route to each of the other switching computers, allowing continuous service when equipment or a connecting line fails.

This system could be used in the same manner as the distributed data processing system network and in addition, provide a data switching matrix. The packet switching system requirements can be handled in three basic methods:

- Leased services from a common carrier
- Company owned processing and switching matrix
- Combination of leased and company owned equipment

The advantage of the packet switching matrix concept is that it provides flexibility of operation where distributed data processing, large volume data transfers, data storage, and data protection are system criteria.

CHAPTER FIVE

System Throughput and Data Flow Analysis

Data communications involves the movement of information from one geographic point to another over some type of communications channel (line). Systems efficiency and the method(s) utilized to move this information is dictated by the individual system or network design criteria. The actual throughput efficiency depends on the best selction of (1) hardware, (2) communications components, (3) transmission media, (4) software structure, and (5) network configuration. These network resources are interrelated and complex, making the selection and structure of a data communications network vital for effective throughput.

The primary emphasis of this chapter will stress basic system design features, data flow and queuing analysis, equipment considerations, and data protection that will affect the integrity and speed at which information moves from one place to another.

Each data communications system application may involve unique software structuring, and variable hardware and communications facilities, data processing and data flow throughput requirements. Many of these variables will be discussed in this chapter.

TRANSMISSION LINE MODES THAT AFFECT THROUGHPUT

There are basically three modes (directions of data movement) through which data are transmitted over a channel: simplex mode, half duplex mode, or full duplex mode. These transmission modes are illustrated in Figure 5-1. Data are transmitted between terminals or between a terminal and a computer in one of these modes. All of these modes affect throughput. The simplex mode is the transmission of data in one direction only, e.g., receive only. The half duplex mode permits data to move in both directions, but in only one direction at a time. The full duplex mode permits data movement in both directions at the same time. This subject is covered in greater detail in Chapter Seven.

FIGURE 5-1
Transmission Modes

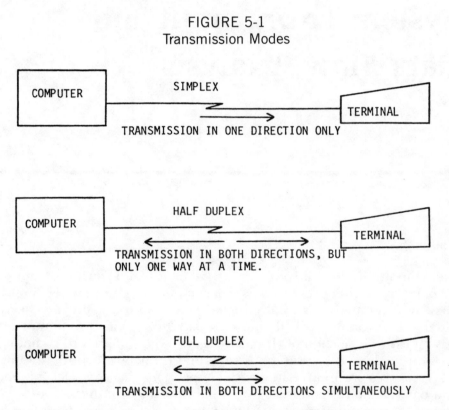

FIGURE 5-1: depicts the three transmission line modes that affect throughput. Simplex is read (receive) only printer. Half duplex is similar to a phone conversation; only one party can talk (send or receive) at a time. Full duplex permits both the computer and the terminal to transmit and receive at the same time.

Some terminals, such as those without memory, known as dumb terminals, transmit in only one direction at a time and do not provide control of the request-to-send signal to the MODEM. Such terminals require full duplex MODEMs even though the line is half duplex.

Other terminals may be configured as full duplex but do not operate in complete full duplex mode. A prime example would be where terminals are designed and configured to operate in an "echoplex" mode. In this type of operation, the computer echoes back to the sending terminal all characters transmitted from the terminal keyboard before they are displayed on a VDT screen or printed to page copy. This permits verification that data sent from the terminal was transmitted to the computer for further processing without error.

FEATURES AND CONSIDERATIONS THAT AFFECT THROUGHPUT

The system applications or functions that require data communication facilities and services may include, but are not limited to, the following:

- Message switching applications
- Data transaction processing
- Data acquisition and collection
- Remote batch processing
- Record update and/or inquiry response (data retrieval)
- Distributed processing
- Packet switching
- Analytical and control signals

Some of the basic system features for consideration in order to provide data communications support may include the following:

- Asynchronous or synchronous timing (sequence and protocols controls)
- Bit, character and/or word storage (buffers)
- Intermediate data storage buffers
- Data code or format conversion
- Data speed rate change flexibility
- Line and system protocol flexibility
- Terminal selection controls
- Data format design criteria
- Data editing features
- Data status control and detection
  - Header information
  - Ending information
  - Control symbol detection and information
  - Parity error detection and controls
  - Line failure detection and controls
  - Carrier failure detection and controls
  - Character overrun detection and controls
  - Time out controls and functions
  - Selection and data transmission retry controls
  - Idle line detection and controls
- Dial-up features
- Queuing functions

- Privacy and security functions
- Operational control functions
- System overload controls
- System failure and recovery functions
- Data retrieval features
- Data tracing features
- Data history files and functions
- Possible data compression features

Each data communications system application may involve unique and variable data processing and data flow requirements. Based on these variable factors, only the most common areas of data communication systems will be discussed.

Figure 5-2 provides an overview of the basic flow of data during input to and output from a message or data switching computer system. A data processing computer could function in much the same manner, but would, in addition, perform data processing functions. However, time consumed in handling communications functions by a data processing computer is time lost for data processing, and this type of system normally is not designed to efficiently handle the communications functions. This is the reason that data communications functions should be performed by a front-end or data switching processor. Because it is designed to handle data communications functions, the data processing computer is left free to handle data processing functions which it is designed to do. A review of the previous list of possible basic communication system features illustrates the many processes that could consume a major portion of the data processor's cycling time, while handling data communication functions.

The number and types of terminals connected to a system will have a major impact on system operation. When only a few terminals are connected to a communications system, the movement of data is normally not a problem. When the number of terminals is increased and/or higher data rates are utilized, the system could become operationally inefficient and continuously overloaded. This consideration is covered further in this chapter.

THROUGHPUT ANALYSIS

Data throughput is a measurement of a system's ability to handle input and output data at a specified rate. Let's assume a system has been designed to handle 10,000 characters a minute (input and output); then that system should have a throughput capability of approximately 10,000 characters per minute. Normally, throughput capability is based on normal operation and under prespecified conditions. Abnormal conditions and any changes applied to the system may have a negative impact on the throughput capability.

Certain software and hardware system design features or types of equipment utilized can aid or hinder system throughput capability. The following are some of the design features or equipment that will affect throughput:

FIGURE 5-2
Communications Data Flow

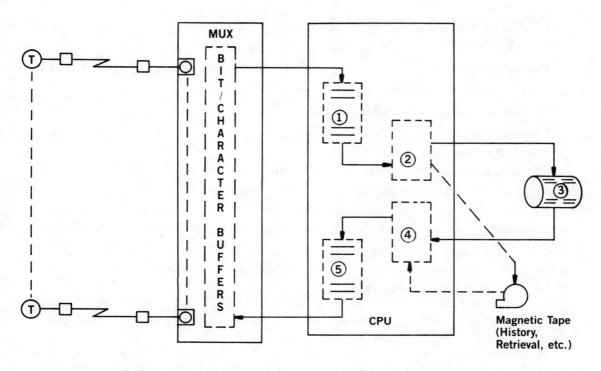

FIGURE 5-2: depicts the data flow from the terminals through the multiplexer and the processing steps as it moves through the Central Processing Unit and peripheral devices back through the multiplexer and to remote terminals.

LEGEND:

CPU = Central Processing Unit

MUX = Multiplexer (Contains bit or character buffers in addition to sequence controls)

⊡ = Line Interface Adapter

▢ = MODEM

⋜ = Communications Line

Ⓣ = Terminal

① = Buffers for Input Data

② = Input Message/Data Queuing, Editing, Processing, Housekeeping, Work Area, etc.

③ = Disk (Queuing, overload, etc.)

④ = Output Message/Data Processing Area

⑤ = Buffers for Output Data

- Types of terminals,
- Terminal bit per second rate and operation,
- Types of communication lines and MODEM capability,
- Communications protocol or handshaking functions,
- Computer line interface adapter and multiplexer,
- Computer mainframe design,
- Computer mainframe cycle speed,
- Computer device cycle speeds (disks, tapes, etc.),
- Computer memory cycle speed,
- Computer mainframe register, device and memory word sizes,
- Computer software design and overhead features,
- Line turnaround problem—this is reviewed in Chapter Seven. This problem illustrates how cycle time can be consumed within the various parts of a system.

In a communications computer, throughput may be expressed in terms of bandwidth. For example, the computer multiplexer may be designed to handle 1,000 characters per second (CPS) or possibly 10,000 bit per second (BPS). This bandwidth would dictate or restrict the number of lines that could be transmitting/receiving data to/from the computer at a given time.

A system with a 10,000 BPS bandwidth may be advertised as having the capability to connect 32 lines, with BPS rates up to 4,800 BPS. The user of this advertised system may connect a mixture of various speed lines, including several 4800 BPS, only to discover that the number of lines allowed to operate concurrently would be limited by the system. This is caused by the multiplexer and computer bandwidth limitation of 10,000 BPS. For instance, only four 2,400 BPS lines could be active concurrently, even if 32 lines were connected. Any of the other connected line services, in excess of the four active 2,400 BPS lines, must be locked out at that moment waiting for service time to become available.

The hardware of a system may allow a given number of line connections at various BPS rates, and then the software system would limit the number of concurrently active lines through terminal selection controls. This limitation will always be dictated by the total system BPS bandwidth capability. In addition, such variables as start of message (SOM), end of message (EOM), error control, symbol detection, and other communication housekeeping functions will reduce the operational bandwidth. The main point to remember is that the actual system throughput capability must be based on the allowable number of concurrently active lines, and not the number of lines that can be connected to the multiplexer.

RESPONSE TIME CONSIDERATIONS

Response time is an indication of a system's ability to accept data input from a terminal, interpret and process the data, and then respond with data output to the terminal, within a specified period of time.

FIGURE 5-3
Inquiry/Response Data Flow

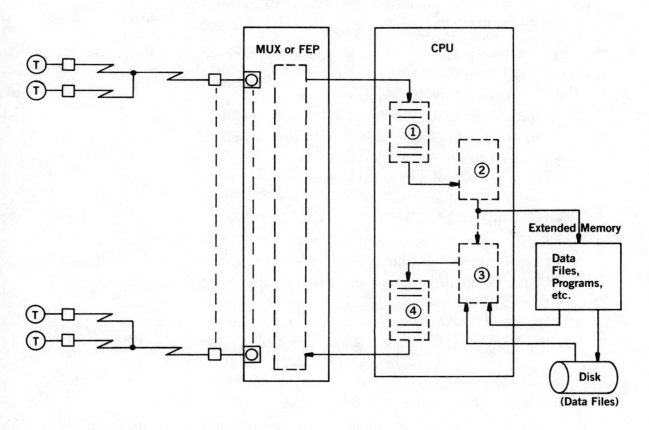

FIGURE 5-3: illustrates how communications functions, data buffering, queuing, and housekeeping functions could be accomplished in a front-end processor. Sorted and preprocessed data would be passed to the main Central Processing Unit.

Figure 5-3 is a brief overview of data flow through a system during an inquiry and response activity. The system could be configured with a front-end as a preprocessor and queuing medium, or a data processor utilizing a multiplexer. As pointed out earlier in this chapter, the front-end configuration will allow for a more efficient operation.

The following factors should be considered when designing a system for inquiry response applications:

- Bit per second rate of terminals and lines
- Type of communication lines—full duplex, half duplex, etc.
- The number of terminals that can be concurrently active
- Terminal selection procedures
- Line protocol and handshaking procedures
- The number of terminals per line
- Line contention factors
- Buffer and queuing techniques—memory or disk, by application types
- Memory access and priority schemes
- Communications hardware and software capability (possible front-end)
- Memory access speeds
- Front-end, multiplexer, mainframe and device cycle speeds
- Hardware characteristics, front-end, multiplexer, device interfaces
- Data processing software design
- Program overlays or storage—memory or disks
- Error handling routines—hardware and software

A major concern within an inquiry-response system is the terminal servicing contention problem. This contention problem can occur in many areas of the system, all resulting in operational inefficiency. One contention problem occurs when multiple terminals are connected to a single line without multiplexer capability. In this situation each terminal must contend with each other for a single line since only one terminal can transmit or receive at any given moment. Data can be intermixed on a single line, without multiplexer equipment, from several terminals concurrently, through the use of sequencing devices at clustered terminal configurations. Even in this situation, only one terminal will actually be operating at any given moment. However, concurrently intermixing data from several terminals will partially help solve the contention problem. Multiplexer equipment, not to be confused with the computer line multiplexer, would almost entirely solve the terminal line contention problem. Multiplexers would allow several terminals to operate concurrently on one line. The use of multiplexers on the line may require additional line connection at the computer multiplexer equipment. This additional line connection requirement is usually the reason multiple terminal connections on a line were initially considered, and this requirement may continue to inhibit the use of multiplexers. Refer to Chapter Ten for information concerning multiplexer equipment, and Chapter Seven for connection examples.

A second contention problem appears at the multiplexer of front-end. The system bandwidth (total BPS rate allowable) will limit the number of concurrently active terminals or lines.

A third contention problem occurs in the buffer area of the front-end and/or data processor. When the data storage buffer area is limited in size and becomes overloaded, the terminal selections for transmitting or receiving must be terminated until the buffer area becomes available. Increasing the data storage buffer areas will solve this problem.

The fourth contention problem occurs within the queuing structure of the front-end or data processor since each input and output must be queued for processing or delivery. As the queues build, each input or output must wait a longer period to be serviced. Hardware cycle speed and design, and software design will be the keys to this problem. Providing individual queues for each application, and then in turn dividing the individual queues into additional parts for multiple processing would also help relieve this problem.

Other contention problems become a part of the overall system design. This includes the media utilized for work area data buffers, data processing, program storage and housekeeping functions. When high-speed memory is utilized for all these major storage areas or processing functions, maximum processing speed can be attained. If slower storage media must be used, such as disk, then processing speed will be reduced.

Many times when inquiry/response systems are designed to provide a response within 3 to 5 seconds after receiving the inquiry, the operational end result, under medium to high system load factors, is a 60- to 90-second response time. The problem, as stated earlier, usually results from (1) too many terminals connected to each line, (2) inquiries being received at a rate greater than the data processor can process them within the time constraints, and (3) a limitation on the number of lines that can be concurrently active. The types and operating speeds of terminals, the types of communication lines, front-end equipment and design, and the data processor operation will all have a determining factor in what number of terminals, lines or inquiries will cause the system to overload. Of course, abnormal conditions will have a major impact on system operation and, in turn, will be a factor in determining when an overload condition will occur. If the condition of lines and terminals (i.e., expected unreliability) is not known, then possibly a 10 percent reduction in the overload level should be anticipated.

QUEUING ANALYSIS

A queue can be defined as an area where data is stored, along with control and tracing information, for future processing. Normally, a queue operates on the basis of first in first out (FIFO). However, when a priority queuing system is used, high priority data will be processed ahead of lower priority data. This will occur even though the lower priority data was in the queue before the higher priority data was received.

Several simulator programs are available that can provide system queuing factor analysis. These programs are designed to provide information concerning data queue conditions under various operational conditions and data rates. The input and output data characteristics, volume and average number of characters per transmission must be available in order to perform this simulation. If all the data activity factors are known, for simulation purposes, a manual analysis can also be performed.

For example, Figure 5-4 and the previous illustration of the transaction (inquiry/response) oriented system could involve a front-end computer and a data processing computer. In this operation, the data processor handles every input and initiates every output, except when error conditions occur. The system will process all normal inputs on a FIFO basis, since all inputs are of similar importance.

As illustrated in Figure 5-4, the single structured queue will build as the number of input transactions exceed the processing capability of the data processor. Assume that it has been determined that the data processor requires a total of two seconds to process each input transaction request. This would include reading the input queue, processing the transaction, writing the response to the output queue and returning to read the next transaction in the input queue.

It can be assumed when input transactions are received at a rate of more than one every two seconds that the input queue will begin to build. This could occur when the allowable number of operating lines are continuously active. The allowable number of active lines will be determined by the front-end BPS bandwidth. As the queues build, the response to each terminal inquiry will take longer. This queue building can be determined accurately when the number and size of each transaction is known, and this activity is determined for low, medium and high peak hours of operation.

As stated earlier, queue building is only a part of the delay problem. Multiple terminal contention on the lines, half duplex operations, line and terminal BPS rates and multiplexer bandwidth all compound the delay problem.

Let's consider a few design features that could help provide a reasonable response time. As illustrated in Figure 5-5, improvements in queue structure could help reduce the queue wait time, but other system areas causing delays would remain. These are listed under "considerations" in Figure 5-5. Additional equipment or software redesign are a matter of cost and operational efficiency trade-offs. A review of Chapters Three, Seven, Nine and Ten may be helpful in determining design alternatives.

The queuing structure illustrated in Figure 5-5 may also be viewed as a priority type queue structure. In a priority system, the various data priorities are separated by queues or by flagging in a single queue. Each of the three queues illustrated in Figure 5-5 could be divided further by allowing priority queuing in each of the three queues. This would result in nine queues if three priority levels are used. In this manner, inputs or outputs could be subdivided by priority and thus allow quicker response to the more important data. A thorough data flow and network analysis will help to determine input and output queue loading, and will provide guidelines for establishing the necessary queue structures.

FIGURE 5-4
Inquiry/Response Using Front-End Processor

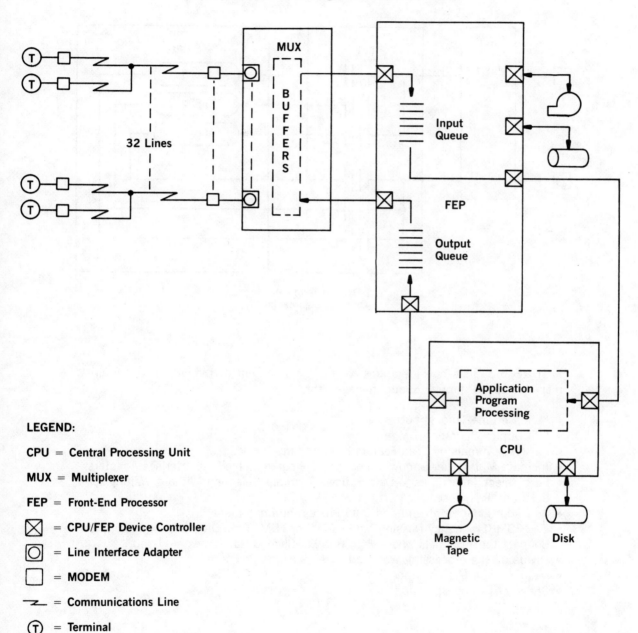

LEGEND:

CPU = Central Processing Unit

MUX = Multiplexer

FEP = Front-End Processor

⊠ = CPU/FEP Device Controller

⊙ = Line Interface Adapter

☐ = MODEM

⌁ = Communications Line

Ⓣ = Terminal

FIGURE 5-4: illustrates a configuration utilizing 1200 bits per second (BPS) terminals operating at half duplex in asynchronous mode. Terminals are selected in a polling sequence. This example is configured in a 32 line with multiple terminals per line connected to a front-end processor through a multiplexer.

FIGURE 5-5
Queuing Structure Using Front-End Processor

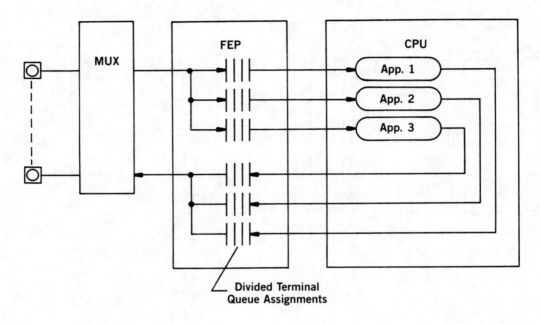

FIGURE 5-5: lists considerations for the improvement of throughput or inquiry response speed through queue management.

- Increase Line Throughput
- Full Duplex Operation
- Assign Terminals by Load Factors to Avoid Line Overload
- Increase Multiplexer Bandwidth or Utilize Programmable Line Interface Adapters
- Fast Select Procedures — Data Follows Terminal Selection Without Waiting for Selection Response
- Add Additional Front-End and Data Processing Equipment
- Use FDM (Frequency Division Modulation) or TDM (Time Division Modulation) to Connect the Terminals where High Bits Per Second Rate Lines are Used
- Divide up the Processing Workload by Application Programs
- Memory Type (Access Speed)
- Speed of Device Operation

LEGEND:

CPU = Central Processing Unit

MUX = Multiplexer

FEP = Front-End Processor

App. = Application

◻ = Line Interface Adapter

EQUIPMENT CONSIDERATIONS TO AID SYSTEM THROUGHPUT

The following is a list of equipment that could affect system throughput where data processing, inquiry-response or any high-volume data transfer is a system function. Equipment reliability, availability, cycle speed, flexibility, and, of course, cost, are the usual considerations. Software must also be properly constructed to take advantage of any highly efficient equipment configurations.

- Line interface adapter (LIA); this unit is line oriented and it would be possible to provide total compatability between the terminal and CPU with this unit. The LIA could be a microcomputer performing many functions for both the terminal and CPU.
- Line multiplexer: similar conditions as the LIA
- Front-end memory considerations
  - Semiconductor memory (best): utilize where possible for frequent housekeeping functions, queuing, data buffers, work areas and other frequently used functions
  - Core (next best): same as semiconductor memory
  - Disk (third choice): when throughput is not paramount for such functions as queuing, overload conditions, data buffers, work areas, file storage, history, etc.
- Data processor memory considerations
  - Semiconductor memory: provides the fastest cycle speed and the greatest number of software processes are performed in this media
  - Core memory: second best area for processing functions
  - Disk (or similar high-speed device): third fastest cycle speed area
  - Magnetic tape: slowest access

When multiple applications or functions are handled by a system, the data queuing may be divided across the various storage media; i.e., inquiry-response would use the memory system, where batch processing would use the disk system. Other operations may be divided across the various storage media in much the same manner. Overload conditions may require memory storage data to be dumped to the disk or, in extreme conditions, magnetic tape may be used.

DATA PROTECTION AND SECURITY CONSIDERATIONS

Data protection normally implies that the system will protect against data distortion or lost data. It does not imply data will not be lost or distorted, but when a loss does occur, the system user should automatically be notified with the necessary information to recover the data. Chapter Eight gives detailed techniques and concepts for data protection.

Basically, the areas to be reviewed for data protection would include the following:

- Terminal error detection capability
- Terminal retransmission capability
- Terminal receiving buffer media and error recovery capability
- Terminal send and receive–computer system error/abnormal detection and recovery procedures
- Computer to terminal normal and abnormal selection procedures
- General communications protocols
- Computer system error detection and recovery features; software and hardware
- Computer system recovery from total failure
- Computer storage media–data recovery from a major failure
- Data format editing and validation routines
- Symbol editing, validation and control
- System generated reports defining the reason for failure
- Development of personnel guidelines for handling system failures
- Data retrieval procedures

Data security is a system provision that allows access to data only by authorized users. Various methods are used to protect data from unauthorized personnel, some simple, some complex. It is a matter of determining the importance of the data under consideration and then developing the necessary data security measures. A review of Chapter Eight will provide an insight to data security considerations. A few security considerations would include the following:

- Key words to identify the terminal attempting to access the data
- Key words to identify the terminal user
- Key words to identify the application program being accessed
- Key words to identify the data being accessed
- Use of code words or symbols derived from the data content or numerical value
- Data scrambling techniques–on-line and in computer storage
- Data scrambling and unscrambling key words or symbols
- Reports to be generated by the system and transmitted to predefined or selected recipients when protected data is accessed
- Selected sequence of key words–changeable as required, manual or automatic
- Key words to be used by computer operators in order to read data from disk or magnetic tape when loading the system
- Time of entry and exit key words: symbols used for access and the terminal and/or operator would be identified in a generated report
- Possible breakdown of the application program into subroutines requiring identifiers

DATA COMPRESSION TO AID THROUGHPUT

Data compression is normally utilized to reduce the necessary data transmission time and to conserve buffer/storage space. When flexible or programmable terminals or intermediate computer systems are used, data compression can be accomplished through software routines. If line transmission time, line contention, or storage areas are not a problem, data compression need not be considered. If the opposite is true, then system design personnel should consider the various areas where data compression could be accomplished. Cost factors will naturally determine how the data compression is accomplished. It may be accomplished in hardware, software, or a combination of both. The following are a few examples of data compression techniques:

- Terminate the transmission of a card (80 character blocks) at the end of valid data.

TERMINATING SYMBOL—CAUSES
TRANSMISSION TO STOP.

| 0 | VALID DATA | 55 | * | FILL CHARACTERS NOT REQUIRED | 80 |

- Terminate the transmission of a printer line at the end of valid date.

TERMINATING SYMBOL—CAUSES
TRANSMISSION TO STOP.

| 0 | VALID DATA | 100 | * | FILL CHARACTERS NOT REQUIRED | 132 |

- Delete the fixed information of a standard form (format on a display screen). Transmit only the fill-in information.

- Compress grouping of redundant characters.

Initial Data =	AAAA	BBBBB	CCCCCCCC	EEE
Becomes	4A	5B	8C	3E

- Eliminate alternate extraneous characters, such as spaces:

FROM—A SP B SP C SP D SP E SP F SP ETC.

TO   —ABCDEF 1010101 0101011— "0" REPRESENTS SPACES—

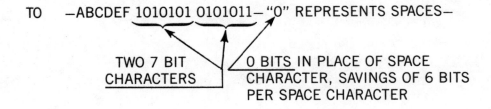

TWO 7 BIT CHARACTERS

0 BITS IN PLACE OF SPACE CHARACTER, SAVINGS OF 6 BITS PER SPACE CHARACTER

- Combine small blocks of data into larger blocks. Identify each individual block with flag characters.
- Use standard word abbreviations to reduce character size.

CHAPTER SIX

System Failure And Recovery Analysis

The most basic approach to minimizing downtime and controlling the network should start with the hardware configuration and software recovery procedures of the host or central site.

Downtime can be costly. As an interactive data network grows, so does the cost of downtime. This cost can be reduced with effective system analysis and recovery procedures. With computers and communications equipment becoming more complex, faster, and more functional in application, procedures to minimize downtime, and for system recovery after failure, are very critical.

The more complex a network grows, the greater its probability for failure. This probability is based upon the fact that there are more communications components, processors, concentrators, terminals, each with an array of semiconductors and switches. As the system grows in complexity, so does the time to isolate and correct problems.

Regardless of the cause of failure, hardware, communications, or software, the user is unable to interact with the system, and suffers from (1) inconvenience, (2) lost revenue, and (3) loss of the customer's good will.

The advent of complex and sophisticated computer systems with new technology in data communications networking has created the feeling of a lack of control, a possible loss of information, and a lack of security among many system users.

Once information enters the computer system, there is a limited amount of readable information to confirm the status of data inputs and data being processed. The end result of the processed data may not reflect the true contents of the collected and processed information. Many times erroneous output information may not be detected for days or weeks.

This chapter discusses weak links in the system, where failure is more likely to occur. Various configurations concepts, which illustrate where these weak links are located, are diagrammed. Design features of hardware and software which will minimize downtime, are examined. Adequate protective features that will help eliminate the problem of lost or incorrectly processed data can be incorporated into most systems. These features will also be discussed in this chapter.

HARDWARE FAILURE ANALYSIS

Computer systems normally consist of the mainframe, device interface, controllers, memories, input/output devices, communication interface equipment and other special equipment required by the system user.

Input/output devices may incorporate a micro- or minicomputer, may be simple or complicated, and may become obsolete in a short period of time. Many times these devices start with a base unit and then are modified to support the individual user's requirements. Modifications may be accomplished via software tables and structures, hardware changes, or possibly a combination of both.

A total system may incorporate a group of minicomputers operating on a monobus/ring bus. The minis may be assigned various functional tasks throughout the total system, with the capability of individual minicomputer reassignment.

System Components Failure Points

Regardless of system configuration or differences, the data protection problems remain and must be considered a major factor in system design. Failed system components, lost data, or improperly processed data will result in increased company operational costs.

Figure 6-1 illustrates the basic system similarities that can be defined, and the failure points, or common areas affected by particular failures, are identified. The numbered areas are defined in the following list.

   1–Terminal and Terminal Interface Adapter (TIA): A terminal failure will normally result in the loss of the terminal or line. Although there have been cases where a single terminal failure caused a total system failure, proper system design would not allow this to happen.

   2–MODEM (Modulator/Demodulator) and Communication Line: Normally, a MODEM or line failure will cause the loss of a single line and any devices connected to that line. The system impact would be similar to a terminal failure. The loss of a multiterminal line could mean the loss of all terminals on that line.

   3–Line Interface Adapter (LIA) or Data Set Adapter: A failure in the line interface adapter should result in the loss of the connected line, MODEM and associated terminals.

FIGURE 6-1
System Configuration Failure Points

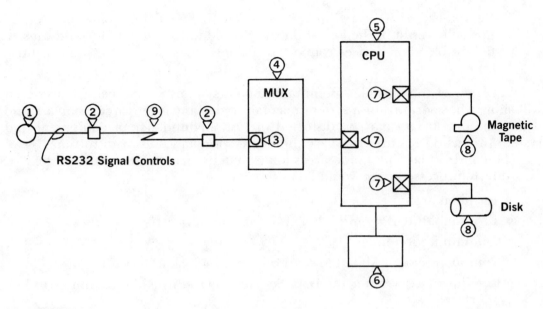

LEGEND:

① **Terminal**

② **MODEM**

③ **Line Interface Adapter**

④ **Line Multiplexer**

⑤ **Central Processing Unit**

⑥ **Memory**

⑦ **Input/Output Device Controller**

⑧ **Input/Output Devices**

⑨ **Communications Line**

4–Line Controller Multiplexer: A partial or total failure of this unit would normally result in the loss of a group of lines or all the connected lines. This unit can also cause a total system failure.

5–Central Processing Unit (CPU): The CPU usually includes the control, arithmetic, and hardware register logic. It may or may not include the memory as an integral unit. A failure in the CPU will normally result in a total system failure.

6–Memory: As a separate unit, a shared unit or extended storage will usually result in a failure of the unit associated with it. This may be the CPU.

7–Input/Output Device Controllers (Multiplexers): A failure of this unit will result in a loss of all connected devices. It could also cause a total system failure.

8–Device Failure (Disk, Tape, Printer, etc.): The failure of a device will normally result in the loss of only the failed unit, although it could cause a failure of other devices connected on the same data, address and control buses.

A review of the possible system failure points of any system being considered will show what portions of a system may fail under any given circumstances, and what amount of data may be distorted or lost. Redundancy of equipment and system protection features can vary the degree of data losses or distortion.

The individual fail point areas of a system that could result in loss or improperly processed data would be as follows:

- Terminal area
- Terminal MODEM (and other transmission devices)
- Communication lines
- Computer system MODEM (and other transmission devices)
- Line interface adapter (or Data Set Adapter)—this is the computer to line interface
- Line multiplexer
- Internal CPU components
- Memory system
- Input/output device controllers
- Input/output devices (disks, magnetic tape, printers, etc.)
- Power, environmental controls, and other related facilities

Cost Trade-Off in Components Failure

Some of the important areas to be reviewed in determining cost trade-offs would be:

- Where and in what parts of a system would the concern for data protection begin and end?
- How important are the data being transmitted or processed?
- Can the system user afford the loss of data?
- Are portions of the processed data more important that other portions?
- What impact will data processing delays have on company operation and profits?
- What additional operations, programming and systems reprocessing costs would result from a system failure?
- What costs will be incurred in all areas because the system is unavailable?

Answers to these types of questions will usually help determine to what extent system recovery, fall back or redundancy configurations should be considered for data protection. It is possible that the cost of data protection could outweigh the costs incurred due to lost or incorrectly processed data. This is an area that must be reviewed thoroughly before a final decision can be made.

COMMUNICATIONS TERMINAL AND LINE ANALYSIS

Beginning with the terminal area, several data protection possibilities could be considered. Figure 6-2 illustrates a typical communications line (facilities), including MODEMs, terminal and multiplexer. Terminal failure analysis can begin with these areas.

FIGURE 6-2
Terminal Area Troubleshooting Analysis

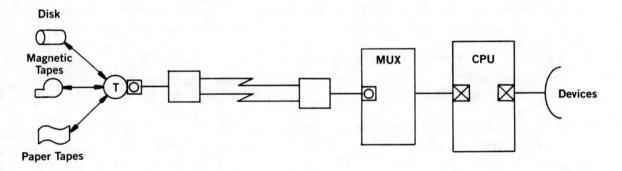

FIGURE 6-2: illustrates how terminal failure analysis may involve isolation of the failed component within the connecting facilities or associated equipment.

LEGEND:

CPU = **Central Processing Unit**

MUX = **Multiplexer (For Line Connections)**

⊠ = **CPU Device Controllers**

◻ = **Line Interface Adapter**

▢ = **MODEM**

〜 = **Communications Line**

Ⓣ = **Terminal and Associated Devices**

A discussion of the terminal area should include the two MODEMs and the connecting line since a failure in any part can cause a loss of the terminal. The first consideration is usually a storage medium at the terminal that provides data protection and storage when the terminal, MODEM or line fail. Battery protected memory, paper tape, magnetic tape (cassette or other small tape systems) or disk systems could be used. These would provide a retransmission capability following recovery from the failure. If a failure occurs during terminal reception, the data must be protected by the transmitting computer system and retransmitted when the problem is corrected.

Other failure protection considerations in the terminal area could encompass the following:

- Fallback Terminal: The redundant terminal may be a transmit or receive unit if the concern for nondelayed data movement is in one direction only. However, the redundant terminal does not solve the MODEM or line failure problem.

- Substitute a Second Terminal: Utilize another terminal located in the same area, building, or across town.

- Courier Service: Mail, air freight, or hand carry the data to the processing center. This is possible if cassette tape or small disk systems are utilized for storage.

- Fallback MODEMs: MODEM failures could be corrected through the use of fallback MODEMs. The problem in the MODEM area is the determination that the MODEM has failed. A MODEM that has "bust back" and test features will aid the maintenance personnel in determining if the unit has failed. This could require testing both ends of the line since two MODEMs are involved and may require personnel capable of running the necessary tests at both ends. MODEM failures could be handled in a manner similar to a terminal failure; this could eliminate the need for duplicate MODEMs. This requires storage facilities at the terminal for retransmission and does not eliminate the data delay. If high speed MODEMs are in use, duplicate MODEMs may not be necessary because high speed MODEMs are very reliable. Failure rates should be available from the MODEM vendors to assist the system designer in making this decision.

- Communications Line: Communications line failures could encompass the MODEMs as they are a natural part of the overall communications line.

As illustrated by Figure 6-3, facility protection can be expensive since duplicate MODEMs and lines could be required. The extent of redundancy should be justified by determining the importance of the data to be transmitted or received. Are delays, or possible loss of data, important enough to justify equipment and line duplication costs? Assuming that certain costs can be justified, the following should be considered:

- Retention of permanent redundant lines and/or MODEMs as illustrated in Figure 6-3. A switching arrangement could be incorporated to allow switching the MODEMs and/or lines in or out.

FIGURE 6-3
Minimize Failure By Communication (Modem and Line) Duplication

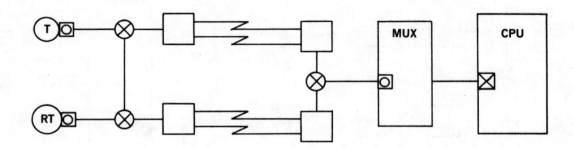

FIGURE 6-3: illustrates how duplicate terminals and line facilities may be used to solve terminal failure conditions.

LEGEND:

CPU = **Central Processing Unit**

MUX = **Multiplexer**

⤴ = **Communications Line (Facilities)**

⊠ = **CPU Device Controller**

◎ = **Line Interface Adapter**

▢ = **MODEM**

⊗ = **Facility Switching Matrix**

(T) = **Terminal**

(RT) = **Redundant Terminal**

• Alternate transmission capability via a dial-up line should be considered. This is illustrated in Figure 6-4. A switching arrangement between the regular MODEM, the dial MODEM and the terminal could be accomplished manually, then, following the dial connection, data transmission could be initiated. This requires the use of an alternate MODEM and Line Interface Adapter (LIA) at the computer end.

When dial-up lines are normally used, a line failure could be corrected by redialing a new connection, although the MODEM problem would still remain as a possible failure point. The use of dial-up fallback lines will reduce the overall costs since a dial-up is only used, and line costs are only incurred, when a connection has been made.

FIGURE 6-4
Alternative Transmission By Dial-Up Lines

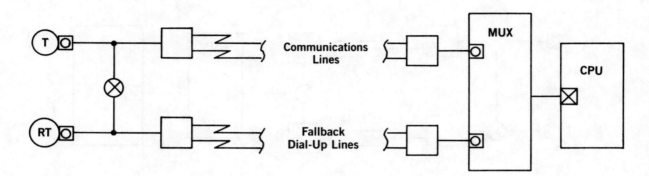

FIGURE 6-4: depicts how dial-up lines may be utilized for fallback capability during line failure.

LEGEND:

CPU = Central Processing Unit

MUX = Multiplexer

◯ = Line Interface Adapter

☐ = MODEM

⊗ = Line Switching Arrangement

⌁ = Communications Line

Ⓣ = Terminal

ⓇⓉ = Redundant Terminal

⊠ = CPU Device Controller

A MODEM allowing data transmissions over either a dedicated line or a dial-up line could be used. This would only require a switching arrangement between the MODEM and the line. This is illustrated in Figure 6-5.

This would also eliminate the need for a second MODEM, provided a reliable MODEM is being used. If automatic dialing is to be utilized, both at the terminal and computer, the line could be swapped by an automatic redial.

MAINFRAME AND ASSOCIATED EQUIPMENT/ANALYSIS

A computer system (mainframe and devices) could serve as a terminal, as an intermediate processing point, or as a central system in a nodal network structure.

FIGURE 6-5
Single Modem Allowing Switching To Dial-Up Lines

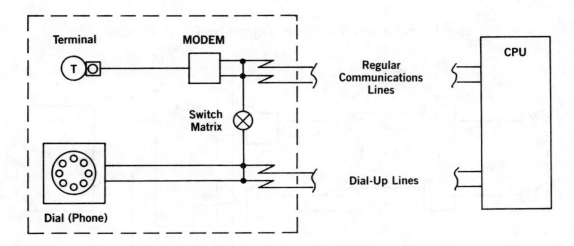

FIGURE 6-5: In this dial-up configuration, the switch and dial equipment are located at the terminal site.

The basic difference would be the size and processing functions assigned to the systems situated at each location. The concern for data protection should exist at each individual location. The following discussions can concern any or all of the individual data processing or switching sites.

Line Interface Adapter

The Line Interface Adapter (LIA) is the first logical point of contact between the terminal, MODEMs, lines and the mainframe. This is illustrated in Figure 6-6. The LIA, being a part of the multiplexer equipment, should be a replaceable unit. The system maintenance personnel should have spare units available for corrective action and downtime should be minimal under these conditions. If spare components are not available or if a new unit does not solve the problem, the capability should exist to connect the line to another LIA and, in turn, reassignment should be accomplished in software tables. The line and terminal would then be restored to service.

Line Multiplexer

The line multiplexer may be a free-standing unit cabled to the mainframe or an integral unit consisting of logic cards plugged into assigned slots located in the mainframe. A failure in the line multiplexer can result in a total loss of all the lines connected to this unit. Refer to Figure 6-6 for an illustration of the multiplexer position in the computer mainframe part of the system.

Restoration of the line multiplexer is normally accomplished through repair by maintenance personnel. The problem with this method of restoration is the lengthy time period required to restore the unit to service. This may involve downtime of several hours or longer.

FIGURE 6-6
Line Interface and Multiplexer Equipment Considerations

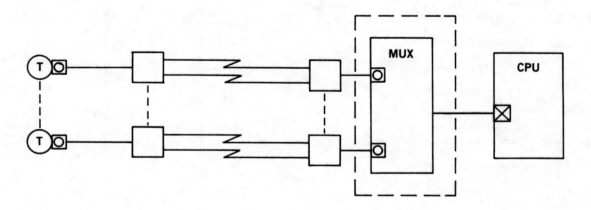

FIGURE 6-6: demonstrates a straightforward line interface and multiplexer configuration to satisfy terminal to multiplexer connection.

LEGEND:

CPU = Central Processing Unit

MUX = Multiplexer

$\boxtimes$ = CPU Device Controller

$\boxed{\bigcirc}$ = Line Interface Adapter

$\square$ = MODEM

$\sim\!\!\!\!\!\!\!\sim$ = Communications Line

$\textcircled{T}$ = Terminal

One solution to the problem would be the addition of a redundant line multiplexer. This could be a fairly simple task or a very complicated one depending on the hardware design concepts. Refer to Figure 6-7 for an example of a dual line multiplexer concept. As illustrated by Figure 6-7, some type of switching matrix would be required to switch the lines from one line multiplexer to the other. On the computer mainframe side two device controllers slots would be required on the mainframe.

A special interface could be utilized where the two line multiplexers would be interconnected together and a single interface connected to one mainframe device controller. The interface could be a logic switching device allowing either line

FIGURE 6-7
Failure Protection Through Switchable Multiplexers

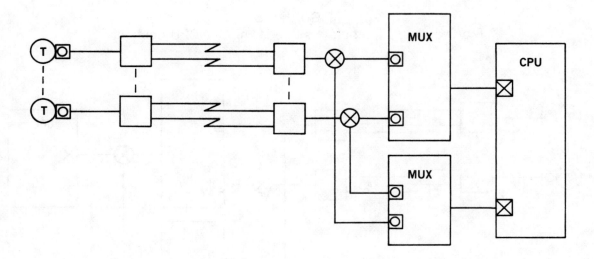

FIGURE 6-7: illustrates how duplication of line multiplexer can provide communications protection in case of the primary multiplexer failure.

LEGEND:

CPU = **Central Processing Unit**

MUX = **Multiplexer**

⊠ = **CPU Device Controller**

◎ = **Line Interface Adapter**

▢ = **MODEM**

〜 = **Communications Line**

Ⓣ = **Terminal**

⊗ = **Multiplexer Line Switching Matrix**

multiplexer to communicate with the single mainframe controller slot. The total cost may be reduced since the switch interface does eliminate the requirement for one device controller and associated cabling. Refer to Figure 6-8 for an illustration of this example. The configuration in Figure 6-8 does create one problem. The interface communications line controller is now a single fail point, where the use of dual line controllers provides dual data paths to the mainframe.

Other types of line multiplexer device controller configurations may be available, such as those illustrated in Figures 6-9 and 6-10. Figure 6-9 shows a loop concept on the line side of the multiplexer. This is more for multiterminal line use than for protective purposes. Loss of the multiplexer will still cause the failure of all terminals.

FIGURE 6-8
Two Switchable Multiplexers Interfacing One CPU Controller

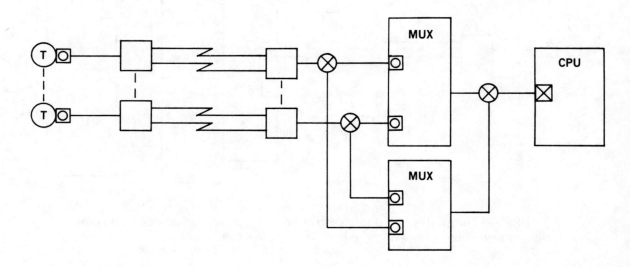

FIGURE 6-8: depicts communications protection through a switchable line that serves two multiplexers utilizing one CPU device controller.

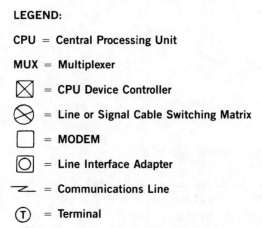

LEGEND:

CPU = Central Processing Unit

MUX = Multiplexer

⊠ = CPU Device Controller

⊗ = Line or Signal Cable Switching Matrix

▢ = MODEM

◖ = Line Interface Adapter

⌇ = Communications Line

Ⓣ = Terminal

Figure 6-10 shows a multisection line multiplexer where the line interface adapters (LIA) operates as individual devices on a multiplexing loop. The LIA can represent both the line interface and multiplexer. This configuration does help

FIGURE 6-9
Local TerminaL Loop Connection Concept

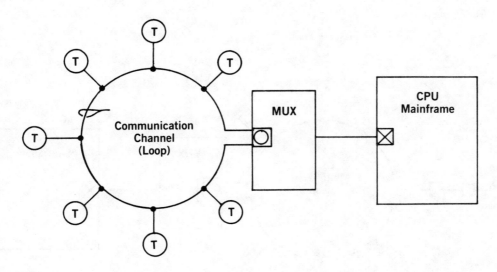

FIGURE 6-9: illustrates a terminal loop, primarily for a local site operation, that simulates multiterminal operation on a single line.

LEGEND:

CPU = **Central Processing Unit**

MUX = **Multiplexer**

⬜ = **Line Interface Adapter**

⊠ = **CPU Device Controller**

Ⓣ = **Terminal**

solve a part of the line interface and line multiplexer failure problem since a spare unit could be placed in service for the failed LIA or multiplexer unit. Sharing the load between the LIA and multiplexer and logic design concepts can create a situation where the failed LIA or multiplexer may easily be replaced. This does not solve the mainframe device controller failure problem since the whole loop is operating through one device controller.

To protect against the mainframe device controller failure, the capability to quickly switch to another controller should be provided. If the data protection requirements dictate the use of redundant line multiplexing units and the costs can be justified, then the example configurations illustrated in Figure 6-11 may be a logical consideration.

FIGURE 6-10
Multi-Section Line Multiplexer For Long Distance Lines

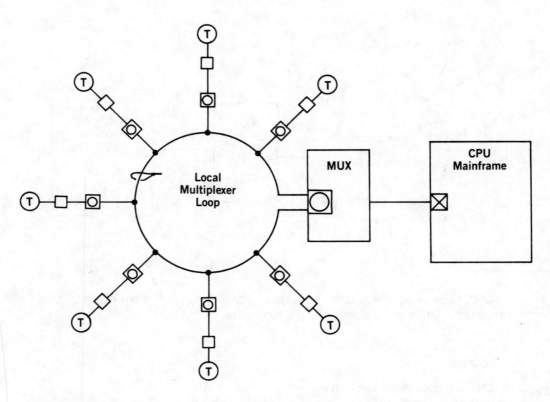

FIGURE 6-10: depicts a loop concept that simulates multiterminal operation on long distance lines.

LEGEND:

CPU = **Central Processing Unit**

MUX = **Multiplexer**

⊠ = **CPU Device Controller**

◎ = **Line Interface Adapter**

▢ = **MODEM**

Ⓣ = **Terminal**

Figure 6-11 also provides a simple illustration of how two programmable line multiplexers could be utilized. Both multiplexers could be on-line, load-sharing the entire system network. Each unit would minitor the adjacent unit's lines and, if a failure occurs, pick up the entire system load. This, of course, requires software support in the mainframe and secondary capability in the line multiplexers. When one multiplexer is forced to interface all the lines, overall system efficiency would be lowered, but servicing of all lines would continue.

FIGURE 6-11
Multiplexers Load Sharing the System

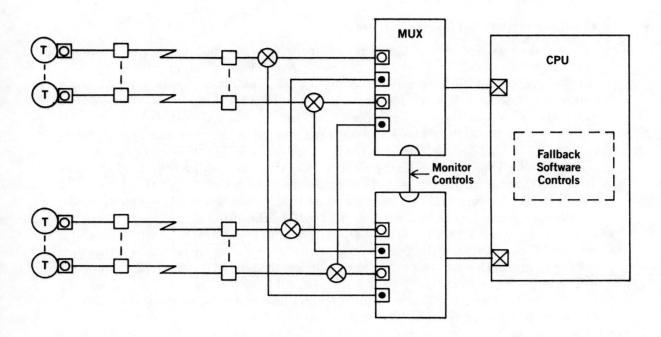

FIGURE 6-11: illustrates two on-line multiplexers which are switchable and each capable of servicing the lines connected to the opposite multiplexer.

LEGEND:

CPU = **Central Processing Unit**

MUX = **Multiplexer**

⊠ = **CPU Device Controller**

◎ = **Line Interface Adapter**

⦿ = **Secondary Line Interface Adapter**
(Allows capability to service all
lines connected to both multiplexers)

⊗ = **Line Switching Matrix**

☐ = **MODEM**

⌇ = **Communications Line**

Ⓣ = **Terminal**

This type of operation would require the use of mostly controlled terminals, since under abnormal conditions the entire system load could cause an overload of a single multiplexer. This occurs because a single multiplexer could be servicing double the amount of lines under abnormal conditions. Controlled terminals would allow the system to dictate when each terminal may transmit or receive. This controls the overall system load and prevents system overload failures.

Central Processing Unit (CPU) and Memory

A failure of a single CPU will result in the total loss of all data processing or switching functions handled by that unit. Normal restoration of the CPU is through repair of the failed CPU component. This repair process requires an unknown amount of system downtime since it is necessary for maintenance personnel to isolate the problem, then take the necessary restoration action.

One solution to the single CPU problem is to provide a redundant CPU. Refer to Figure 6-12 for an example of a simple two-CPU configuration. The fallback or redundant CPU must have the capability to access the line multiplexer and all other associated input/output devices. This would require a switching arrangement of some type, either manual or automatic. The type of switching arrangement would be a determining factor in the amount of system downtime.

Switching the CPUs in or out of service would be accomplished following the failure; the standby unit program would be loaded with the current tables, files and modules, and would be connected to the devices and then placed on-line. In order to allow quick recovery and to avoid the possibility of lost data, restart tables and other necessary software modules must be maintained by the original on-line unit, and then utilized by the standby restoral unit.

Restoration in this manner will result in some downtime but it should be a great deal less than the time required to repair a failed CPU. The actual downtime would be determined by the number of necessary steps required to place the standby unit on-line.

An ideal system arrangement would have the standby unit assume on-line status automatically. This would require an arrangement where each CPU could monitor the on-line status of the adjacent CPU. The standby CPU would be maintained in a program mode enabling it to perform a restart, assuming an on-line status, when the present on-line CPU fails. This of course would require that both CPUs have a capability to access all input/output devices automatically, and the software table structures, pointers, and stored data must be accessible by either CPU. This two-CPU arrangement could be carried a step further as illustrated in Figure 6-13.

Both CPUs can maintain an on-line status, sharing the system load, and if necessary, either CPU could automatically assume the processing load of the total system when one of the CPUs fails. Also, one of the CPUs could be used for off-line processing during low data processing and switching periods. In this dual configuration the necessary software programs must be available in each CPU for the total system configuration, and all input/output devices must be accessible from either CPU.

In order to accomplish a switchover following a failure of one CPU, all the data or messages being processed, including files and tables, must be accessible through

FIGURE 6-12
Redundant CPU Configuration

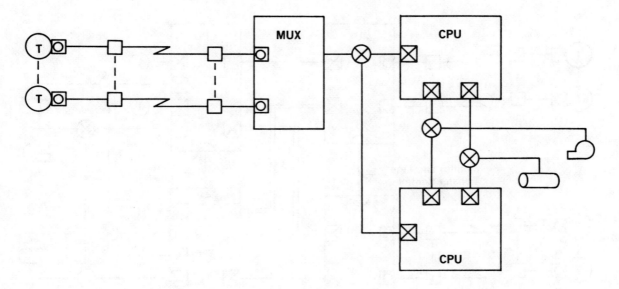

FIGURE 6-12: shows a redundant CPU configuration where each CPU can be connected to a single multiplexer unit through a switchable arrangement. The input/output devices are also switchable.

LEGEND:

CPU = **Central Processing Unit**

MUX = **Multiplexer**

⊠ = **CPU Device Controller**

◯ = **Line Interface Adapter**

⊗ = **Signal and Control Cable Switch Matrix**

☐ = **MODEM**

⚡ = **Communications Line**

Ⓣ = **Terminal**

either CPU. This will permit the functioning CPU to do a restart and protect the failed CPU's data. Processing efficiency would be lowered, but data would be protected and processing could continue.

Device Controllers, Input/Output Devices and Extended Memory

Read and/or write storage devices usually consist of magnetic disks, magnetic strips, memories, magnetic tapes, card machines, scanning units, paper tape,

FIGURE 6-13
Dual CPU On-Line Configuration

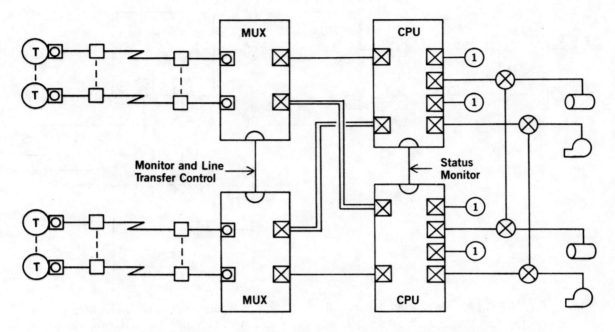

Monitor and Line Transfer Control

Status Monitor

FIGURE 6-13: illustrates a dual CPU and multiplexer operation where all units operate on-line. When a failure occurs, one CPU can assume the entire line load and device operation through the switchable matrix. A line switch and monitor arrangement as illustrated in Figure 6-11 would be used on the line side of the multiplexers.

LEGEND:

CPU = **Central Processing Unit**

MUX = **Multiplexer**

⊠ = **CPU Device Controller**

◎ = **Line Interface Adapter**

⊗ = **Switching Matrix**

= **Secondary and Fallback Multiplexer Connection**

☐ = **MODEM**

∿ = **Communications Line**

Ⓣ = **Terminal**

① = **Possible Fallback Device Controller to be Connected to the Opposite CPU Devices.**

printers, keyboards, etc. Any one of these devices can fail and create a data protection problem; some might be insignificant, while others cause a major or total system loss.

Paper tape, card machines or scanners retain a copy in a printed or punched form which can be used for fallback purposes. Merely rerun the original information, if it is not mutilated, to obtain the necessary output data.

Loss of a disk or magnetic tape unit may only mean that the disk platter or magnetic tape reel need to be placed on another device and the programs rerun. Software restart features must be available and tables and pointers maintained to allow programs to be reentered and the data to be retrieved in its original form. This also requires that a fallback disk or tape device be available to the system for recovery purposes. If only one device is available, the system would be in a failed mode until the device is repaired or restored.

Input/output device failures could be caused by either the device controller or the device itself. Also, a single device failure could cause the loss of several devices. This is a very important point because of the "daisy chaining" concept used to connect devices to the mainframe. This is illustrated in Figure 6-14.

FIGURE 6-14
Daisy Chaining Devices to Mainframe

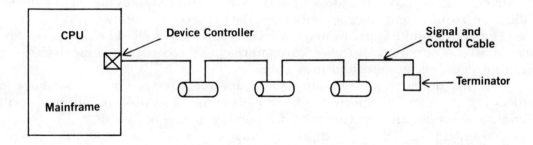

If a disk to be utilized for restoration is on the same signal, control and data bit cable (daisy chain connection) with the device that failed, then the restoration device may also be in a failed state. This type of total failure can occur because of the common connection of all devices on the daisy chained buses, the entire string being connected to one CPU controller. In this situation, the total disk system could be in a failed condition, if only the one string (daisy chain) of disks is available to the system.

To avoid this problem, two device controllers could be used. The fallback unit used for restoration should be on a separate device controller and cable daisy chain link, as illustrated in Figure 6-15. This does increase cost because another controller is being utilized. This would be another case of cost versus data protection justification.

FIGURE 6-15
Daisy Chaining Backup Configuration

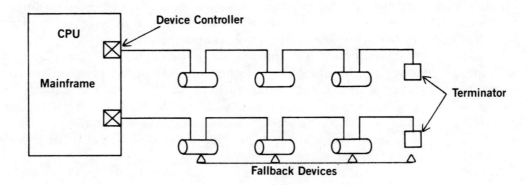

Rather than have a disk sit idle just for protection purposes, it may be logical to perform load-sharing in the same manner as previously described for the CPUs. This could allow quicker recovery since it would not be necessary to move the disk platters to another unit. A copy of all transactions could be recorded to both disks. This would allow complete redundancy since the data is available from two separate disk units. This also entails the necessary software to support a dual write and read system capable of recovering after a failure. Of course, this does double the device utilization requirement since all important data is recorded on two devices.

The above could apply to magnetic tape devices as well. The magnetic tape area may be as important as the disk area since data is recorded to these devices for future processing, storage, and protection.

External memory systems are usually utilized for temporary storage and processing and should be protected by records retained on disks or any equivalent device. This would also provide restart capability in case of failure.

Redundant recording to disks and tapes, prior to releasing the raw or processed data, can create a throughput problem. The system data throughput will be regulated by the speed of the recording device. Because of this, it is important to review this requirement very carefully. Normally it is sufficient to provide redundant protection to a separate power-protected memory or a disk with follow-up to tape. When a failure occurs, the separate memory or disk will provide a recovery path and this would avoid system regulation by the magnetic tapes. A total redundant system may appear as illustrated in Figure 6-16.

In this system, both CPUs can be placed on-line in a load-sharing mode and have the capability to access all devices. A copy of each transaction can be recorded to two disks. All tables, pointers, data restart programs, and other important software modules would be recorded to two disks. If either one of the disks fails, a copy would be available on the redundant unit. The adjacent system component would be placed on-line in place of the failed unit.

The cost of a system of this nature could be high depending on the types of hardware utilized. However, in today's market, low-cost minicomputers could be used to supplement the main system. Figure 6-16 illustrates where the minicom-

FIGURE 6-16
Minicomputer Supplement to the Main System

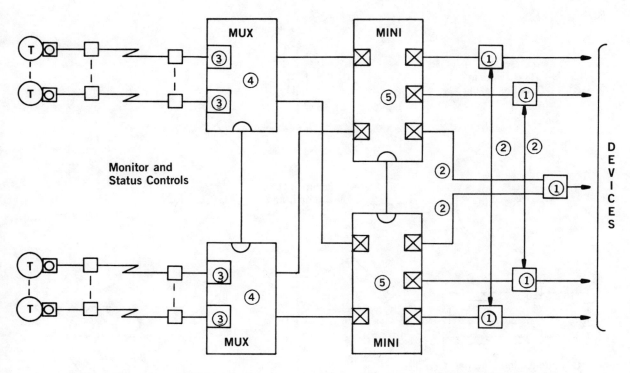

FIGURE 6-16: amplifies Figures 6-11 and 6-13 with minicomputers instead of large mainframe computers being used in a dual on-line configuration.

LEGEND:

① = **Programmable Interface and Device Management**

② = **Alternate Device Sharing Methods**

③ = **Programmable Line Interface Adapters**

④ = **Programmable Multiplexer and Data Storage**

⑤ = **Load Sharing Minicomputer and Software System**

▢ = **MODEM**

Ⓣ = **Terminal**

◉ = **Line Interface Adapter**

⊠ = **CPU Device Controller**

puter could be used within the system. In addition, one could consider the ring processing (monobus) capability of many available minicomputer or major computer systems. This is illustrated in Figure 6-17.

FIGURE 6-17
Ring Processing (Monobus) System

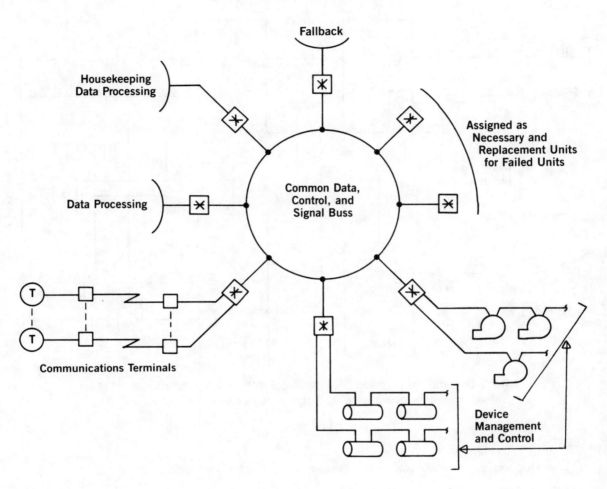

FIGURE 6-17: depicts a ring processing configuration with interchangeable mini-processing units identified by an asterisk. The miniprocessors could be reassigned functions as necessary.

Each minor system of the overall major system would be assigned a given function. These functions could consist of communication tasks, device management, table structures, controls, application processing or any other functions necessary to accomplish the overall system requirements.

A failed minor unit could be removed from the system and the function assigned to another unit. A subsystem unit would be assigned the task of maintaining redundant restart files, tables and other necessary data to allow system recovery in case of a subsystem failure. This would be necessary where the failed unit is unable to recover. The weak link in this system is the single bus electrically connecting the units.

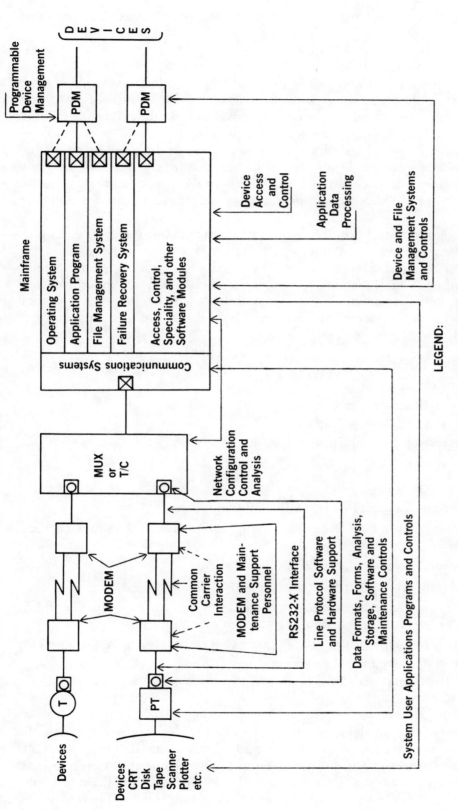

FIGURE 6-18
System Failure Points for Software Analysis

FIGURE 6-18: illustrates failure points for software analysis. There are multiple areas in which system failure can occur. Most system failure and recovery procedures require software and hardware maintenance analysis and cooperative recovery actions by all involved parties.

SOFTWARE ANALYSIS

When data protection is a system requirement, the software system must be designed with this requirement as a major consideration. Failure of hardware components, failure detection, automatic removal of the failed unit, fallback recovery, hardware and software redundancy requirements, ease of device replacement, and software restart tables, files and pointers must be designed into the total software system. The software design should include failure recovery routines and other special routines to recover stored data where total recovery and restart is not possible. Figure 6-18 illustrates the various possible failure points for software analysis.

Where data communications is one of the system functions, software support must be provided to recover from a terminal, MODEM, communications line, line interface adapter, or multiplexer failure. For normal operation, usually a table structure consisting of the following typical entries would be maintained for each input and output line terminated into the system. Normally, even when a total system failure occurs, the system can recover by identifying the following status of each terminal device at time of failure.

- Time of data input
- Time of data output
- Input terminal device identifier
- Output terminal device identifier
- Code set utilized by the terminal device
- Input line type (type of device and protocol)
- Output line type (type of device and protocol)
- Header format identifier (type of format being used)
- Data sequence numbers (input and output)—numerical count of each transaction
- Internal system storage data tracers
- Abnormal data tracers for intercept reasons
- Symbols detected during each transaction—SOM, End of Header, STX, EOM, and other important data format symbols
- Character counts—or amount of data processed for the terminal device when failure occurred
- Pointers identifying active terminal devices
- Core or memory storage assignments

CPU and input/output device failure recovery can be handled in much the same manner as the communications line and terminal media since the CPU primarily is a data processing and transfer point for the communication terminals and the input/output devices. Recovery of the CPU is accomplished through tables and pointers stored on the input/output device recording media. Therefore, the input/output devices—disks, magnetic tapes (or equivalent)—are the primary areas that need to be protected. Disks would be the normal area for storage of the failure recovery tables and pointers. Not only the storage of information data, but data in various degrees of manipulation, some programs, records, files, tables, and pointers, and any other important information the user cannot afford to lose, should be protected. The table structures necessary to protect and recover data could consist of the following typical entries:

- Pointers identifying the processing status of each program module at the time of failure (allows for rollback to the last valid cycle prior to failure),
- Active input/output devices and the assigned functions,
- Time of all data transfers,
- Input/output device identifiers,
- Format assignments for each input/output device,
- Data storage tracers for each active program module,
- Core or memory assignments for all variable data information,
- Data map identifying type and position of all data stored on each input/ output device and the program module to which the data is assigned.

In order to protect these information and program data entries, the previous discussion in the hardware section on disk data protection would apply. The software requirements would entail the ability to write dual copies on disks and/or tapes, and then be able to utilize either copy in case of a failure.

It would also be necessary to accomplish recovery of the failed device to resume the dual copy operation. The software files would also be utilized for this purpose. Recovery would entail the writing of, or copying, the stored information from the operational device to the device being returned to service. Dual copy operation would continue once the restoration is complete.

We will not attempt to design failure detection or recovery software since every system has its own unique requirements. The main point in recovery software design is to be aware of every step in every processing cycle in motion, store entries identifying each step, identify the beginning and end of each processed entry and store these entries in a protected area to allow recovery if a failure occurs.

The protective and recovery software may be more comprehensive than the normal processing software. Usually about 25% of the software design work is for the normal processing routines and 75% of the design work entails error, protection and recovery software routines since every normal process could result in many different abnormal conditions. Each abnormal condition could require a different recovery procedure, depending on the particular point of failure in the processing cycle. Therefore, it would be necessary to store a pointer for each step in every process cycle that would enable the system to return to the last valid process point prior to failure. This results in a high percentage of the software design work being applied to the abnormal routines. Abnormal software should be a major design criterion when system specifications are compiled and/or provided by the vendor supplying software.

OPERATIONS ANALYSIS

Operational procedures in the event of a system component, input/output device, subsystem, communications terminal, or major system failure are as important as any other phase of system procedures. A procedural failure on the part of an operator may result in lost or improperly processed data. It is very important that documented and possibly step-by-step procedures be compiled to guide operations personnel through all possible types of system failure. An operator's manual, utilizing some type of binder that allows easy addition of pages, should be utilized since procedures will be revised frequently.

The system procedures should encompass all possible equipment or software failures that can affect system operation. These procedures would normally cover the following areas as a minimum:

- A terminal MODEM, communications line, or line interface adapter failure should be identified through a report to the operator's console identifying the type of failure. These reports could identify such problems as:
  - The failed line and the terminal(s) on that line
  - No response from the terminal
  - Parity error
  - Continuous character on input (invalid character)
  - Idle or data stream stopped on input (time-out)
  - No response to dial (dialing control–third attempt)
  - Line interface adapter failure
  - Clear to send not detected from MODEM
  - Carrier detect not received from MODEM
  - Other individual MODEM signals utilized, but not normal
  - Time-outs for various controls
  - Synchronous binary control signals abnormal; many of these controls are available, but all may not be utilized
- Other special system identifiable failures
- Input/output device failure, including the line multiplexer

Input/output devices would include any units connected through an input/output device controller. These could be disks, magnetic tape, card reader/punches, magnetic recording strips, optical readers, keyboard/printers, printers, and other various input/output devices. Software-generated reports should identify the failed unit and provide information giving the cause of failure. These reports could include the following information:

- Identify the failed input/output device,
- Identify the reason for failure:
  - Parity error,
  - Data transfer errors and failure errors,
  - No response from the input/output device,
  - Time-out and the operational function attempted,
  - Data overrun,

  –Abnormal response from the input/output device,
  –End of tape reached,
  –Tape marks detected,
  –Rejected document,
  –Input/output device out of service.

• Other special responses that may be available from the input/output devices in use,

• The abnormal signals generated by the various input/output devices are identified by the device specification available from the supplying vendor. Others can be designed into the software as necessary for system failure control.

• CPU or Memory failure would normally be identified through a parity error, with a resulting restart of the software system for total system recovery.

Operator procedures should outline the operator steps to be performed to protect the data within the system and the steps necessary to restore the failed device or component. System recovery in many instances where redundancy is utilized should be automatic. Where recovery is automatic, a report should identify what abnormal condition occurred, the failed device, and reason for device failure. Follow-up operator action would then be necessary.

In order to maintain an efficient system operation, the user should establish a comprehensive procedural manual, insure its accuracy, continuously perform necessary updates, and see that the operational personnel understand and follow the procedures. The manual should be indexed, easy to read, and available.

SYSTEM FAILURE AND RECOVERY MANAGEMENT ANALYSIS

System management begins from the initial idea of a system through the day the system is terminated and/or a new system is assuming the operation. A part of management responsibility should be to ensure that data protection is incorporated into the system. This entails the ability to recover from any type of failure in one manner or another without the loss of data. Management personnel should review Chapters One, Two, and Thirteen for a better understanding of system analysis, design, and documentation considerations.

Management supervision is necessary in all aspects of system design, documentation, coordination, testing, implementation, cutover, and follow-up system operation. In many cases during system development, data protection is an area that usually ends up being a minor part of system design. Many personnel involved in the system design activities tend to primarily worry about the normal requirements and treat abnormal requirements as secondary or minor functions. Normal and abnormal functions should receive equal considerations. Management may discover that many personnel can perform efficiently when designing normal system functions, but will perform inefficiently when designing abnormal system handling functions. Many times it is necessary to change one's thinking in order to handle the abnormal design tasks.

Many systems are in operation today that will totally fail because of a communications terminal malfunction. Other system input/output device failures may cause a total system failure. A communications terminal or input/output device should never cause a system to fail without the ability to perform a system restart. Temporary system failures can be handled easily if a total system restart can be performed. When a total system failure results without restart ability, then system design concepts were inadequate. These system failures happen because abnormal handlers were considered a minor requirement during system design. Of course, multiple failures or those occurring in the CPU may cause a loss of the system, but efficient abnormal routines should protect the data and allow follow-up recovery.

CHAPTER SEVEN

Line and Communication Terminal Engineering For a Data Communications System

The communications terminal equipment area becomes one of the important service areas when system operational efficiency is considered. The terminals and associated equipment must be selected in consideration of economics, efficiency, functional features, availability, ease of operation and compatibility with the total system.

A terminal that provides the necessary operational features, is cost-effective, and is system compatible, may not function efficiently when communicating with the existing computer system. This inefficiency may be due in part to the manner in which the terminal communications protocol (electrical interface) was designed. Terminal-computer protocols vary in accordance with the equipment manufacturer's design. Some systems offer terminal protocols flexibility while others do not. A system user may not have the opportunity to dictate the type of system protocols available, but may have some influence to cause improvements in the operational protocol efficiency.

Among the many problems that must be worked out in the network design phase are (1) transmission data code compatibility, (2) communication line protocol compatibility, and (3) the equipment's electrical interfacing requirements. The different types of protocol are a problem area for the network designers. Communication protocol is a set of procedures and rules that permit different communications facilities and components, and computer equipment to communicate and exchange data among dissimilar equipment, code sets, and transmission speeds. The function of the protocol procedures and rules involve framing bits or characters, numbering of messages, and line, timing, and start-up controls in the resolution of conflicts and transmission problems.

There are various code sets and communications protocols available. Selecting the most efficient code set and protocol must be weighed very carefully. Besides the more obvious technical problems that must be resolved, there will be many managerial decisions to be made concerning which code sets and protocols will benefit system throughput. This chapter will deal with the various types and efficiencies of code sets and terminal-computer protocols that will assist the system designer in arriving at the most efficient operation possible.

EMULATION

Emulation is the art of configuring a communications terminal to communicate with different types of computer system terminal protocols. Integration of microelectronics has simplified the tasks of emulation for terminal manufacturers. This new electronic medium has made it possible for terminal manufacturers to easily emulate other vendors' terminals, therefore making it possible for the user to be selective in procuring terminals. Usually an emulation mode of operation is considered because the terminal under review is not manufactured by the vendor supplying the mainframe equipment.

Emulation in a communication terminal environment is not necessarily a stopgap measure as it possibly would be in the case where old software systems are run on newer computer equipment. A communication terminal is usually selected for its operational features; emulation makes it possible to be selective. This should enable a user to select the most efficient terminal to meet the system operational and cost requirements.

Reasons for Emulation

Terminal emulation should be considered for the following reasons:

- The central system (mainframe) vendor does not manufacture terminals.

- A communication terminal offered by a vendor, other than the vendor supplying the mainframe equipment, provides the same basic features at a reduced cost and provides maximum on-line time.

- A communications terminal offered by a particular vendor provides features not available from the terminal distributed by the vendor providing the mainframe equipment.

- Peripheral data processing is a system requirement and it is necessary to utilize a micro- or minicomputer system. This peripheral system will communicate with the central system, using the central system protocols. In this case peripheral terminal (computer) equipment selection precludes use of the central system vendor terminal equipment.

- The terminal will communicate with two or more different computer equipment communications protocols. This requires the ability to change protocols in accordance with the particular computer system connected at the time.

COMMUNICATIONS LINE AND TERMINAL CONSIDERATIONS

The selection of terminal equipment should include a study and parallel selection of the communication line components and computer interfaces, all complementing the overall system operational requirements.

One of the main requirements of any terminal is the movement of a given amount of information in a specified period of time. This same requirement would dictate the communications line requirements. Usually there are two major considerations that should be considered in the terminal to computer configuration. These considerations are time and contention.

Time is consumed to perform a function and contention occurs when terminals compete for a shared line or available computer cycle time. A computer may run out of data terminal servicing time, therefore causing delays in communications and other data processing. A functionally efficient terminal and associated facilities (line) will permit more time to be available for servicing other terminals and other data processing.

Line contention, where multiple terminals share a single line and where too many lines are terminated in the computer system, can result in servicing delays that may extend for several minutes. This may or may not be a problem; but if the system performs inquiry-response functions, it's a major problem. Many other factors influence the problem, but system protocols can help or compound the problem.

There are various types of communications lines available, each type permitting certain data rates. Basically, the following types of communications lines are available from the various communications companies:

- Low speed lines, 0-150 Bits Per Second (BPS) (leased lines),
- Medium speed lines, 300-9600 Bits Per Second (BPS) (leased lines),
- Dial-up lines, 150-9600 Bits Per Second (BPS) (leased lines on an intermittent time basis),
- Wide band lines, through 50 Kilo Bits Per Second (KBPS) (leased lines),
- Lines composed of two or more 50 KBPS.

There are other types of sophisticated communications lines, but they are not directly applicable to this discussion. The choice between leased or dial-up lines would normally be based on an analysis of the data load to and from a terminal or group of terminals. If this analysis of data movement indicates high line utilization, leased lines would be the most logical choice. If low line utilization was indicated, low-speed leased lines or dial-up lines would be the logical choice.

Line costs will usually be one of the most expensive areas of the total communications system. Dial-up lines could normally be utilized for data rates of 9600 BPS and below. Rates higher than 9600 BPS would usually dictate utilization of leased lines. There are other terminal and communications line considerations, such as full duplex operation, line conditioning, line noise and interference, and echo suppressors, all of which may be a problem when using dial-up lines.

System expansion cost can be reduced when the terminal, MODEM, and communications lines are completely matched when the initial system is configured. Terminal operation of data rates higher than 150 BPS would require the use of at least a voice grade line. This line, with proper conditioning, can normally be used at data rates up to 9600 BPS. The system designer should consider a line capable of 9600 BPS as a source of possible expansion. The line could support more than one terminal since the line capability could be divided between two or more terminals through the use of multiplexers or special MODEMs. This is discussed in greater detail later in this chapter.

Line data rates of 150 BPS can support low speed teletype, teletype compatible CRTs, monitoring or metering devices, analog signalling, or other special low speed devices. A 150 BPS rate may be exactly as stated if a binary type of signalling is used. This would be the case where only numerics or binary patterns are used to provide information.

Where teletype terminal types are used, the total transmission code bits that are available are not all used for information. There are start, stop, and parity bits used to control and synchronize the transfer of information. These bits do not represent useful information.

A comparison of two transmission code sets is illustrated below using a Baudot and ANSCII Code set.

Baudot Code

5–information bits per character

1–start bit per character

1–stop bit per character

A total of 7 bits is needed to transfer a single alphanumeric character over a communication line. Using a 100 BPS terminal and line operation, the following rate of character transfer would result (calculations assume all bits are of equal length):

Example: $100 \div 7 = 14.28$ Characters Per Second (CPS)

In most cases the stop bit is longer than the other bits. This would have an additional impact on the total data transferred. If the start or stop bits were not required, the character transfer would be as follows:

Example: $100 \div 5 = 20$ CPS

ANSCII Code

Using the ANSCII Code set for 100 BPS asynchronous operation, the following would result:

7–information bits per character

1–parity bit

1–start bit

1–stop bit

$100 \div 10 = 10$ CPS.

Assuming a normal ANSCII Communications Terminal operating at a 150 BPS (the low speed line maximum), we could arrive at the terminal's maximum capability. The total character transfer rate would be 15 CPS, 900 Characters Per Minute (CPM), or 54,000 Characters Per Hour (CPH). This does not take into account possible parity errors or line and communication terminal controls; these will be discussed later in this chapter.

If the above data rate, using the low speed line, would not handle the data transfer requirements, the next choice would be the medium-speed voice grade line. This communications line could handle the normal medium speed communications terminal rates such as:

300 BPS	2400 BPS	9600 BPS
1200 BPS	4800 BPS	
1800 BPS	7200 BPS	

The data rates above 2400 BPS usually result in higher communications line costs since high speed MODEMs are more expensive and line conditioning is necessary. Also, error rates tend to rise. Line conditioning can be accomplished in the MODEM or may be provided through the common carrier. There are several levels of line conditioning available and the level selected should be the one required to handle the data rate. Network (line) conditioning is covered in Chapter Eleven.

The higher data rates, beginning with 2400 BPS, usually utilize the synchronous mode of data transmission. The lower data rates could also utilize this mode, but it is usually not necessary since the purpose of the synchronous mode of operation is to increase the data transfer rate.

The synchronous mode does not require the start or stop bits. The parity bit may also be eliminated through the use of other parity checking schemes. This is important when one considers the time consumed by those bits. A comparison of asynchronous to synchronous is presented in the following paragraphs utilizing the ANSCII Code Set. Different terminal and MODEM characteristics are required when transmitting in asynchronous or synchronous modes, but the communications line could be of the same type.

Asynchronous Versus Synchronous

Asynchronous 2400 BPS @ 10 Bits Per Character (BPC) = 240 Characters Per Second (CPS). Synchronous (start and stop bit deleted): 2400 BPS @ 8 BPC = 300 CPS. Synchronous (start, stop and parity bit deleted): 2400 BPS @ 7 BPC = approximately 343 CPS.

Synchronous operation does require the use of synchronous characters. These additional 7- or 8- bit characters are not useful data, but are required for synchronization. The number of synchronous characters varies by terminal types, but usually at least three are required preceding transmission of data and one is required in the data stream at predetermined intervals. This reduces the total data transfer rate, but not to the degree of that caused by an asynchronous mode of operation.

An example of this synchronous operation would be as follows: 2400 BPS @ 8 BPC = 300 CPS, 300 CPS minus 1 synchronous character per second = 299 CPS. The three initial synchronous characters would also be subtracted from the total data transfer.

CONFIGURATION OF THE LINES
AND COMMUNICATIONS TERMINALS

Data transfer requirements normally dictate the location of terminals and the number of terminals at each location. Performance efficiency and economics should be the determining factors in how the facilities (lines) are routed and connected to terminals. Efficiency of terminal operation is covered under a separate topic later in this chapter.

The rules for the selection of the terminals and communication lines are not always clearly defined. System design factors based on system analysis and other pertinent data should be the guiding factor. Each terminal and line requirement must be looked at individually, as well as collectively, to determine the overall requirement to ensure the best routing, connection method and type of line to use, while maintaining the lowest cost possible.

Lease or dedicated lines incur a fixed monthly charge, where dial-up lines incur a connection and time-of-use charge each time the service is utilized.

High dial-up line usage may result in the total cost exceeding the monthly charges for leased lines. If system analysis and experience indicates that this may happen, then leased lines should be considered. Leased lines offer many other options not available with dial-up lines. These options will be presented later in this chapter.

Some of the possible reasons a line and terminal network configuration analysis should be performed are listed below:

- Overall line costs
- MODEM and other line component costs
- Possible host or central system overload caused by:
  - Terminal selection procedures
  - Line and terminal protocols
  - Data format
  - Data editing
  - Code conversion methods
  - Fixed terminal types
  - Failure recovery methods
  - Overall communications processing software design
- Network support criteria
  - Monitoring
  - Error statistics
  - Data volume statistics
  - Maintenance test devices and tools
  - Maintenance diagnostics
  - Redundant or replacement lines and equipment
- Decentralized data base or processing requirements
- Requirement of a terminal to support multiple application types

- Point of entry text editing and processing requirements
  - Data verification
  - Error-free data transmission
  - Data protection and storage
- Provide a system that meets the user's requirements
- Provide a cost-effective, responsive and operational efficient system, with high throughput capability

Some of the areas to be considered during system network design should include the following:

- Points to be connected
- The type of applications to be supported
  - Communications
  - Inquiry/response
  - Batch
  - Conversational
  - Data base or record update
  - Remote data base or processing
  - Other applications as required
- Data Volume
  - Normal load factor
  - Peak load factors
- Response time requirements
  - Inquiry/response
  - Conversational
  - Data base update
  - Batch
- Data protection requirements
  - Parity error detection and correction procedures
  - System restart procedures
  - System reload (start-over) procedures
  - Redundant equipment or data protection areas
- Data formats
  - Possible variations in order to support multiple applications
  - Consider the most efficient formats to support the user and system operation
- Data compression
  - Conserve line usage time
  - Conserve system handling and processing time
- Line and communications terminal protocols
- Computer equipment availability
  - Mainframe

       –Communications multiplexers–programmable
       –Line interface units–programmable
       –Device capability–programmable
       –Mini- or microcomputer equipment
       –Microprogrammable computers
       –Firmware
       –Expansion capability–modular design

- Software availability to support the overall system requirements
  - Ease of program design
  - Ease of program enhancement
  - Ease of program maintenance
  - Modular design

- Communications terminal equipment
  - Uncontrolled
  - Controlled
  - Firmware
  - Programmable
  - Micro- or minicomputer
  - Device availability
  - Programming or software capability
  - Will it support the present and future expansion requirements?

- MODEM and other data communications equipment

- Common carriers—providers or communication lines
  - Telephone companies
  - Western Union
  - Specialized common carriers
  - Foreign
  - User supplied

- System support requirements
  - Hardware (central system)
  - Software (central system and terminals)
  - Facility (line) equipment
  - Communications terminals
  - Redundant equipment (spares and fallback)

- Consideration of the most efficient and cost-effective network design

Line and terminal network design should always be accomplished with the total system requirements in mind. This is necessary since there are many different methods of connecting the terminals. In many cases, once the total network requirement is known, lines and the associated equipment can be configured in such a manner so that lines may be shared by several terminals. This sharing of lines can in effect reduce the cost of the overall network since the lines are usually the most expensive part of any network.

Figures 7-1 through 7-10 in this chapter provide some examples for consideration when connecting the various types of equipment in a terminal, line and

Terminal, Line and Computer System
Network Considerations
(Figures 7-1 through 7-10)

FIGURE 7-1
Terminal Network Consideration — Single Line

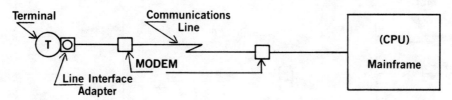

FIGURE 7-1: depicts a single terminal line with two-way communications between terminal and computer.

FIGURE 7-2
Terminal Network Consideration — Shared Line

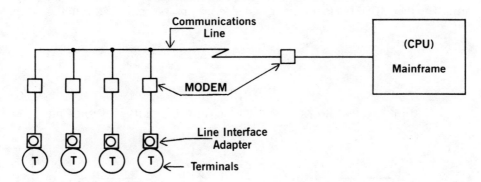

FIGURE 7-2: allows multiple terminals to share a single line with only one terminal being able to transmit or receive at any given time.

FIGURE 7-3
Terminal Network Consideration — Direct Distance Dialing

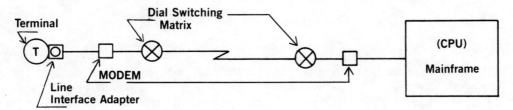

FIGURE 7-3: allows direct distance dialing facilities with single terminal and single line.

FIGURE 7-4

Terminal Network Consideration – Frequency Division Multiplexing

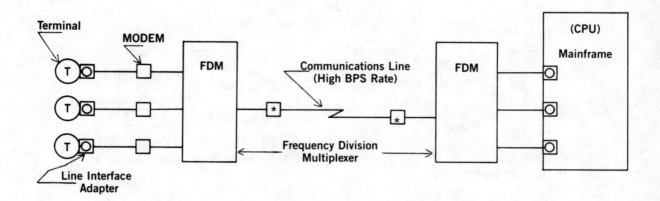

FIGURE 7-4: illustrates concurrent terminals transmit and receive capability with a single line connection between FDMs and multiple line connections at the main-frame. The two MODEMs identified by an asterisk may be combined with the FDMs.

FIGURE 7-5

Terminal Network Consideration – Time Division Multiplexing

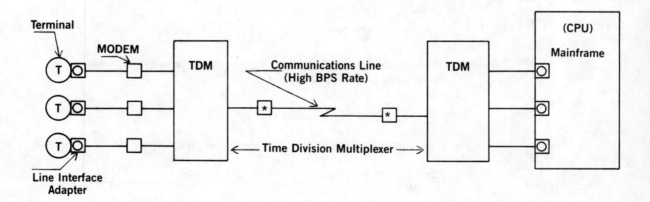

FIGURE 7-5: allows concurrent terminals to transmit and receive with a single line connection between TDMs and multiple line connections at the mainframe. The two MODEMs identified by an asterisk may be combined with the TDMs.

FIGURE 7-6
Terminal Network Consideration — Multiterminals, TDM, and Single Line

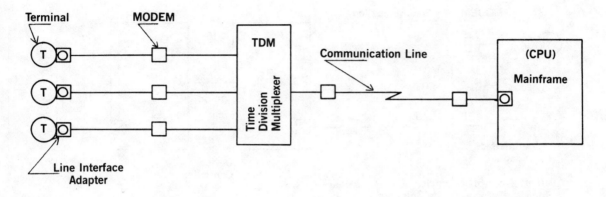

FIGURE 7-6: allows concurrent terminals to transmit and receive with a single line connection between TDM and the mainframe. In this illustration, the time division multiplexing functions are preformed by the mainframe (hardware or software).

FIGURE 7-7
Terminal Network Consideration — Concentrator

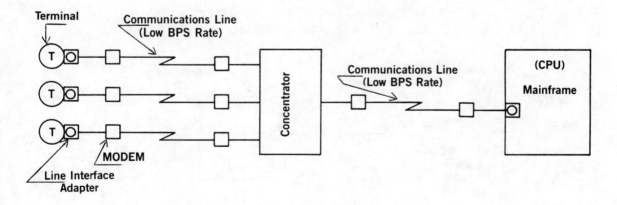

FIGURE 7-7: illustrates concentrator possibilities for (1) data storage and transfer only or, (2) processing, data storage, and transfer or, (3) a complete data processing center. This configuration permits concurrent terminals to transmit and receive if buffering is available in the concentrator. It also allows for single line connections to the mainframe.

FIGURE 7-8
Terminal Network Consideraton — Front-End Processor

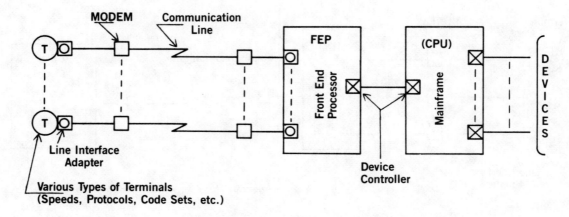

FIGURE 7-8: depicts a configuration using a front-end processor to assume all data communication functions. The front-end can be connected via a device controller (channel) or a communications line. The FEP is capable of data storage and data processing functions prior to passing data to the mainframe or terminals.

FIGURE 7-9
Terminal Network Consideration — Programmable
(Minicomputer) Terminals

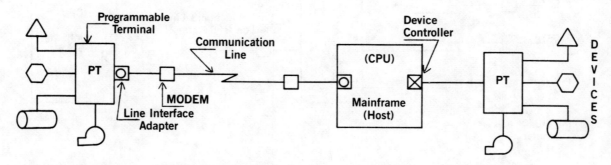

FIGURE 7-9: illustrates a configuration using minicomputer programmable terminals which may be connected via line interface adapter or a device controller. The minicomputer terminal can perform peripheral data processing and provide pre-processing or post-processing at distant points.

FIGURE 7-10

Terminal Network Consideration – Distributive Processing

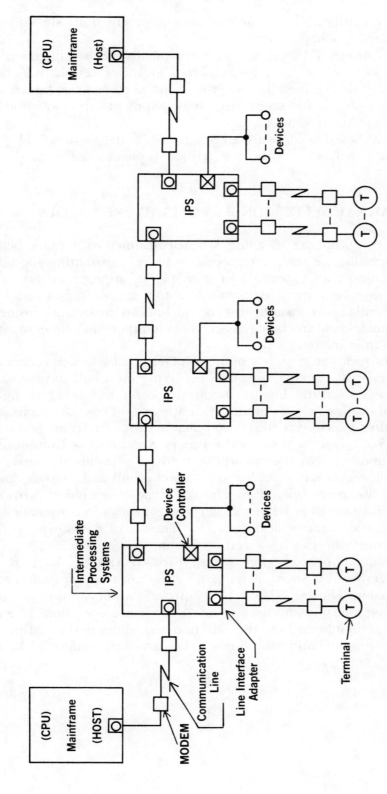

FIGURE 7-10: illustrates a distributive processing configuration which operates under the control of the main (host) or primary system. This configuration reduces storage and processing requirements at the host computer site. It distributes the workload to the users' functional areas and it reduces the communications requirements.

computer network configuration. The various equipment units shown in these figures are described in Chapter Ten.

Figures 7-11 through 7-14 provide an overview of various connection modes and equipment that may be used to connect a group of terminals. The total estimated cost can be determined by using the common carrier cost factors for the various lines to be utilized, and cost factors for equipment can be obtained from common carriers and other vendors.

One point that should become apparent after reviewing Figures 7-11 through 7-14 and applying cost factors, is the cost reduction possibilities through proper network design.

TERMINAL SELECTION BY POLLING PROTOCOLS

Terminal selection (polling or calling) is time consumed without the benefit of moving data. Normally, the selection process includes transmitting the terminal select code, validating the response and then taking appropriate action. This follow-up action may be normal data movement or an abnormal action. This selection process would also consume times on the line, an important consideration where multiterminal lines are being used. The multiterminal line situation is described later in this chapter.

Figure 7-15 provides an overview of a typical terminal selection sequence and response. Consider this sequence of events occurring on a half duplex or a full duplex line. A review of the line turnaround section will bring to light the importance of full duplex lines or other efficient selection considerations.

There are other selection methods completely different from the one illustrated in Figure 7-15. One of these is the Binary Synchronous Communication (BSC) mode of operation. No attempt will be made to show all the possible BSC events and controls since a very complex sequence of events and controls can occur during normal or abnormal operation. The BSC type of operation provides the system designer with a variable means of selection control and manipulation of the data exchanges between communicating points. The use of BSC normally implies synchronous and medium- to high-speed operation.

Every terminal and/or computer system protocol can be diagrammed to provide a clear overview as to what will happen during terminal selection sequences and data transmission. Figures 7-16 and 7-17 provide an illustration of a typical computer (terminal) selection and the transmit and receive operation. The system design specification should include the selection sequences illustrated in such a manner to ensure complete understanding on the part of the vendor and the user.

**Network Design Considerations
(Figures 7-11 through 7-14)**

FIGURE 7-11
Network Design Consideration – Half Duplex Operation

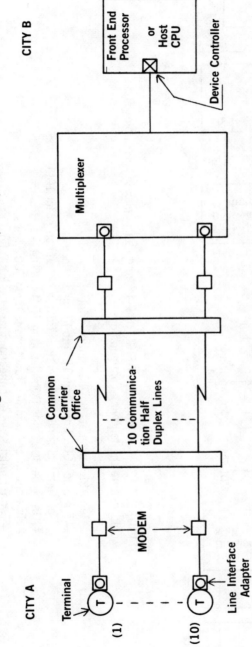

FIGURE 7-11: identifies cost considerations for a 10-terminal network. The 10 terminals may be automatic send/receive (ASR) with keyboard, paper tape and printer. To connect the terminals to the CPU or FEP would require ten 1006 type lines at (X) miles each from terminal to processor and 20 terminal service connections from the common carrier. Ten low-speed asynchronous line interface adapters and ten multiplexer ports would also be required. Throughput requirements are 150 characters per second or 15 characters per second per terminal.

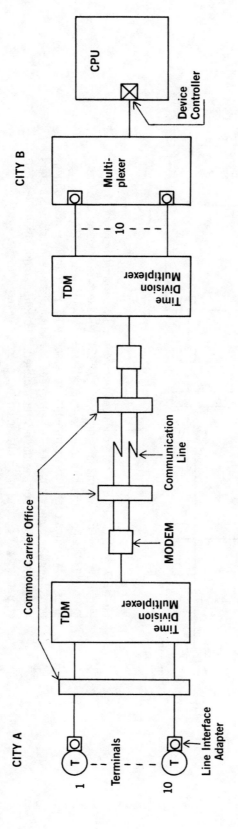

FIGURE 7-12
Network Design Consideration — Full Duplex Operation

FIGURE 7-12: is an upgrade of FIGURE 7-11 from half duplex to full duplex and would require the following configuration:

—Ten ASR terminals (keyboard/tape/printer)
—Ten type 1006 lines from TDM to terminals (local)
—Ten terminal service connections from common carrier for 1006 type lines
—One type 3002 line (X) miles from TDM to TDM
—Two circuit conditioning functions for type 3002 lines
—Two terminal service connections for type 3002 lines
—Two time division multiplexers capable of handling 10-150 BPS lines
—Two MODEMs for 2400 or 4800 BPS capability
—Ten Asynchronous low-speed line interface adapters
—Ten multiplexer ports
—Throughput requirement is 150 characters per second with memory, hardware, and software management requirements in the CPU

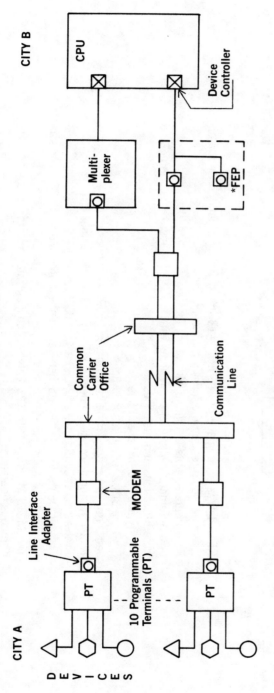

FIGURE 7-13
Network Design Consideration – Programmable Terminals

FIGURE 7-13: is an upgrade of FIGURE 7-12 to a programmable terminal environment which would require the following configuration:

—Ten programmable terminals all in one location and sharing one communications line
—One type 3002 line (X) miles from City A to City B
—Eleven terminal service connections from common carrier
—Eleven circuit conditioning functions (possible requirement)
—Eleven MODEMs for 2400 to 4800 BPS capability (dictated by terminal types)
—One synchronous medium speed line interface adapter
*Optional programmable (front-end processor) operating as a single device or on a multiplexing loop
—One multiplexer port
—Throughput requirement is 300 to 600 characters per second (dictated by terminal types)
—Multiple terminals sharing a single line
—Memory, hardware, software, terminals, and network management under the control of the CPU
—Line sharing equipment in common carrier's office

FIGURE 7-14

Network Design Consideration – Data Concentrator

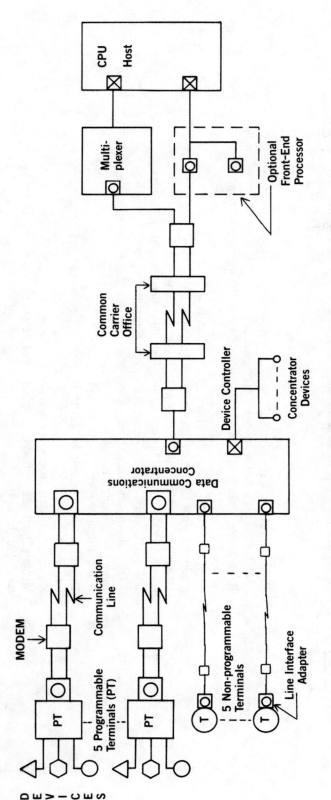

FIGURE 7-14: is an upgrade of FIGURE 7-13 incorporating a data concentrator. This structure would require the following configuration:

—Five programmable terminals with varied locations and line distances
—Five automatic send/receive terminals with keyboard, paper tape, printer, and varied locations and distances
—Five type 1006 low-speed lines
—Six type 3002 medium-speed lines
—Ten terminal service connections for type 1006 type lines
—Twelve terminal service connections for type 3002 type lines
—Twelve circuit conditioning functions for 3002 type lines
—Two MODEMs for 4800 BPS between concentrator and host CPU for synchronous operation
—Ten MODEMs for 2400 BPS between concentrator and terminals for synchronous operation
—One minicomputer for concentrator functions
—Throughput requirement is 600 to 1200 characters per second between the concentrator and the host CPU
—Memory, hardware, software, and other system control features are in concentrator and host computer

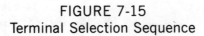

FIGURE 7-15
Terminal Selection Sequence

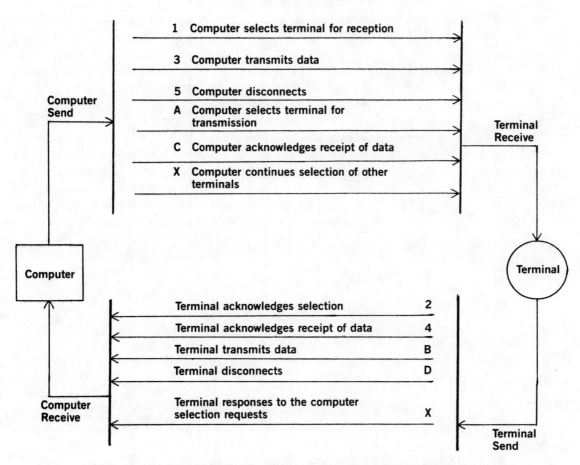

Figure 7-15: depicts an example of a computer to terminal and terminal to computer communications and the sequence for the terminal selection. In this example the computer to terminal sequence is 1, 2, 3, 4, 5 and the terminal to computer sequence is A, B, C, D. (This sequence of events assumes normal operation.)

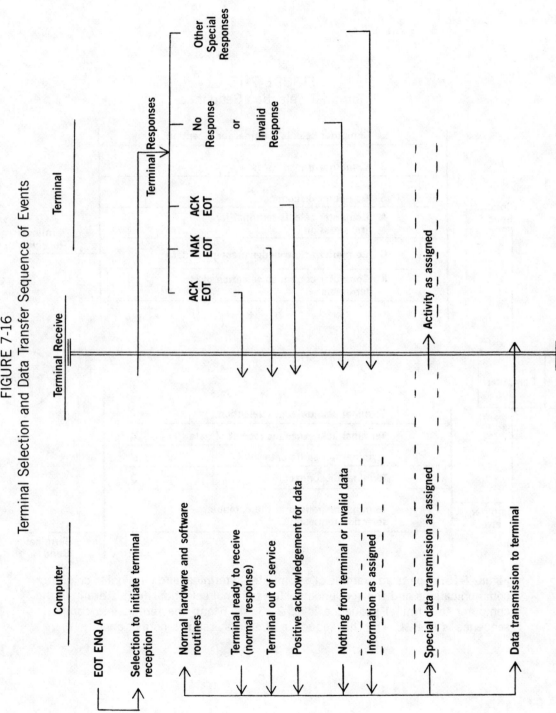

FIGURE 7-16
Terminal Selection and Data Transfer Sequence of Events

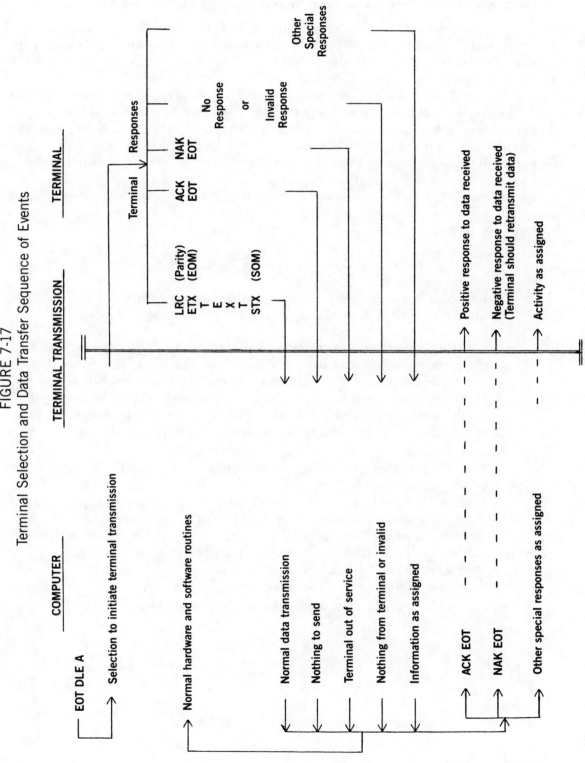

FIGURE 7-17
Terminal Selection and Data Transfer Sequence of Events

Communications Terminal Selection and Configuration Considerations

System protocol methods play an important part in network configuration. It is necessary to analyze the effect of terminal selection when determining the data movement capability of each line connection. This consideration is very important when multiterminal lines will be used.

Figures 7-18 through 7-20 illustrate the effect that terminal selection may have on the system's ability to utilize the full capability of a given line. Lost line time due to selection requirements can be a limiting factor and may result in the line being incapable of handling the data transfer requirements. The problem is compounded when processing time consumed by the central system is added to the lost time caused by the line and terminal.

Some of the areas that should be reviewed when acquiring terminals, line equipment, and designing communications handling software and hardware, would be as follows:

- Terminal Selection Procedures (Protocols):
  - Polling/calling sequences.
  - Response from the selected communications terminals.
  - Special functions controls as required.
  - Error controls.
  - Quick selection: implies a poll or call is transmitted to a terminal and the response is the data stream rather than a response indicating that the terminal is ready to transmit or receive. The acknowledgment from the central system is for the data. Transmission to the terminal would work in a similar manner. The selection would immediately precede the data and the terminal would acknowledge the data.

- Central system:
  - Selection cycles—variable in accordance with each terminal's requirement.
  - Selection weight factors—selection of a particular terminal may be two, three, or more times more frequent than of some other terminals,
  - Dynamic selection weight factors—system automatically varies individual terminal selection in accordance with system load factors.
  - Overall associated system processing functions.
  - Communications processing software.

- Consider sequences that can be changed or eliminated.

- Full duplex operation.

Terminal Selection and
Configuration Considerations
(Figures 7-18 through 7-20)

FIGURE 7-18
Terminal Selection and Configuration Consideration — Noncontrolled

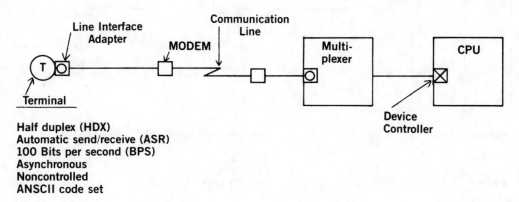

Half duplex (HDX)
Automatic send/receive (ASR)
100 Bits per second (BPS)
Asynchronous
Noncontrolled
ANSCII code set

Terminal Line Capability

10 characters per second (CPS)
600 characters per minute (CPM)
36,000 characters per hour (CPH)

FIGURE 7-18: This example assumes 200 character data blocks or 3 blocks per minute or 180 blocks per hour with a total data transfer equal to the sum of send and receive at half duplex operation. Error control reduces transfer rate and no terminal selection controls are utilized. In this example, the line and terminal capability is fully utilized. Review FIGURE 7-21 for an illustration of lost time caused by selection and error controls.

FIGURE 7-19
Terminal Selection and Configuration — 100 BPS Controlled

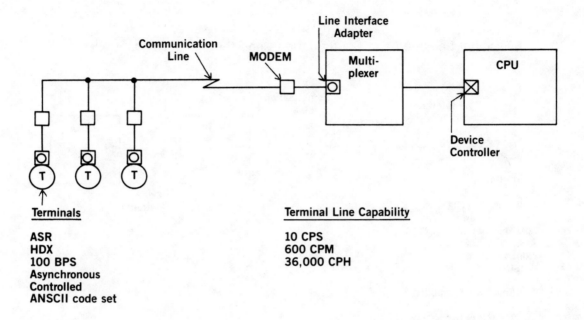

Terminals

ASR
HDX
100 BPS
Asynchronous
Controlled
ANSCII code set

Terminal Line Capability

10 CPS
600 CPM
36,000 CPH

FIGURE 7-19: This example assumes 200 character data blocks with the following characteristics:

—Poll (terminal transmit) EOT DLE A   Response = 5 char time
—Call (terminal receive) ENQ A ENQ DC2   = 4 char time
—Motor start-up time delay
  (750 milliseconds)   = 8 char time
—ACK (send or receive + line
  turnaround time   = 3 char time
—Possible ACK for call prior to
  computer transmission   = 2 to 3 char time
—Error control (repeat data block)

Lost line time of approximately 16 to 19 character time will occur for every data block sent or received because of selection, data verification controls, and line turnaround. This lost time will result in the total line capability being reduced to less than 3 blocks per minute as shown in FIGURE 7-18. Software routines required for selection and error controls will cause additional lost line time. Error retransmission will cause additional lost time.

FIGURE 7-20
Terminal Selection and Configuration Consideration — 300 BPS Controlled

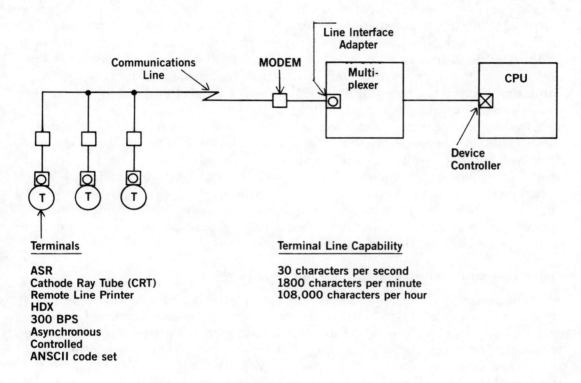

Terminals

ASR
Cathode Ray Tube (CRT)
Remote Line Printer
HDX
300 BPS
Asynchronous
Controlled
ANSCII code set

Terminal Line Capability

30 characters per second
1800 characters per minute
108,000 characters per hour

FIGURE 7-20: This example assumes 200 character data blocks with the following characteristics:

—Selection for terminal transmit	= 3 char time
—Selection for terminal receive	= 3 char time
—Response (terminal to receive selection)	= 2 or 3 char time
—ACK for data transmitted and line turnaround time	= 3 char time
—Error control (repeat data block)	

Without controls, the maximum terminal(s) capability would be 9 data blocks per minute or 540 data blocks per hour. Errors causing repeat of data must be subtracted from the maximum capability. Selection controls as indicated above will reduce the maximum capability to approximately 5 data blocks per minute or 300 per hour. Software routines required for selection controls, line controls, and error controls cause a further reduction in total capability. A change to 2400 BPS and synchronous operation (8 bit characters), minus the necessary synchronous characters, would result in the following operation (approximately): 87 data blocks per minute or 5,220 data blocks per hour.

LINE TURNAROUND PROBLEM

During the process of terminal selection and data transfer, when half duplex lines are used, it is necessary to frequently turn the line around for communication purposes. Take the case where the computer is transmitting to a terminal. The computer seizes the line and calls the terminal; then the computer releases the line and the terminal seizes the line and responds; then the terminal releases the line and the computer seizes the line and transmits the data (1 block); then the computer releases the line and the terminal seizes the line and acknowledges the data; then the terminal releases the line.

In the above sequence of events the line was turned around three times during the transfer of one block of data. The time consumed to turn the line around is time lost for data transfer. The amount of time lost during line turnaround sequences will be determined by the type of equipment used, since there is a large variation in equipment capabilities. This capability should be illustrated in the equipment descriptions or specifications and should be made available to the system designer. Every part of the system plays a part in the lost time created during selections and data transfers.

Definition and Analysis of Turnaround Problem

The response time problems and the part played by the system equipment is shown in Figure 7-21. Figure 7-21 represents an inquiry message received from the terminal and in turn a response message transmitted from the computer to the terminal. The times quoted in milliseconds represent typical system software and equipment operation times. These quoted times may be too long for some of the more sophisticated equipment, but on the other hand, the time is optimistic for other types of equipment and software used in many systems. Also, system load factors are not considered in this example. Loading the system usually increases the time consumed by the central system.

A review of Figure 7-21 will show the line was seized and/or turned around a total of seven times during the exchange of one inquiry and response message. Consider the case of block by block transmission, which would occur if a batch of data is being transmitted from a terminal. The line would be turned around before and after each block of data, as illustrated in the following example:

	MILLISECONDS
(C) RTS CTS	200MS
(C) Poll Transmission	X
(T) RTS CTS	200MS
(T) Block of Data (300 Characters)	1200MS
(C) RTS CTS	200MS
(C) ACK	36MS
(T) Block of Data (300 Characters)	1200MS
(C) RTS CTS	200MS
(C) ACK	36MS
ETC. - - - - -	

WHERE: (C)   = Computer
         RTS   = Request to Send
         CTS   = Clear to Send
         (T)   = Terminal

An analysis of the line time consumed during the block by block transmission would show a major part of the line time is consumed in controlling the line and acknowledging the data.

Solutions and Design Considerations

Terminal operation, line control, and the central system functions can be efficient when proper design concepts are followed. Mainframe equipment, multiplexers, line interface adapters, MODEMs, terminals, line types, and software design all have an important part in problem resolution.

If full duplex lines are used instead of half duplex lines, which is possible if the computer hardware and software can support full duplex operation, every line turnaround could be eliminated. The computer and terminal could hold up Request to Send (RTS) at all times when a single terminal line is being used. When a multiterminal line is being used, the terminal could hold up RTS only if the response to the computer output will be returned prior to any other terminal on the line being selected for an input. If another terminal is allowed input prior to the response being returned to the first terminal, then the terminal RTS signal cannot be held up. In this case, approximately half of the line turnarounds could be eliminated. The computer could always hold the RTS signal in an up condition.

If the terminal and computer operational modes will not permit holding up the RTS signal, then other means of eliminating the turnaround problem must be considered.

One consideration would be as follows: When the terminal or computer is receiving, the receiving device could anticipate the response requirement and raise the RTS signal prior to the completion of data input. This could occur during some period of data transmission where this action would not cause a problem.

A major part of system design, where communications with terminal equipment will be a system function, should include an analysis of the line control methods and procedures. Proper design of line devices and equipment components can aid in solving the turnaround problem. MODEMs are available that will provide a quick turnaround, thus cutting down on lost time. Design of the line interface adapters and supporting software can be a major factor. These areas play a major part in all functions of network control. Full duplex operation can solve the problem in many cases. Chapters Three and Five cover communications hardware and software principles and can provide additional information concerning this subject.

FIGURE 7-21
Line Turnaround Analysis

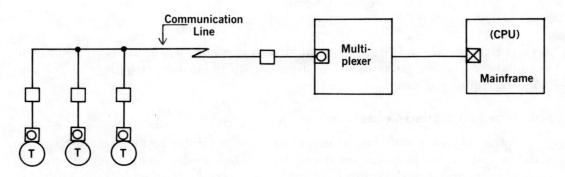

LEGEND:
Ⓣ = **Terminal**
◎ = **Line Interface Adapter**
▢ = **MODEM**
⊠ = **CPU Device Controller**
C = **Computer Operation**
T = **Terminal Operation**

The following is an example of the response time problem for terminal inquiry and follow-up computer response for controlled terminals.

	FUNCTION	MILLISECONDS
C	Selection Rate Time	250
	— Interupt Handlers	
	— Selection Module Cycle	Time = X
	— Program Scheduling	
	— Software Routines	
C	MODEM — Request to Send, Clear to Send	200*
C	Transmit Poll to Terminal: SYNC SYNC SOH AAX EOT CRC CRC	30
T	MODEM Turn Around — Request to Send, Clear to Send	200
T	Terminal Transmit: SYN SYN SOH — Header Info — STX — Data (Inquiry) EOT CRC CRC	60
C	MODEM Turn Around — Request to Send, Clear to Send	200*
C	Acknowledgment to Terminal	30
C	Computer Processing Time (Inquiry Processing)	
	— Module Scheduling	
	— Edit Program	
	— Code Conversion	Time = Y
	— Processing Modules Run Time	
	— I/O Processors	
	— Communications Processing	
C	Selection Rate Time (Similar to Poll Transmission Processing)	250
C	MODEM — Request to Send, Clear to Send	200*
C	Transmit Call to Terminal (Approximately Same as Poll)	30
T	MODEM Turn Around — Request to Send, Clear to Send	200
T	Acknowledgment to Computer for Call	30

FUNCTION	MILLISECONDS
C MODEM Turn Around — Request to Send, Clear to Send	200*
C Response to Terminal (300 Characters)	1000
T MODEM Turn Around — Request to Send, Clear to Send	200
T Acknowledgment to Computer for Data	30

FIGURE 7-21: illustrates an example of line turnaround analysis of response time problem for terminal to computer transmission of 24 bits per second over half duplex circuit operating in synchronous mode with selection controls. Those functions indicated by an asterisk could be eliminated by continuously holding up request to send at the computer providing all transmissions are between computer and terminal. Full duplex operation could eliminate all MODEM request to send, clear to send requirements, under controlled conditions. As illustrated in this example, approximately 1400 milliseconds was consumed in the process of activating the MODEM for transmission.

CHAPTER EIGHT

Data Transmission Codes And Error Handling Techniques

Communications between mainframe components and external devices or terminals requires the use of data codes, data formats, and error controls in order to control and protect the flow of data and to allow the necessary editing and processing. Data flow efficiency and protection is usually determined by the types of codes used and the error control procedures designed into the system. Data structure or format of the data has an impact on the internal software editing, processing, and integrity of the data as it is processed and transmitted through the system.

Modern computer systems permit the sharing of data bases by many users simultaneously and permit on-line programming, job execution, and data file interactions from remote terminal locations. It is necessary to isolate programs that are running (in execution) and to protect their working memory and permanent data files from being destroyed or modified by accident or by deliberate actions. Systems must be designed so that not only proprietary and confidential information is protected, but personal information in data bases must be safeguarded as well.

This chapter discusses the efficiencies, advantages, and disadvantages of various transmission code sets and how they affect data manipulation and throughput. Different methods and schemes for error detection and correction techniques are included along with concepts and ideas on data and private information protection.

TYPES AND EFFICIENCIES OF CODE SETS

Data codes are composed of a group of bits formatted in a particular pattern to represent an alpha or numeric character or symbol. A bit is the smallest element of information and the term bit is derived from the contraction "binary digit." Computers operate in binary. The binary digit is represented by a "0" bit and "1" bit. The 0 represents an "Off" or "No" condition, while the 1 represents an "On" or "Yes" condition. The binary bit represents the presence or absence of an electrical pulse. Bits are usually manipulated in the computer in 8-bit bytes.

A byte is a grouping of bits that are treated as a unit. A byte normally consists of 8 bits. A byte could represent one alphanumeric character, or 2 decimal digits, or 8 binary digits, or any other configuration necessary to fulfill system data requirements. When a bit grouping is assembled for communications purposes, the result is generally termed an alpha character, a number set, a special symbol or control symbol.

Baudot Code

The Baudot Code set is 5 bits in length allowing 32 possible unique code combinations to represent characters. In the English language there are 26 letters, 10 numbers, and approximately 10 special symbols used for punctuation, formatting, and control symbols. This count represents 46 characters. The 5-bit code does not allow enough unique combinations to satisfy this number of characters. To remedy this problem, shift characters were added to the Baudot Code. These shift characters are designated for upper and lower case. In this manner, Baudot machines operate similar to a typewriter with its upper and lower case. The shift characters increase the code capability to 64 combinations (excluding upper and lower shift characters) since the same bit combination can be used twice, in upper and lower case.

As seen in Figure 8-1, in addition to the two shift codes, there are six character codes which exist in either upper or lower case. These six codes may be classed as control codes since they allow machine controls to be transmitted but do not convey any printed information. After assigning the six control codes, the remaining combinations were assigned to the alphabet in lower case and the number set and special symbols in upper case. There are three widely used variations of these special symbols in use today: communications (narrative text), weather symbols, and fractions.

The efficiency of the Baudot Code is very high from the standpoint that there is a code assignment for each unique grouping of bits. For the narrative type of communication, the code performs very well and is frequently used. For general data transmission though, this code loses some efficiency due to a mix of alphanumerics and numerics. For example:

- A stock number for an item is A1B2C3D4.

- The stock number encoded for transmission in the Baudot Code would require the following manipulations on the keyboard: Ltrs Shift A, Figs Shift 1, Ltrs Shift B, Figs Shift 2, Ltrs Shift C, Figs Shift 3, Ltrs Shift D, and Figs Shift 4.

- Insertion of letters shift and figures shift characters has reduced the overall data throughput efficiency by 50 percent.

FIGURE 8-1
Baudot Code Set Example

Character Case		Bit Pattern					Character Case		Bit Pattern				
Lower	Upper	5	4	3	2	1	Lower	Upper	5	4	3	2	1
A	—	0	0	0	1	1	Q	1	1	0	1	1	1
B	?	1	1	0	0	1	R	4	0	1	0	1	0
C	:	0	1	1	1	0	S	'	0	0	1	0	1
D	$	0	1	0	0	1	T	5	1	0	0	0	0
E	3	0	0	0	0	1	U	7	0	0	1	1	1
F	!	0	1	1	0	1	V	;	1	1	1	1	0
G	&	1	1	0	1	0	W	2	1	0	0	1	1
H	#	1	0	1	0	0	X	/	1	1	1	0	1
I	8	0	0	1	1	0	Y	6	1	0	1	0	1
J	Bell	0	1	0	1	1	Z	"	1	0	0	0	1
K	(	0	1	1	1	1	Letters (Shift) ↓		1	1	1	1	1
L	)	1	0	0	1	0	Figures (Shift) ↑		1	1	0	1	1
M	.	1	1	1	0	0	Space (SP) =		0	0	1	0	0
N	,	0	1	1	0	0	Carriage Return <		0	1	0	0	0
O	9	1	1	0	0	0	Line Feed ≡		0	0	0	1	0
P	0	1	0	1	1	0	Blank		0	0	0	0	0

1 = Mark Condition
0 = Space Condition

Hollerith Code

The most popular code used for DP punched card operations is the Hollerith Code. (See Figure 8-2.) There are other versions of the code where three or more number punches per card column are assigned a variety of graphic or scientific notations. The alpha, numerics and special symbols of the Hollerith Code are shown in Figure 8-2.

The efficiency of the Hollerith Code is very low since there are 4,096 possible unique combinations of bits in each column and only 100 or so code assignments are utilized in the code set. The fact that the card is standard in industry and that it provides the flexibility of many new code assignments has kept this code set popular.

FIGURE 8-2
Hollerith Code Example

Character	Card Code Punches	Character	Card Code Punches
A	12-1	#	3-8
B	12-2	$	11-3-8
C	12-3	%	*5
D	12-4	&	12
E	12-5	"	*6
F	12-6	(	*9
G	12-7	)	*0 (zero)
H	12-8	*	*8
I	12-9	+	*12
J	11-1	,	0-3-8
K	11-2	-	11
L	11-3	.	12-3-8
M	11-4	/	0-1
N	11-5	:	*4
O	11-6	;	*3
P	11-7	=	*1
Q	11-8	?	*0-1
R	11-9	@	4-8
S	0-2	□	*2
T	0-3	¢	*4-8
U	0-4	Tab	12-5-9
V	0-5	Pch On	4-9
W	0-6	Pch Off	12-4-9
X	0-7	Delete	12-7-9
Y	0-8	EOT	7-9
Z	0-9	Idle	11-7-9
Upper Case	9-6	Bypass	0-4-9
Lower Case	12-9-6	Restore	11-4-9
0	0	±	*3-8
1	1	≠	0-2-8
2	2	≢	*0-2-8
3	3	✄	*11-0
4	4	√	*12-0
5	5	Rdr Stop	5-9
6	6	EOB	0-6-9
7	7	Backsp	11-6-9
8	8	+0 (zero)	12-0
9	9	−0 (zero)	11-0
Space	Blank	CR + LF	11-9-5
Linefeed (LF)	0-9-5		

FIGURE 8-2, continued

*	= Upper case	≠	= Record Mark
Pch	= Punch	≢	= Group Mark
EOT	= End of Transmission	Rdr	= Reader
EOB	= End of Block	CR	= Carriage Return

Binary Coded Decimal (4 Bits)

In data processing, the internal processing code selected for the computer is one which most nearly represents the pure binary numbers adaptable to computer hardware. Pure binary numbers were too difficult for humans to work with when dealing with decimal numbers. In order for humans to be effective working with decimal numbers in binary notation, the pure binary representations were modified to represent numeric numbers in a code set known as binary coded decimal (BCD). As shown in Figure 8-3, numeric numbers are represented by a 4-bit BCD code. These numeric code assignments follow the mathematical binary digit weights with exception of the 0 (zero).

FIGURE 8-3
Binary Coded Decimal Example
(Numerics Encoding)

Numeric (Decimal)	Equivalent (Binary)	BCD Code
0	0	1010
1	1	0001
2	10	0010
3	11	0011
4	100	0100
5	101	0101
6	110	0110
7	111	0111
8	1000	1000
9	1001	1001
10	1010	0001 1010
11	1011	0001 0001
15	1111	0001 0101
16	10000	0001 0110
255	11111111	0010 0101 0101
256	100000000	0010 0101 0110

Binary Coded Decimal Interchange Code (6 Bits)

One shortcoming of the BCD code was that there were no representations for the alphanumerics or punctuation symbols necessary for interchange of most information. This deficiency was fulfilled by the development of the Binary Coded

Decimal Interchange Code (BCDIC). There are, as in the case of the Baudot Code, many variations of code assignments within this code set as required by the users. One variation is the BCDIC graphics as shown in Figure 8-4.

BCDIC is a 6-bit code and therefore has the capability of 64 unique combinations for code assignments. All 64 codes are used in this set, which makes BCDIC very efficient. As can be seen in Figure 8-4, the 26 alpha characters, 10 numerics, and 26 special functions are accommodated.

FIGURE 8-4

Binary Coded Decimal Interchange Code Example

B I T S			3	0	0	0	0	1	1	1	1
			2	0	0	1	1	0	0	1	1
			1	0	1	0	1	0	1	0	1
6	5	4									
0	0	0		SP	1	2	3	4	5	6	7
0	0	1		8	9	0	#/=	@/'	:	>	√
0	1	0		SP	/	S	T	U	V	W	X
0	1	1		Y	Z	=	,	%/(	γ	\	+++
1	0	0		—	J	K	L	M	N	O	P
1	0	1		Q	R	!	$	*	]	;	
1	1	0		&/+	A	B	C	D	E	F	G
1	1	1		H	I	?	.	¤/)	[	<	‡

Commercial Usage /
Scientific Usage

Example:

Bits: 6 5 4 3 2 1

1 1 0 0 1 0 = LETTER B

0 0 0 0 1 1 = NUMBER 3

Extended Binary Coded Decimal (6 Bits)

The Extended Binary Coded Decimal (EBCD) Code, sometimes called Paper Tape Transmission Code (PTTC), was developed to add a parity bit to the BCDIC Coded character. This redundant bit is used in checking the validity of the character after it has been transmitted. As shown in Figure 8-5, the EBCD code set has two code assignments, upper or lower case, similar to the Baudot Code. This code set also has the capability to utilize a special bit preceding the data bit allowing a shift to occur upon reception of each character.

The shift codes extend the number of code assignments from 64 to 128, except that many of the control codes are assigned in both cases. The efficiency of the EBCD code is very high. With the upper and lower case functions, the number of codes available is doubled. The throughput of this code when handling data is good because the numerics are kept in lower case as opposed to the upper case in

FIGURE 8-5

Extended Binary Coded Decimal Example
(Paper Tape Transmission Code)

BITS 3 2 1 \ 6 5 4	0 0 0	0 0 1	0 1 0	0 1 1	1 0 0	1 0 1	1 1 0	1 1 1
0 0 0	SP / SP	: / 4	2	' / 6	= / 1	% / 5	; / 3	7
0 0 1	-	M / m	K / k	O / o	J / j	N / n	L / l	P / p
0 1 0	¢ / @	U / u	S / s	W / w	? / /	V / v	T / t	X / x
0 1 1	+ / &	D / d	B / b	F / f	A / a	E / e	C / c	G / g
1 0 0	* / 8	PN / PN	∅	UC / UC	(/ 9	RS / RS	" / #	EOT / EOT
1 0 1	Q / q	RES / RES	EOB / EOB	BS / BS	R / r	NL / NL	! / $	IL / IL
1 1 0	Y / y	BY / BY			Z / z	LF / LF		/ '	PRE / PRE
1 1 1	H / h	PF / PF		LC / LC	I / i	HT / HT	7 / .	DLE / DLE

Upper Case \ Lower Case

Example:

Bits:	P	6	5	4	3	2	1	(P = Parity Bit)
	0	1	0	1	0	1	1	(P = letter "E")
	1	1	0	0	1	0	0	= number "9"

NON-PRINTING CHARACTERS

LF – Line Feed
HT – Horiz. Tab
EOT – End of Transmission
EOB – End of Block
UC – Upper Case
LC – Lower Case
IL – Idle
PRE – Prefix
DLE – Delete

SP – Space
PN – Punch On
RES – Restore
BY – Bypass
PF – Punch Off
BS – Backspace
RS – Reader Stop
NL – New Line

Baudot Code. In this way there is no need for the shifting functions required when transmitting stock numbers as used in the earlier example.

In addition to the high efficiency of the EBCD code set, it makes provision for a number of machine function codes to improve the man-machine interface. Such characters as HT (Horizontal Tabulation), BS (Backspace), and DLE (Delete) are format effectors which are very useful in editing and checking data prior to actual transmission. Several communications control functions are provided in EBCD. Line-handling routines such as framing the data into blocks with the use of the EOB (End of Block) code, framing messages or other complete transmissions with the EOT (End of Transmission) code are very helpful to communication operations. Character synchronization during synchronous transmissions have been accommodated through the IDLE code. This IDLE code is used preceding and during actual data to provide this synchronization. Because of their importance, these control characters are assigned the same meaning in both cases of the code.

Extended Binary Coded Decimal Interchange Code (8 Bits)

This Extended Binary Coded Decimal Interchange Code (EBCDIC) is an 8-bit code and has the capability of 256 unique code assignments. Of this number, only about half are used, causing EBCDIC to be very inefficient. The code set does provide for both upper and lower case alpha characters without the bother of shift functions as in the case of EBCD. As can be seen in Figure 8-6, there are several areas of unassigned codes where unique symbols can be assigned on a local basis. This gives the code set a wider flexibility than most at the expense of efficiency. The EBCDIC code set does have many of the control codes mentioned previously but does not inherently have a parity bit. The parity bit can of course be added on an individual basis.

American National Standard Code for Information Interchange (7 Bits)

The American National Standard Code for Information Interchange (AN-SCII) was developed as the standard code for information interchange in the United States. This code set or variations of it has now been adopted worldwide and it is becoming a world standard code set. ANSCII is a 7-bit code and has provision for a parity bit. The ANSCII code is illustrated in Figure 8-7 and Table 8-7. The maximum possible number of unique code combinations (omitting the parity bit) is 128. Notice that the code set has provision for both upper and lower case alpha characters, numerics, a general number of special symbols used as format effectors and for punctuation, and finally, the most extensive set of control characters of any of the codes discussed.

FIGURE 8-6

Extended Binary Coded Decimal Interchange Code Example

BITS 8 7 6 5 → / ↓ 4 3 2 1	0000	0001	0010	0011	0100	0101	0110	0111	1000	1001	1010	1011	1100	1101	1110	1111
0000	NUL				SP	&	-									0
0001							/		a	j			A	J		1
0010									b	k	s		B	K	S	2
0011									c	l	t		C	L	T	3
0100	PF	RES	BYP	PN					d	m	u		D	M	U	4
0101	HT	NL	LF	RS					e	n	v		E	N	V	5
0110	LC	BS	EOB	UC					f	o	w		F	O	W	6
0111	DEL	IL	PRE	EOT					g	p	x		G	P	X	7
1000									h	q	y		H	Q	Y	8
1001									i	r	z		I	R	Z	9
1010			SM		¢	!			:							
1011					.	$	,	#								
1100					<	*	%	@								
1101					(	)	_	'								
1110					+	;	>	=								
1111						¬	?	"								¤

PF – Punch Off
HT – Horiz. Tab
LC – Lower Case
DEL – Delete
SP – Space
UC – Upper Case

RES – Restore
NL – New Line
BS – Backspace
IL – Idle
PN – Punch On
EOT – End of Transmission

BYP – Bypass
LF – Line Feed
EOB – End of Block
PRE – Prefix
RS – Reader Stop
SM – Start Message

FIGURE 8-7
American National Standard Code for
Information Interchange

B I T S			7	0	0	0	0	1	1	1	1
			6	0	0	1	1	0	0	1	1
			5	0	1	0	1	0	1	0	1
4	3	2	1								
0	0	0	0	NUL	DLE	SP	0	@	P	`	p
0	0	0	1	SOH	DC1	!	1	A	Q	a	q
0	0	1	0	STX	DC2	"	2	B	R	b	r
0	0	1	1	ETX	DC3	#	3	C	S	c	s
0	1	0	0	EOT	DC4	$	4	D	T	d	t
0	1	0	1	ENQ	NAK	%	5	E	U	e	u
0	1	1	0	ACK	SYN	&	6	F	V	f	v
0	1	1	1	BEL	ETB	'	7	G	W	g	w
1	0	0	0	BS	CAN	(	8	H	X	h	x
1	0	0	1	HT	EM	)	9	I	Y	i	y
1	0	1	0	LF	SUB	*	:	J	Z	j	z
1	0	1	1	VT	ESC	+	;	K	[	k	{
1	1	0	0	FF	FS	'		L	\	l	|
1	1	0	1	CR	GS	-	=	M	]	m	}
1	1	1	0	SO	RS	•	>	N	^	n	~
1	1	1	1	SI	US	/	?	O	—	o	DEL

EXAMPLE: $\textcircled{P}$ = Parity
Bits: $\textcircled{P}$ 7 6 5 4 3 2 1
    1 1 0 0 0 0 0 1 = letter "A"   (Odd Parity)
    0 0 1 1 0 0 1 0 = number "2" (Odd Parity)

TABLE 8-7
ANSCII Code Set Abbreviations

ABBREVIATION (DEFINITION)	FUNCTION
NUL (Null)	The all zeros character, used for time or media fill.
SOH (Start of Header)	A communication control character, used at the beginning of routing information.
STS (Start of Text)	A communication control character, used at the end of header or start of text.
EXT (End of Text)	A communication control character, used at end of text or start of trailer.
EOT (End of Transmission)	A communication control character, used at end of transmission, i.e., end of call.
ENQ (Enquire)	A communication control character, used as a request for response, "who are you."
ACK (Acknowledge)	A communication control character, used as an affirmative response to a sender.
BEL (Bell)	A character used to call for human attention.
BS (Backspace)	A format effector, moves a printing device back one space on the same line.
HT (Horiz. Tab)	A format effector, moves a printing device to the next predetermined position along a line.
LF (Line Feed)	A format effector, moves a printing device to the next printing line.
VT (Vertical Tab)	A format effector, moves a printing device to the next predetermined printing line.
FF (Form Feed)	A format effector, moves the paper to the next page.
CR (Carriage Return)	A format effector, moves the printing device to the left margin.
SO (Shift Out)	A control character, code characters which follow are not in the code set of the standard code in use.
SI (Shift In)	A control character, code characters which follow are in the code set of the standard code in use.
DLE (Data Line Escape)	A communication control character, used to change the meaning of a limited number of contiguously following characters.
DC1, DC2, DC3, DC4 (Device Controls)	Characters for the control of auxiliary devices, i.e., start, pause, stop.
NAK (Negative Acknowledge)	A communication control character, used as a negative response to a sender.
SYN (Synchronous Idle)	A communication control character, used for character synchronization in synchronous transmissions.

TABLE 8-7, continued

ETB (End of Trans-....... mission Block)	A communication control character, used to indicate end of a block of data.
CAN (Cancel)............	A control character; disregard the data sent .
EM (End of Medium).....	A control character; end of wanted information recorded on a medium.
SS (Start of Special...... Sequence)	A control character; as named.
ESC (Escape)	A control character, used to extend code.
FS, GS, RS, US (File..... Group, Record, Unit Separators)	Characters for control purposes.
DEL (Delete)	Used to erase in paper tape punching.
SP (Space)..............	A format effector, used to separate words.

ERROR ISOLATION ANALYSIS

When processing or transmitting information, error may be created by an equipment failure, line degradation or human error. Some parts or components of a system are more reliable than other parts. Statistics have shown that the central processor, built from solid state electronic components, has the least expected error rate.

Peripheral equipment such as a magnetic tape drive, disks, and card reader/ punch equipment are partly mechanical and, therefore, subject to more errors and adjustments than solid state devices with no moving parts. Mechanical wear and maladjustments can cause a greater number of errors or a higher error rate than the electronic computer. The communications line (facilities) has the next greatest error rate due to noise, environmental, and physical interferences. The highest error rate producer of the system is the human operator. On the average, humans tend to make about one mistake for every 100 operations.

ERROR DETECTION TECHNIQUES

There are basically three types of error detection and subsequent corrective action schemes: (1) the flagged error type signifies that an error has been detected, (2) the feedback type is one in which the receiver sends a message back to the sender requesting a retransmission of errored blocks of data, and (3) the forward error correcting type is one in which the receiver corrects any errors that have occurred through use of unique data encoding.

There is a fourth type called "Echo Check" that might be classified as an error detection system. In this type, the central processor "echos" each character received back to the terminal for display to the operator. This type is quite popular in systems using cathode ray tube (CRT) terminal devices. The speed limitations of the system are obvious as is the inefficiency. Fifty percent of the capability of the communication line is used to echo check the transmitted data.

Parity Checking

Parity is the technique of adding noninformation or redundant bits to a group of bits that represent a character or block of characters. There are three popular types of parity checking schemes: (1) vertical redundancy checking (VRC) or character parity checking, (2) horizontal redundancy checking (HRC) or block parity checking, (3) cyclic redundancy checking (CRC) which is a bit stream parity testing scheme.

The efficiency of data transfer or throughput of a communication line or system is based on the number of information-carrying bits versus the total number of bits transferred, including the parity or redundant bits. The greater the number of parity bits inserted into a segment of data for checking purposes, the lesser the efficiency of the data transfer operation. The efficiencies of the following error checking and correcting techniques will be stated, using the more popular codes and variations of each, for purposes of comparison.

Vertical Redundancy Checking

Vertical Redundancy Checking (VRC) or character parity checking is the technique of adding a bit position to each character of a code set. The parity bit will contain a 1 or 0 as is needed to produce the convention being used, i.e., odd or even numbers of 1's per character. Note that in Figure 8-8 the parity bit, the eight-bit position, is set to a "0" or "1" to maintain an odd number of 1's for each character.

When using VRC as the only parity checking scheme, it is possible that a burst of noise on a transmission line could change two bits of data in succession and the error would not be detected. This becomes especially true as data speeds are

FIGURE 8-8
Vertical Redundancy Checking Example

| Bit Position # | Information Characters | | | | | |
	#1	#2	#3	#4	#5	#6
1	0	1	0	0	1	0
2	1	0	0	0	0	1
3	0	0	1	1	0	1
4	0	1	1	1	1	0
5	0	0	0	0	1	1
6	0	0	0	0	0	0
7	1	1	1	1	1	0
Parity	1	0	0	0	1	0

increased toward the maximum capacity of the line. The higher the bit rate is, the more susceptible the bits are to degradation, which is caused by excessive noise on the line. The character parity check will fail to detect the error if two bits within the same character are changed by some type of interference. For example: the number 3 in Figure 8-8 could have the 1's in bit positions 3 and 4 dropped in transmission. The receive parity check would not show the error. The efficiency of VRC when using the ANSCII 8-bit code set would be 87.5% (7 information bits plus a parity bit, $7 \div 8 \times 100\% = 87.5\%$).

Horizontal Redundancy Checking

Because of the failure of VRC when two bits are changed in the same character, additional redundancy checking is often applied. One of the techniques used is horizontal redundancy checking (HRC). HRC involves inserting a character at the end of a fixed length block of data characters, such that the sum of each horizontal bit position of the block is made into odd or even parity. For this reason, HRC is sometimes known as block parity. As shown in Figure 8-9, each bit position of all characters in the block is computed "horizontally" through the block and the proper bit inserted into the block parity character, including the character parity bit positions. This block parity character is now appended to the data block for transmission over the communication line.

Now if a noise burst were to change two bits in the same character on the transmission line, the block parity check by the receiver will detect the error. Although highly improbable, there is a remote chance that four bits can be changed within a data block and the HRC system will fail. The failed bits would have to be in some pattern of two bit positions of one character and the same two bit positions of another character, as shown in Figure 8-9, for an HRC failure to detect the error. The efficiency of HRC for a typical length block of 80 characters, using the ANSCII code set with a character parity bit, would be 87.3 percent.

FIGURE 8-9

Horizontal Redundancy Checking Example

Bit Position #	#1	#2	Information Characters #3	#4	#5	#6	Block Parity Character
1	0	1	0	0	1	0	1
2	1	0	0	0	0	0	0
3	0	0	1	1	0	1	0
4	0	1	1	1	1	0	1
5	0	0	0	0	1	1	1
6	0	0	0	0	0	0	1
7	1	1	1	1	1	0	0
Parity	1	0	0	0	1	1	0

Cyclic Redundancy Checking

The previous techniques have all been based on having a data stream composed of discreet characters of some code set. In some cases, the data to be transferred will be a stream of binary digits as in the case of digitized graphics. In order to minimize undetected errors in this type of data transfer, a technique known as cyclic redundancy checking (CRC) can be used for error detection. CRC essentially uses a polynomial value known to both sender and receiver for operation on the data to be transferred. CRC is a 16-bit polynomial which is exclusive-OR'ed to each group of 16 bits within a block of data.

At the conclusion of the operation by the transmitter on a fixed length block, the remainder of the exclusive-OR operation is appended to the block of data and transmitted to the receiver. The receiver performs the same operations as the sender and then compares the remainder computed with the remainder received from the transmitter. Any nonzero result of the comparison indicates an error in transmission of the data. The efficiency of CRC for an 80-character block is approximately 96.7 percent.

ERROR CORRECTION TECHNIQUES

The intent in applying detection schemes is to enable the correction of errored data. The simplest form of data correction is the flagging technique. In this case, the errored data is not corrected within the data system but is corrected by the human operator. In another method, many terminal equipments and central computer processing systems employ VRC and, when a parity error is detected, merely insert an asterisk, question mark, or other distinctive character code in place of the errored character. When the data is narrative text intended to be acted on by human operations, the flagging system works very well. There may be times, however, when the data is such that the flagging method will not work. Examples might be stock numbers on salesmen's orders or money counts in the financial industry. In these cases, error correction by a "feedback" technique may be employed.

One of the most used feedback systems involves blocking the data into predetermined blocks of data, performing both VRC and HRC on the block, and, if found in error at the receiver, a message is returned to the sender requesting retransmission of the errored block. In the ANSCII code set there are two control characters assigned for this feedback message, the ACK (affirmative reply) and the NAK (negative reply). When the receiver detects an error in the block, it responds with NAK, otherwise the positive response ACK is sent.

During the discussion of error detection schemes and transmission efficiencies, the assumption was made that no errors were occurring and the throughput was based on the fact that only redundant bits were inserted for checking. In actual practice, there will be errors that these schemes are designed to detect, and if retransmission is the means of correcting the errors, the throughput of the system will be affected by the retransmission as well. There are two primary time delays in throughput: the wait time for feedback response and the time to resend any block found in error.

Many elaborate calculations have been made to optimize the length of the data block to reach the most efficient means of transmitting data. The trade-off is between a longer block for greater efficiency when no errors are occurring and a shorter block which will take less time to retransmit when errors occur. Two of the more popular block lengths are 80 and 160 characters, which correspond to the contents of one or two DP punched cards.

The wait time lost in feedback systems is caused by several different transmission and operational functions: (1) the electrical propagation time from sender to receiver, (2) time required by the receiver to generate a response, (3) turnaround time required by the MODEM or line when using half duplex transmission, (4) propagation time for the signal to be returned back to the sender, and (5) the time consumed by the computer system in processing the data. This send and wait type operation has been labeled block-by-block transmission. Techniques for continuous transmission of the blocks without the wait time delays have been developed. This method requires full duplex transmission lines and two blocks of data storage per line direction at each terminal or computer.

Figure 8-10 shows the block-by-block transmission with the wait periods labeled "W" while Figure 8-11 shows the continuous mode transmission. As shown in Figure 8-11, the second block in continuous mode is started toward the receiver while waiting for the response to the first block. The first block is kept in a storage area by the sender until the response is returned from the receiver indicating the data block was received correctly. Since there will be two blocks in this storage, there have to be two affirmative responses assigned in the code set to tell the sender which block to retransmit when an error occurs. In this example, ACK I is used for correctly received odd-numbered blocks and ACK II is used in response to correctly received even-numbered blocks. The response sent for a block received in error is aptly named ERR.

There are some situations when there isn't time to resend errored data. In such cases, some form of receiver or forward error correction is required. All forward error correction (FEC) schemes work on the principle of sending additional or redundant bits with the information carrying data bits in order that the receiver can detect an error and, in turn, correct the error as well. Under normal operation, the efficiencies of these systems are inherently lower than the previous detection schemes because of the greater number of redundant bits required to detect and correct the error.

Hamming Code

An example of one FEC technique is the application of a coding scheme developed by Hamming. These coding schemes require the data bits to be arranged in fixed-length blocks. The bit count in a block may be any number resulting from the following calculations: Block length 2^H-1, where H is the number of redundant or "Hamming" bits to be added for correcting an error at the receiving terminal. In the example shown in Figure 8-12, the Hamming code block

FIGURE 8-10
Block-By-Block Transmission

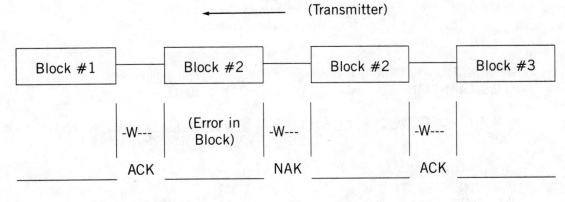

(Transmitter)

| Block #1 | Block #2 | Block #2 | Block #3 |

-W---   (Error in Block)   -W---   -W---

ACK   NAK   ACK

(Receiver Response) ⟶

W—Wait period due to propagation and line turnaround.

FIGURE 8-11
Continuous Mode Transmission Example

(Transmitter)

| Block #1 | Block #2 | Block #3 | Block #2 | Block #3 | Block #4 |

(Error in Block)

ACK I   ERR   ACK II   ACK I

(Receiver Response) ⟶

size has been selected as 12 bits, although a maximum of 15 bits could have been used with the 4 Hamming bits selected.

FIGURE 8-12

Hamming Code Operation

INFORMATION BLOCK   8   7   6   5 4 3 2 1 (Bit Positions)
TO BE TRANSMITTED   0   1   0   1 0 0 1 0 (Data Bits)

HAMMING CODED   12 11 10 9 8 7 6 5 4 3 2 1 (Bit Positions)
BLOCK   0   1   0 1 (H) 0 0 1 (H) 0 (H)(H) (Data Bits)

CALCULATION OF $5_{10} = 0101_2$
HAMMING BITS BY $9_{10} = 1001_2$
TRANSMITTER $11_{10} = 1011_2$
   EXCLUSIVE-OR FUNCTION $\longrightarrow$ $= 0111_2$

HAMMING CODED   12 11 10 9 8 7 6 5 4 3 2 1 (Bit Positions)
BLOCK TO BE   0   1   0 1 (0) 0 0 1 (1) 0 (1)(1)
TRANSMITTED

HAMMING CODED   12 11 10 9 8 7 6 5 4 3 2 1 (Bit Positions)
BLOCK RECEIVED   0   1   0 [0](0) 0 0 1 (1) 0 (1)(1)
WITH ERROR

EXCLUSIVE-OR   (H) $= 0111_2$
CALCULATION AND $5_{10} = 0101_2$
ERROR TEST BY $11_{10} = 1011_2$
RECEIVER $\longrightarrow$ $1011_2 = $ >Bit Number 9 Missing

(H)   = Hamming
0   = Data Bit
[0]   = Bit Error
1   = Data Bit

The Hamming code block is composed of 8 information bits plus 4 Hamming bits. The Hamming bits are placed in the data block in positions which are numbered in integral powers of two, i.e., bit positions 1, 2, 4, and 8. The Hamming bit configuration is computed by an exclusive-OR function of the binary numbers representing the 1-bit positions in the remaining 8 information bits. In the example, the 1 bits are located in bit positions 5, 9, and 11 of the Hamming coded block. The results of the exclusive-OR function of binary values constitute the value to be inserted into the Hamming bit positions with the least significant digit to the right.

Next, the assumption is made that one bit was dropped when the 12 bit Hamming block was transmitted to the receiver. The receiver performs the exclusive-OR function on the Hamming bits and all the block bit positions containing 1's. The result, in the example, is not zero which indicates that an error has occurred. The decimal value of this nonzero result is the actual block bit position which is in error. The receiver can now change the errored bit in position 9 from the 0 which was received to a 1, thus correcting the error at the receiving site. An error in one of the Hamming bit positions will be detected and identified in the same manner. Two errors in the block will yield a nonzero result of the computation at the receiver but the bit position in the block will be meaningless. Three errors could escape detection. The error detection efficiency of this code can be made quite high by increasing the number of Hamming bits.

Bose-Chaudhuri and Hocquengham Codes

The codes developed by Bose and Chaudhuri are a general class of Hamming type codes. Hocquengham was also responsible for independently developing similar codes, hence the acronym BCH. BCH codes are derived by dividing the information bit stream by a constant polynomial known to both sender and receiver similar to the CRC technique. The resultant remainder for the sender's computation is appended to the data block for the receiver to perform a comparison.

The size of the data block is selected in the same manner as the Hamming code with the exception that the number of redundant bits used by BCH coding can be some integral multiple of those used in the Hamming code. This allows the detection of error counts up to the number of redundant bits used in a single block. The polynomial selected for use in BCH coding is one that will generate as many remainders as possible. The efficiency of the BCH codes approaches 98 percent for error rates of 10^5 using blocks as large as 2,047 information bits.

ERROR DETECTION AND CORRECTION IMPLEMENTATION

The most efficient areas for implementation of these error detection and correction techniques are shown in Figure 8-13. The code sets in use which have no inherent provision for VRC can be modified to include the parity bit for transmission, but this would generally require extensive hardware or software revisions and is therefore not recommended. Error handling schemes can be implemented quite easily through the use of integrated micro logic or via large scale integration (LSI) electronic memory.

The system designer must analyze the system protection requirements and weigh these protection considerations against data transmission efficiency and overall costs. Trade-offs usually result due to this analysis, but one should never overlook the total effect erroneous data may have on the overall system operation.

FIGURE 8-13
Error Detection and Correction Implementation

ERROR DETECTION CORRECTION TECHNIQUES	COMPUTER SYSTEM IMPLEMENTATION	TERMINAL SYSTEM IMPLEMENTATION
VERTICAL REDUNDANCY CHECKING	HARDWARE	HARDWARE
HORIZONTAL REDUNDANCY CHECKING	HARDWARE	HARDWARE
CHARACTER INTERLEAVING	SOFTWARE	SOFTWARE
FORWARD ERROR CORRECTION HAMMING/BCH	HARDWARE OR SOFTWARE	HARDWARE OR SOFTWARE

APPLICATIONS AND FUNCTIONAL DATA FORMAT CONSIDERATIONS

A properly prepared data format will be a major factor in system operational efficiency where data editing, file or data base update, data manipulation, forms, reports, graphics, communications, or other special data output requirements are a system's criteria.

The data format determines processing time consumed to perform the necessary data manipulation to produce the end result product. Every computer instruction performed uses a specified period of time. The number of instructions performed can be held to a minimum through properly formatted data.

Regardless of whether the system operation is simple or complex, data formats have the same importance. It is merely a matter of designing the format to fit the need. Figure 8-14 provides a model of a format that could be compressed or expanded to meet most system communication requirements.

Data processing systems utilize more of a table structure format and are usually designed to enable user manipulation of the table format or structure. This implies that the fields or sections of the data format can be rearranged to meet the individual needs. This type of structure changing is not normally performed when communicating between computer systems and terminals or remote computer devices. However, compression or expansion of the number of fields, while maintaining the position of certain fields, is common practice.

The use of a data format control effector allows a system to use a variable data format, allows compression or expansion of the number of fields, and reduces the

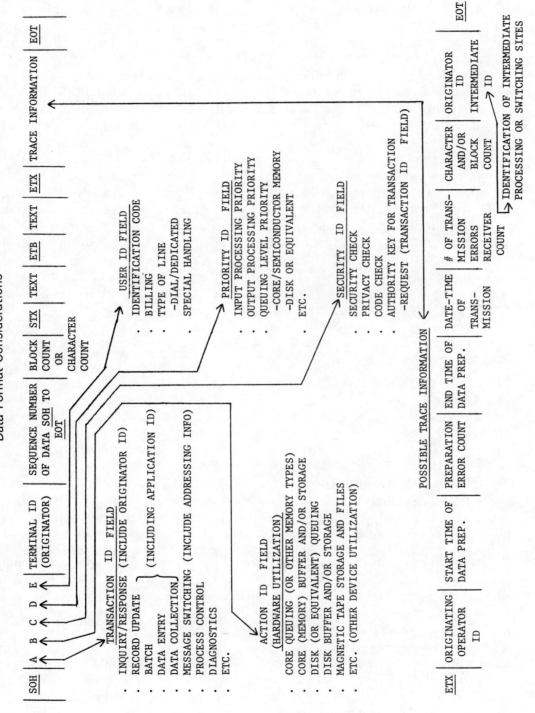

FIGURE 8-14
Data Format Considerations

system editing requirements. Only those fields having meaning for the particular transaction type would be used and edited, thus eliminating the requirements to edit unused information. The use of transaction controls also allows a remote system or terminal to handle more than one type of data or activity. In Figure 8-14, the data format control effector would be the transaction ID field.

Each data format type under consideration must be specified and documented to insure that the system is efficiently designed and all personnel fully understand the different format controls. If three different types of transactions will be handled by a terminal, then it is possible three different data formats would be used.

Many symbols could be used to control transmission and act as data format delimitors. Some are standard symbols in the industry and easily or already designed into most equipment, such as the SOH, SP, STX, ETX, BS, NUL, and EOT from the ANSCII code set. The SOH and EOT symbols (delimitors) define the beginning and end of valid information. The STX and ETX symbols define the beginning and end of the data to be processed. The STX plays a double role since it also defines the end of the data header fields. The ETB symbol defines the end of blocks; the STX symbol could be used for start of each block. The SP symbol is used to separate the control fields. The abbreviations are defined in Table 8-7 (ANSCII Code Set Abbreviations).

The *Transaction* ID field designates the type of transaction the data represents (see Figure 8-14). This field would consist of from one to X number of characters and could encompass such transactions as:

- Inquiry-Response
- Record Update
- Data Collection
- Batch
- Intermediate Process (satellite processing)
- Message Switching
- Diagnostic Process
- Process Control

The *Action* ID field designates how the data is to be routed and stored within the computer system. Some types of transactions require high-speed handling and would use core or Electronic Storage Memory, where other transactions may utilize disk or magnetic tape storage. Communications environment would use core or Electronic Storage Memory for Inquiry/Response and high-priority messages and disk for low-priority messages. Other data processing activities such as Record Update or Process Control, may use core (memory) for processing where a batch environment may use disk for processing. The *Action* field would be used to control this processing activity. This field would consist of one to X number of characters.

The *Security or Privacy* field (optional) would be a confirmation check, if necessary, on the input transaction. If the system supports many unrelated users, or wishes to restrict access to information between company departments, this field could be used. Different key symbols would be assigned to each user. The key would be confirmed prior to allowing access to the data required. This field would consist of one to X characters (see Figure 8-14).

The *Priority* ID field (optional) would be used to designate the importance of the data and the processing category in which it should be placed. In message switching, this field would designate the queuing level. This field would normally consist of one or two characters.

The *User Identification* field is used to identify the particular data originator for billing, data output, type of line (dial/dedicated WATS/Telex, etc.) and other unique data handling processes. This field would consist of one to X number of characters.

The *Terminal Identification* field (Originator) provides an additional security password, privacy check, or permanently assigned originator (terminal) ID. This field could supplement the previous security and privacy field by requiring an additional key word identifying the terminal and particular user. This field would consist of one to X number of characters.

The *Input Sequence Number* would be used to provide a sequential number of each input transaction. Loss of a number would indicate lost data. The transmitting device or operation would insert the number prior to inputting the data to the computer. This field would normally consist of three or four numbers.

The *Block or Character Count* field would indicate the number of blocks or characters contained in the data stream. This number would be checked following reception of the data to confirm that the number of blocks or characters is correct. This field would normally consist of two to four numbers.

Trace Information. These fields of information would enable the system or receiving device to identify transmission and reception time, system processing time, number of errors that occurred during transmission or processing, or during operator handling, provide operator identification and other pertinent system information. In communications, this information could be appended to the output data or message. The *Input Sequence Number* and *Block Count* in the header could be a part of the trace information.

The prime point to consider during format development is attainment of the highest operational efficiency possible. The data format should be one of the major design criteria during the system design and development phases in order to achieve high operational efficiency.

DATA PROTECTION

Data protection cannot be overemphasized as a major system design consideration. Many systems simply lose data due to inadequate software or hardware design, causing inaccurate or missing data during final output.

Some of the field included in the data format example, Figure 8-14, were placed there to provide data protection for user validation and for the detection of errors and lost data. Data can still be rearranged, lost, or incorrectly processed without a parity error being detected. For this reason, it is important to determine other means of detecting errors to supplement parity error detection schemes.

Parity detection schemes, as discussed previously in this chapter, are not 100 percent foolproof. Some parity detection schemes, or a multiple of these schemes, are better than others, but still may require other protective measures for complete data protection.

Some protective measures that may be considered in addition to the error detection schemes could include:

- Total character count confirmation from SOH to EOT.

- Block count—either by a number representing the total number of blocks or insertion of a sequential number in each block.

- Sequence numbers identifying each input of data from individual devices or terminals, incrementing for each valid transmission.

- Sequence numbers identifying each output from the computer system to an individual device or terminal, incrementing for each valid transmission.

- Retry counts for input or output attempts to or from devices or terminals. This count would enable maintenance personnel to detect problems and take corrective action prior to total failure.

- Repeat numbers or important words contained in a transmission and add this additional information as an addendum to the data transmission, although this adds additional data and becomes a time-consuming measure.

- Use key words, check digits, or numerical symbols to confirm numerical values contained in the data.

- Use key words to identify the data originator, a device, terminal or person in case of failure.

- Echo back all data to the originating terminal. This is expensive, time-consuming, and should use full duplex operation. Also, this process does not confirm computer processing or output data quality.

DATA VALIDITY CHECKS

Certain tests can be performed to insure validity of the data control fields located with the data stream. Refer to Figure 8-14. The primary purpose of testing data fields is to confirm that the proper number of alphanumeric characters exist in each data control field and to ensure that the separator symbols are correct and are placed properly.

Data validity tests should definitely be performed when communications is a system function. All data input to the computer portion of the system should be tested for parity errors, security as necessary, and validity of control fields.

When a data format field validity test fails, appropriate action should be taken. When an error is detected, the input data from SOH through EOT should be intercepted and routed to a location where the reason for failure can be determined and corrected. If the data transmission involves large amounts of data, possibly only the header section, from SOH through STX (see Figure 8-14), would be intercepted. The intercepted data could be routed back to the originator or to a service position located at the central site. Some type of tracer information should be appended to the intercepted data to identify the reason for interception.

Each control field starting with the SOH through STX (see Figure 8-14) could be identified and tagged as the reason for failure, such as:

- Transaction ID field,
- Action ID field,
- Security or privacy fields,
- Priority ID field,
- User ID field,
- Terminal ID field,
- Data sequence number,
- Block count,
- Format field separators, symbols or delimitors including the STX, ETX, or EOT.

Interception could also occur during data output when continuous parity errors or other types of errors result due to a malfunction. This data should also be routed to a service position for handling.

Continuous attempts to output data when a malfunction prevents normal operation, should not be allowed. The data should be intercepted and routed to a service position for manual handling.

DATA SECURITY AND PRIVACY

The continuing search for an economical and usually quicker method to accomplish the necessary data processing requirements has created many shared system concepts. These shared systems may be provided by a vendor who provides data processing services to all types of users, or the shared system may be a company-owned system which provides processing services for the various company departments.

This sharing of system resources does create the problem of data security and privacy. The system designers and users must arrive at a mutual system concept that will provide adequate data security or privacy. This concept may be simple, such as retaining the programs and raw data on tapes, disks, cards, etc., and placing these units in service at processing time. When processing is complete, the units are removed and retained by the user. This method does require retention of disk, tape reels, cards, etc., by each user. Also, it is necessary to collect the raw data by other means than the shared system. Many problems can arise with this operational concept. There is the possibility of the disks, tapes, cards, or devices being mishandled. Who provides the operators for each processing session? If a common group of operators is utilized, who guarantees the security and privacy of the data? What protective measures are taken to insure protection of the various storage units? How is the raw data collected? Is some sort of duplicate system needed to collect the data? If the raw data is collected on the shared system, what protective measures are taken to insure security of data?

The above comments and questions, as well as others which could be asked, bring out several facts. A computer system that is manually shared as indicated above:

- Is inefficient.
- Would result in redundancy of computer hardware, storage units, and devices.
- Could not adequately insure the security and privacy of the data.

Steps could be taken to improve a manual operation by incorporating some of the common security and privacy measures, but these still would not solve the system's inefficiencies, possible mishandling, or redundancy requirements.

The more efficient shared systems provide a means of collecting data in addition to the processing of data. These systems, depending on whether they are unrelated user systems or individual company systems, also provide various methods for data security protection.

The concern of the system designers and users varies in accordance with the importance of the data and this should dictate the implementation of adequate security measures to protect the collected and processed data.

The normal methods entail using key characters or words to identify the entering or requesting terminal and user. The appropriate data and/or application programs assigned to the user are then made available when the check is affirmative.

In addition to requiring an identification of the terminal and user, the appropriate collected data base and application program could each require a key word for identification. This could involve four or more necessary key words in order to access and cause the processing of the data. These key words may identify such items, functions, or areas as follows:

- Terminal identification,
- User identification,
- Check digits computed through the use of a constant or variable polynomial,
- Line port identification,
- Transaction identification,
- Data base identification,
- Intermittent key words scattered in the data,
- Applications programs identifications,
- The data base and application programs may also be in identifiable sections.

Another precautionary measure that could be utilized is the use of a pre-assigned terminal or user polynomial to scramble the data during transmission and storage. A reverse procedure would be used to unscramble the data during processing. This polynomial could require a key for the unscrambling function.

Black boxes are available to scramble data on the line, but usually it is unscrambled upon reception and stored in clear text. This will not protect the stored data, but will provide protection during transmission.

CHAPTER NINE

Communications Terminal Requirements Analysis

Terminal operational functions and the interface relationship to data communications network and computer systems were discussed in Chapters Seven and Eight. Normally, a terminal is selected for its efficiency and functional requirements instead of cost. When more consideration is given to cost than to performance, the results can be inefficient operations, both from performance and user satisfaction. In today's market, flexible terminals, both in cost and performance, are available to meet most requirements.

Determining the terminal requirements is not an easy task. Three areas of intense analysis are required: (1) terminal architectural features, (2) terminal operational features, and (3) the human features.

This chapter will discuss these various features and review certain functional characteristics, types, and utilization of terminals. It will contain a number of checklists for reviewing the various types of terminals available and to aid the analyst in the selection of terminal equipment. The greater part of this chapter will be heavily slanted toward the characteristics of and functional requirements for an intelligent terminal environment.

TERMINAL TYPES

Many types of terminals are available and they range from: (1) general purpose typewriter-like terminals, (2) general purpose CRT, (3) special purpose CRT for stock quotation, (4) medium and high-speed input devices–card reader, paper tape reader, optical scanner, (5) graphical input/output, (6) key entry systems, to full-blown intelligent terminals with their own independent software and peripheral subsystems. The problem in selecting a particular terminal is determining the characteristics and functional requirements to meet the required application. Most terminals will operate in an uncontrolled or controlled mode or a combination of these modes.

Uncontrolled

This type of terminal does not require selection for either transmitting or receiving and, therefore, operates without polling/calling features. It is free to transmit any time without being selected or asked by the receiving device or computer. When transmission is initiated in either direction, the receiving device (terminal or computer) must be available for receiving the incoming data. If the receiving unit is not available for data input, the result may be lost data. Normally this type of operation is used with low-speed Automatic-Send-Receive (ASR) terminals and display terminals.

Controlled

A controlled terminal requires an initial selection or polling sequence prior to transmitting or receiving data. A controlled terminal may be locally programmable and offer other flexible features or it may be a nonintelligent terminal, used only as a display device or other simple input/output activities.

In a controlled terminal system environment, the polling station or computer contains all the required software, firmware, and electronics to control the terminal's activities. This is necessary for confirmation of the terminal's status, such as: (1) selection of individual terminal, (2) number of concurrently operating terminals, (3) error control, (4) overload controls, (5) terminals that have data to transmit, (6) terminals that are available to receive data, and (7) other transmit or receive functions as required.

Nonintelligent Terminals

Terminals that contain no programmable software and just enough electronics to transmit and receive data to and from another device or computer are thought of as nonintelligent terminals. Many CRT terminals within this category may contain switches that allow the user to change the rate at which data is transmitted or received. Also, other options may be available that will allow the selection of different word size, type of parity, number of lines displayed, separate numeric keyboard, answer back capability, and other nonprogrammable switch-controlled functions.

A nonintelligent terminal could be used efficiently within an inquiry/response type system. Several areas (to name a few) where these terminals may be used are: (1) police departments, (2) banks, (3) schools, (4) airlines, (5) inventory and control applications, (6) collections, (7) accounts receivable/payable, (8) hospitals, and (9) insurance companies. These users normally require a terminal for inputting questions (inquiries) into a system and then expect a quick answer (response) back from the system.

Intelligent Terminals

An intelligent or smart terminal is normally software or firmware programmable or a combination of both. Application software is usually stored on cassette tapes or disk units. These terminals can perform preprocessing functions, perform data editing, provide data format controls, handle preformatted forms, provide file management features, store data, and perform many other software functions, as required by the user.

When processing was centralized, remote terminals did not require intelligence or programmability. The host or central processor contained all the intelligence and controlled all functions of the nonintelligent terminal. With distributed processing and other applications that required certain preprocessing prior to the data being passed to the host processor, an intelligent terminal became a necessary unit. Generally, the intelligent terminal would support such preprocessing functions as: (1) data entry, (2) central system inquiry, (3) local data management, (4) batch communication, (5) local document and report generation, (6) distributed and, in some cases, word, processing. To support these requirements, the intelligent terminal must perform certain functions for communications protocols, accept data for preprocessing, and update and share data base information.

The user should review five major areas when selecting an intelligent terminal: *communication, usability* (flexibility), *memory, cost,* and *hardware* characteristics. The various questions to be satisfied under these five categories are:

- Does the terminal's *communications*
  - Support a well-recognized protocol?
  - Allow for future support of different and higher levels of protocols?
  - Include automatic polling?
  - Contain a standard interface?
  - Permit both batch and interactive communications?
  - Handle varying data rates?

- Does the terminal's *usability* (flexibility) include
  - Support for user-oriented languages?
  - Cursor control for error correction (if required)?
  - Capability to detect errored signals?
  - Programmable function keys?
  - A mixed language capability?
  - Support for simultaneous operations?

-Capability for clustered configuration?
-Software compatible with other network elements?

- Does the *memory* include
  -A portion dedicated to machine overhead?
  -A portion dedicated to data communications?
  -A portion dedicated to vendor or user supplied software?
  -Capability to expand memory?
  -Double buffering for faster data handling (throughput)?

- Does the terminal *cost* include
  -Application software?
  -Maintenance or warranty?
  -Any components external or internal to the terminal (MODEMS, printer, slave CRT, etc.)?
  -Hardware and software diagnostics?
  -Cabling/hardware necessary to connect to another terminal/CPU?

- Does the terminal's *hardware* have
  -Up-to-date processor architecture?
  -Easy/direct access to memory?
  -An uninterruptible power supply?
  -A data security scheme?
  -Both secure and open data bases?
  -Capability to support other terminals?
  -A standard keyboard?

Communications and software functions are becoming more efficient and easier to handle. This, plus data base sharing, will open up new areas of applications that will continually increase user acceptance of intelligent terminals.

PROGRAMMABILITY AND INDEPENDENT PROCESSING

For a number of years, intelligent terminals have been viewed as input/output devices, with a certain amount of application firmware and indicator lamps which signal a terminal malfunction, to sophisticated host-interactive terminals providing multiple functions via a user-programmable language. Regardless of the category in which these terminals are placed, if distributed data processing is to be accomplished, the terminal must be capable of some programmability, provide for local independent processing, and handle communications protocols.

The majority of intelligent terminal manufacturers claim programmability, but many of them do not support a problem-oriented easy-to-use programming language. Some consider user-programmability as the ability of a user to reprogram his microprocessor or microcomputer at an assembler language level. True programmability is considered the ability to locally program from the terminal's keyboard or a related input/output device. This is the first requirement of an intelligent terminal.

The second requirement of an intelligent terminal is the ability to assume a portion of the host's data processing workload. To do this, the terminal must contain a processor and the necessary storage medium in order for the terminal to assume that portion of the user's data requirements which would normally have been performed by the host computer.

Finally, in a distributed data processing environment, the intelligent terminal must have data communications capability. The user often incorrectly assumes that any terminal will contain the latest state of the art communications technology. The smart user will insist that his terminal support one, if not all, of the higher-level protocols such as high-level data link control (HDLC), synchronous data link control (SDLC), and American National Standard Institute (ANSI) X25 packet switching techniques. Some manufacturers feel that HDLC and SDLC protocols are not the most efficient for intelligent terminals and that more efficient industry standards will emerge.

CLUSTERING

Intelligent terminals may be used as stand-alone systems or configured in clusters. A stand-alone terminal may be divided into one of three applications: single purpose, multifunction, and general purpose. A single purpose terminal is designed for a single application, i.e., payroll accounting, with software designated to that task. A multifunction terminal performs a number of specified functions, with software dedicated to the various functions of the system. A general purpose terminal system offers a wide variety of different applications with software geared to each unique function or application.

On a cluster of intelligent terminals, each terminal could serve one specific application. One terminal may be used for data entry, another for batch application, and yet another for form or report generation. In a clustered environment, each terminal user also has stand-alone capability, including interactive communications through the MODEM and remote access to the host computer.

Through the multiple interfaces, each terminal has its own memory and processor, making it possible to reconfigure the system as required. Flexible configuration capability at the terminal should allow for concepts that encompass many local processing requirements as well as on-line communications interactions with the host computer.

Some stand-alone intelligent terminal systems may include a separate microprocessor dedicated exclusively to communications. In a clustered environment, communications intelligence may be contained in a controller outside or separate from the physical terminal but interconnecting all the terminals in the cluster.

Clustering may also include a configuration where a number of intelligent terminals are configured with a group of nonintelligent terminals via a common computer bus connection. One or more of the intelligent terminals could be designated as a control unit for the nonintelligent terminals.

MICROPROCESSOR OR MINICOMPUTER TERMINAL

A terminal designed around a microprocessor or minicomputer contains firmware, software, or both, and is locally programmable either from the keyboard or by conventional means. The terminal will encompass those functions and the flexibility, to a limited degree, that are available in a small computer system. However, a terminal built around a microprocessor will normally be less flexible and more limited in its processing functions than a minicomputer terminal configuration. The microprocessor (computer-on-a-chip) is usually designed for a single operational function or limited application requirements. In many cases, the microprocessor contains memory and input and output functions integrated on the same chip. The minicomputer terminal system could be a preprocessing center, a data processing center, a distributed processing center, a data switching center, or perform other functions of a typical medium- or large-scale computer.

PORTABLE TERMINAL

The portable terminal is designed to be moved or carried from one location to another. It may be designed to be carried in a suitcase or briefcase type carrying unit. An acoustical coupler will normally be used to allow the standard telephone (desk or pay phone) to be used for transmitting or receiving data to and from a host computer. The device may be a simple keyboard and printer or may provide a transmitter, utilizing perforated paper tape or cassette tape. The advent of the microprocessor has made it possible to design many types of portable terminals.

TERMINAL OPERATIONAL CONSIDERATIONS

Whether the requirement is for a terminal system expansion or a totally new terminal system, the terminal configuration requirement should be geared to the user's operational requirements.

Table 9-1 is a checklist to aid the analyst in selecting the necessary terminals and to weigh the many factors against the user's requirements and needs. On the left side of the Table are suggested considerations that should aid in terminal selection; on the right side are suggested analysis factors to weigh the many terminal considerations against the user's requirements and needs.

TABLE 9-1
Checklist for Terminal Requirements

CONSIDERATIONS	ANALYSIS FACTORS
TYPE OF TERMINAL APPLICATIONS	TYPE OF TERMINAL
• Interactive 　—Time Sharing 　—Conversation • Batch File System • Data Communication 　(Teleprocessing)	• Intelligent (Some Local Processing) • Nonintelligent • Cost

TABLE 9-1, continued

CONSIDERATIONS	ANALYSIS FACTORS
LOCAL DATA PROCESSING REQUIRED • Computational (Scientific) • Record/File-Oriented (Batch) • Inquiry Response (Interactive) • Data Communications (On-Line) • System Redesign • Remote Processing	**PROGRAMMABLE/FIRMWARE TERMINAL** • Use of Existing Software • Programming Language • Combination of Software/Firmware • Reprogramming Required • Record Redesign • Conversion of Existing Records • Software Modularity • Memory Required • Cost
PHYSICAL INTERFACE • Terminal to Computer • Terminal to Communication Line • Terminal to Off-Line Device • Transmission Mode • Transmission Code	**TERMINAL COMPATABILITY WITH SYSTEM** • Protocol • Code Format • Buffering • Half Duplex • Full duplex • Synchronous/Asynchronous • Cost
PROCESSING RATE OF TERMINAL • Data Inputs (Per Min/Hr) • Data Reception-Output (Per Min/Hr) • Response Time • Time Restraints (Other)	**THROUGHPUT AND DATA VOLUME** • Eliminate Unnecessary Data • Redesign Record Format • Compression of Data • Priority Polling • Speed of I/O Devices • Cost
ACCEPTABLE ERROR RATE • Incoming Data • Outgoing Data • Loss of Data Protection	**DATA VALIDATION TECHNIQUES** • Error Detection Schemes • Error Correction Schemes • Visual Display • Error Flagging • Data Recovery Procedures • Operator Intervention • Desk Checking • Cost

TABLE 9-1, continued

CONSIDERATIONS	ANALYSIS FACTORS
NUMBER OF TERMINALS REQUIRED • Type of Terminal Per Location • Input Devices Linked to Terminal • Terminal/System Layout • Back-up Equipment	**CONFIGURATION** • Multistation Terminals Link • Single Terminal Link • Need for Redundant Equipment (Backup) • Cluster Arrangement • Input Stations Per Terminal • Sharing of Memory • Building Space/Modifications • Cost
ACCEPTABLE ACQUISITION COST • Hardware • Software • Documentation • Communication (Line) • Supplies (Disk Packs, Forms, Etc.)	**TYPE OF ACQUISITION** • Purchase • Lease • Lease/Purchase Arrangement • Systems House Contractor • Equipment Manufacturer • Third Party • Cost
ACCEPTABLE MAINTENANCE COST • 24 Hour Service • Part Time (Scheduled) • Part Time (On Call) • Response Time	**TYPE OF MAINTENANCE** • In-House • Vendor Supplied • Third Party • Spare Parts Requirements • Cost
TRAINING REQUIREMENTS • Equipment Operation • Software (If not In-House Developed) • Maintenance (If not In-House Maintained) • At Contractor's Plant • On-Site	**TRAINING PERFORMED BY** • In-House • Vendor • Third Party • Cost

SPECIAL TERMINAL PERIPHERAL FEATURES
• Printers
  —Form Width
	PRINTERS/GRAPHIC, CRT/PAPER TAPE/CARD EQUIPMENT
	• Printers
	  —Impact Non-Impact Printer

TABLE 9-1, continued

CONSIDERATIONS

- —Platen type
- —Individual/Continuous Form Feed
- —Upper/Lower Case
- —Number of Carbons Needed
- —Desirable Speed
- • Graphic/CRT Devices
  - —Display Alpha & Numeric
  - —Lines and Curves
  - —Special Keyboard
  - —Scroll (Forward/Backward)
  - —Special Cursor/Pin Control
  - —Ambient Illumination (On Site)
  - —Special Symbols
- • Paper Tape/Punch Card Equipment
  - —Coding Scheme
  - —Punching Speeds

SPECIAL FEATURES
- • Transmit Message to Multiple Locations
- • Unattended Operation
- • Automatic Terminal Identification
- • Passwords
- • Dial-Up and Line Network Compatability
- • Multipoint Control Capability
- • Multiplexer/MODEM/Line Interface
  - —Rack, Wall, or Desk Mounted
  - —Portable
- • Environmental
  - —Heat
  - —Power
  - —Air Conditioning
  - —Lighting
  - —Dust/Dirt
  - —Housekeeping Practices
  - —Noise

ANALYSIS FACTORS

- —Line or Character Printing
- —Other Special Printing Features
- • Graphic/CRT Devices
  - —ALPHA/Numeric
  - —Graphic Data
  - —Size of Display Area
  - —Characters Per Line
  - —Lines Displayed
  - —Brightness
  - —Character Resolution
  - —Refresh Rate
  - —Keyboard Layout
- • Paper Tape/Card Equipment
  - —Meets Desired Features
  - —Compatible with Existing Devices
- • Cost

CANDIDATE TERMINAL EQUIPMENT
- • Ability to Provide/Meet Capabilities/Requirements
- • Upgrade Capability
  - —Terminal's Buffer
  - —Software Within Processor Limits
  - —Processor Speed
  - —Data Transmission Speed
  - —Ability to Add Input Devices
  - —New Applications/Functions
  - —Better Data Line Utilization
- • Mean Time to Failure/Repair
- • Special Software/Equipment to Secure Data
- • Installation
  - —Site Survey/Preparation
  - —Team Members
  - —Schedules
- • Other Capabilities/ Requirements as Determined in the Analysis and Evaluation

TABLE 9-1, continued

CONSIDERATIONS	ANALYSIS FACTORS

• Data Security
• Physical Security
• Equipment Reliability
• Implementation Plans
• Expansion Capability
  —Hardware/Firmware
  —Software
  —Building/Space
	of the Terminal Equipment
	• Cost

VISUAL DISPLAY TERMINAL SELECTION CONSIDERATION

If the terminal hardware is to be a self-contained display system with its own memory and a cluster of input and output slave display stations, then a careful analysis of the architectural features for the visual display terminal should be made. In addition to those considerations and "analysis factors" contained in Table 9-1 that are applicable to visual display devices, the following should be considered when selecting a visual display terminal system:

- Display capacity (screen size)
- Number of lines displayed
- Characters per line
- Size of characters (height and width)
- Forms handling capability
- Character or code set
- Character generator
- Internal storage capacity
- Refresh rate (phosphor, blinking rate, intensity, memory)
- Keyboard layout
- Special function keys
- Editing and character format control
- Cursor control and positioning
- Erase features (line, character, page)
- Line roll up or down features
- Paging in or out features
- Split screen features
- Cluster capability
- External storage or devices
- Firmware or hardwired

- Print (hardcopy) capability
- Character or bit per second transmission rates
- Communication interface features (compatibility; synchronous/ asynchronous; HDX or FDX; RS232; control modes)
- Maintenance availability

TERMINAL HUMAN FACTORS

Every terminal, regardless of how automatic its functions, requires an operator to provide data inputs, manipulate the console and devices, and perform other routine functions. A simple terminal may only require keyboard operation and tearing off the printer hardcopy, but a complex programmable terminal can require many operational functions. The architectural design and operational functions of the terminal should be designed for ease of operations; make it easy for the operator to do the right thing and difficult to do the wrong thing.

A large number of terminal failures are caused by operator personnel and this is not necessarily due to inexperienced personnel. Even if inexperienced operator personnel were eliminated, a problem could still exist due to terminal design. Many times, certain designed features of a terminal cause personal frustration. This may occur because the various controls, keys, switches, and buttons are difficult to operate or manipulate. If the terminal has too many control switches, lights, bells, buzzers, etc., it may appear difficult and frustrating to new operators. An irritated operator may take his or her frustrations out on the terminal.

The other problem may be the procedures necessary to service the various devices. This would include such areas as disk platter removal and replacement, cassette tape or reel removal, or replacement and handling of card machines, printers, paper tape punches, operator consoles, and other connected devices. The terminal and all connected devices should be designed for ease of operator handling and protected against misuse where possible.

Operational procedures and directives should be compiled and be readily available to the operator personnel. These should be step-by-step, clearly written instructions covering any circumstances that may arise and also instructions for servicing the various devices.

Another consideration is the operational reliability of the terminal. This enters into the realm of maintenance activities, but is still an important factor in operations efficiency. A terminal that is easy to operate, provides operator assistance features, gives reliable continuous service, provides quiet operation and has soft color tones will be more acceptable to the operator than a terminal that falls short in these categories.

In addition to the other human consideration factors given under this topic, the following should be considered in the selection of a terminal device:

- Ease of operation
- Ease of maintenance
- Ease of moving from one area to another

- No sharp or pointed edges
- Pleasing color
- Size
- Acceptable noise
- Reflections
- Glare
- Position of operator's:
  - Arms
  - Hands
  - Fingers
  - Torso
  - Head, when operating terminal
- Printing characteristics—size, sharpness, error correction features, number of lines on screen, etc.
- All controls software readable
- CRT high intensity (less eye strain)
- Status indicators:
  - What is system status—normal or abnormal?
  - Is system inoperative?
  - How long has the system been down?
  - Is the computer waiting for data?
  - Has my input been received?
  - Is computer working on my data, etc.?

SOFTWARE CONSIDERATIONS

Programmable terminals offer a wide variety of programming languages and methods required to program the terminal. Most of these terminals are provided with an assembler and in some cases a cross-assembler. This usually allows assembly work to be accomplished on a larger computer. Assembling on an outside computer can eliminate the need for various devices at the terminal, such as card reader-punches and printers.

Application software programs that are available from vendors will vary from terminal to terminal. The type and flexibility of software must be determined when considering terminals to meet the user's system requirements. Another consideration is the vendor maintenance support for software packages and the availability of program enhancements, and the quality of software documentation provided with the terminal system.

If the user intends to develop his own applications program, close analysis should be given to the task in terms of time, manpower and equipment to ensure milestones are met and that there are no costly overruns. In many terminals a limited instruction set and limited memory storage space causes lengthy program run times, making large application tasks difficult to accomplish. Some of the languages supported by the various programmable terminals would include:

- Assemblers
- Symbolic compiler
- Cobol
- Fortran
- Basic
- Tal (terminal application language)
- Hardwired–strappable
- Electronic–chip logic programming
- Firmware wired microprograms
- Others

TERMINAL COMMUNICATIONS INTERFACE REQUIREMENTS

Matching the terminal configuration to the computer system or communications requirements involves meeting the requirements of the user applications, the requirements of the host computer, and the requirements of the communications facilities.

Some of the basic considerations in matching a terminal to these requirements are listed below:

- Terminal line interface (RS232, etc.)
- Code set
- Synchronous or Asynchronous operation
- Half duplex or full duplex operation
- Line speed requirements–characters per second or bits per second
- Controlled or uncontrolled terminal operations
- Polling/calling requirements
- Parity error detection and/or correction requirements
- Dedicated or dial-up line
- Data format controls
- Terminal to connected device protocol disciplines
- Individual terminal device selection from the host computer
- Data transmission characteristics
  - Block by block
  - Block transmission size
  - Continuous block mode
  - Binary synchronous control operation
  - Binary bit stream (transparent modes)
  - Etc.

MAINTENANCE

Maintenance support for a terminal is a vital consideration and should not be overlooked when selecting one. A terminal that is inoperable because of a failed component cannot support the user functions, and can be very costly in terms of lost sales, unbalanced inventory or delayed billing. It should be determined what type and level of maintenance support is available for each terminal under consideration. Most terminal suppliers can provide different levels of maintenance support, including a maintenance contract that may be included in the terminal lease. The level of maintenance negotiated will usually determine the cost of the maintenance coverage.

Several factors will determine the adequacy of maintenance coverage provided by the terminal supplier (manufacturer, third party, or systems house). These would include:

- Terminal reliability–average time between failures
- Warranty period
- Location of maintenance service centers
- Number of maintenance technicians available to service the terminals
- Assigned location of the maintenance technicians
- Qualification level of the maintenance technicians
- Average response time for users' maintenance calls, i.e., 4 hours, 8 hours, 24 hours, 48 hours, etc.
- Average time to repair the terminal after the maintenance technician has arrived
- Availability of spare parts
- Method of repair—plug-in components or hardwired component, or replace terminal device
- Training for user maintenance personnel (this may be a requirement when the terminals are purchased and the user will perform the maintenance)

DIAGNOSTICS

Terminal malfunctions can be classified primarily into four categories: (1) operator errors, (2) hardware errors, (3) communications line errors, and (4) possible software caused errors.

Of these sources, the most common are operator induced errors. The reasons for operator errors are numerous and they far exceed errors induced by the communications line, hardware, or software. Most operator errors are caused at the time data are induced into the system. Good local procedures to avoid operator errors should include: (also refer to the section on "Terminal Human Factors")

- Simple, uncomplicated data entry procedures
- A quiet working environment
- Good operator training programs
- Strict procedures for programmed entry formats, e.g., record and field layout, characters per position/columns within fields
- Desk checking for programmed format entry
- Mod-X check digits within entered data
- Etc.

Some terminals are more susceptible to failures than others. For instance, a hardcopy type of terminal is more likely to malfunction than a CRT terminal. This happens because the hardcopy terminal has mechanically moving parts while the CRT terminal is electronically operated. When a problem does arise in any terminal, the local vendor's technical representative is usually called to correct the problem. Considering the high labor costs, this routine practice can be very expensive.

Diagnostics can be provided that will help identify many of the failures that may occur at a terminal. This allows a large number of the failure problems to be identified prior to calling maintenance repair personnel. In this manner, the repair personnel will have been briefed during the phone call as to the problem and what diagnostics were run. This can mean considerable savings on maintenance over a period of time. Diagnostics are proven trouble-shooting techniques for installed terminals, particularly when these terminals are utilized in distributed processing networks and data communications.

The cause of a terminal problem can come from anywhere in the system. The problem can reside in the MODEM, the terminal software, host computer, communications lines, and the operator. Regardless of the source of the problem, it will first be noticed at the terminal. The terminal serves as a thermometer and is the "window" into a user terminal system. Remote diagnostics are tools to aid the operator in isolating a problem and to serve the service engineer in restoring a faulty terminal. Diagnostics also provide management with the means to monitor: (1) The quality of service, (2) The adequacy of field response time, (3) The reliability of a vendor's software, and (4) The effectiveness of an entire system in meeting user needs.

TYPICAL INTELLIGENT (PROGRAMMABLE) TERMINAL CONFIGURATION

A programmable or intelligent terminal is configured through the assembly of various components of hardware, electronics, and software. An example of a possible terminal configuration is provided in Table 9-2. A fictitious programmable terminal has been selected for this example.

TABLE 9-2
Terminal Technical Specifications Example

CONSIDERATIONS	SPECIFICATIONS/REQUIREMENTS
PROCESSOR	
—Main memory (bytes)	8-64K
—Word length (bits)	16
—Addressable registers	5
—Cycle time (u sec)	1.5
—Number of I/O channels	3 multiplexer
—Max. devices per channel	8 on each device channel
AUXILIARY STORAGE	
—Medium	Disk files (removable)
—Storage capacity (bytes)	3M to 6M
—Transfer rate (CPS)	200 K (20-usec rotation)
—Other features	IBM 2311/2314 compatible
SOFTWARE	
—Languages supported	Fortran (OS-DOS/loader)
—Terminal emulation	IBM BSC (1130, 2770, 2780; IBM Hasp III)
—Utility routines	File, test, edit, diagnostic, debug, Math, I/O control
PERIPHERALS	
—Card reader	Optional (300 CPM-51/80-Col)
—Line printer	Optional (200 LPM-96 ANSCII)
—Magnetic tape	Optional dual tape cassette
—Other features	Data comm. interface/MODEMS
KEYBOARD ENTRY	
—Console layout	2260/entry typewriter/ANSCII
—Code generated	64/128 ANSCII with parity
—Manual controls	Program functions, numeric pod, cursor, edit, TTY graphics

TABLE 9-2, continued

CONSIDERATIONS	SPECIFICATIONS/REQUIREMENTS

DISPLAY UNIT

—Configuration	Cluster (8-16-24)
—Screen capacity (char)	960 to 1,920
—Lines and char per line	12 x 80; 24 X 80
—Display character set	64 or 96 ANSCII (Including L C)
—Editing facilities	Char/line insert or delete, 4X cursor, erase—EOL or EOS, home

PAGE PRINTER

—Platen/print mechanism	2 optional ACX read out (Pin Fed)
—Line length (char)	13-132 (adjustable)
—Rated print speed (CPS)	30-165 (50-100 LPM)
—Printable char set	64/96-ASCII (U C or L C)
—Other features	Horizontal/vertical format controls

LINE TRANSMISSION FEATURES

—Interface	RS232
—Data rate (BPS)	110-1800 (asynchronous), 2000-9600 (synchronous), clock optional
—Operating mode	HDX/FDX (IBM BSC)
—Line code	EBCDIC, ANSCII, BCD/PTTC
—Error code	VRC/LRC, Automatic re-transmit
—Bell system data set (MODEM)	103, 201, 202, 203

An intelligent terminal cluster may be configured with part of one terminal's memory dedicated to communications protocol. This arrangement eliminates the need for a controller because one terminal performs multifunctions, including handling all protocol requests. Dedicating a portion of memory to communications is practical if enough memory is available to perform the other terminal functions.

We can expect continuing technological improvements in communications protocol for future intelligent terminals. Other technological considerations are emerging that may impact the current architecture of intelligent terminals. Some of these technologies include: additional micro/minicomputer applications, gas plasma display devices, multifunction software, a universal standard interactive language, and voice recognition terminals.

CHAPTER TEN

Network, Modem And Multiplexer Components

Data communications technology has progressed from the component level to the system or network level. This came about because users wanted vendors to become more involved with the problems of line quality and to do communications control. They wanted integrated product lines and plug-compatible components that are efficient, cost-effective and problem solving. The vendors are shifting away from traditional components such as independent MODEMs and multiplexers to more sophisticated components and systems for networking. The traditional lines between products are coming down; manufacturers of one kind of component are absorbing functions of neighboring components into their new product lines. Modern technology, which combines the classical MODEM and time-division multiplexing functions into a single component, is an example of "absorbing functions."

The classical 1970s data communications system configurations are evolving into hierarchical levels of integrated components for network control. The user is presented with data communications components, facilities, and systems that are greatly different from those of the 70s. On most of the traditional component lines, new or vastly improved components and systems are available such as tech control, MODEMs, and multiplexers for data communications monitoring and control.

This chapter provides information concerning component characteristics, areas of equipment design, and operational functions which will aid system designers in the development and configuration of their individual systems. It is primarily devoted to discussing the characteristics of the MODEM and multiplexer as to types, functions, and their "life-giving" interface to other components of the network.

MODEMS (MODULATOR-DEMODULATOR)

A MODEM of some type is a normal part of most communication lines. Figure 10-1 provides a simple pictorial overview of the related components required to configure a communication connection between a terminal and a computer. A review of Figure 10-1 will be helpful during the course of reading this chapter. Low-speed data and all speeds of digital operation can and may be performed without a MODEM. Pure digital (DC pulses) normally utilize other types of equipment which provide the necessary phase generation and multiplexing.

There are many types of MODEMs on the market with various unique capabilities, but they all have certain operational features in common. These would include conversion of digital signals to analog signals, and analog to digital, a process known as Modulation-Demodulation. MODEM is a contraction of modulator-demodulator. The MODEM is required to interface standard RS232 signals and provide controls and other required features to interface and operate on common carrier lines.

The basic types of modulation that can be performed on an analog signal are: Amplitude Modulation (AM), Frequency Shift Modulation (FSK), Phase Modulation (PM), or a combination of these types and utilization of side band features. It is not necessary to be concerned how the modulation is accomplished, but rather be concerned about the cost and capability of a MODEM to operate efficiently at the required bit per second (BPS) rate.

The BPS capability of the MODEM may be restricted by the type of communication line utilized. This restriction is caused by the usable frequency band width capability of the various common carrier line offerings. For example, a Voice Grade Line has a maximum usable band width of approximately 2700 Hertz (Hz). This creates a limitation on bit rates above 9600 BPS on a Voice Grade Line. Line conditioning is required to attain the rates up to 9600 BPS. The line conditioning requirements are specified and dictated by the MODEM manufacturer and common carrier.

To achieve bit capacities of 4800 BPS, 7200 BPS, and 9600 BPS, which is done frequently today, some form of multiplication with the MODEM must be performed. To increase MODEM bit capacity to 4800 BPS, the technique known as di-bit modulation is used. Using the example of AM, two bits are modulated at one time. As shown in Figure 10-2, the number of levels needed for di-bit AM are the number of states that two bits can have when taken two at a time. To maintain an ability to detect a failed line when there is no carrier, a fifth level (calling zero volts

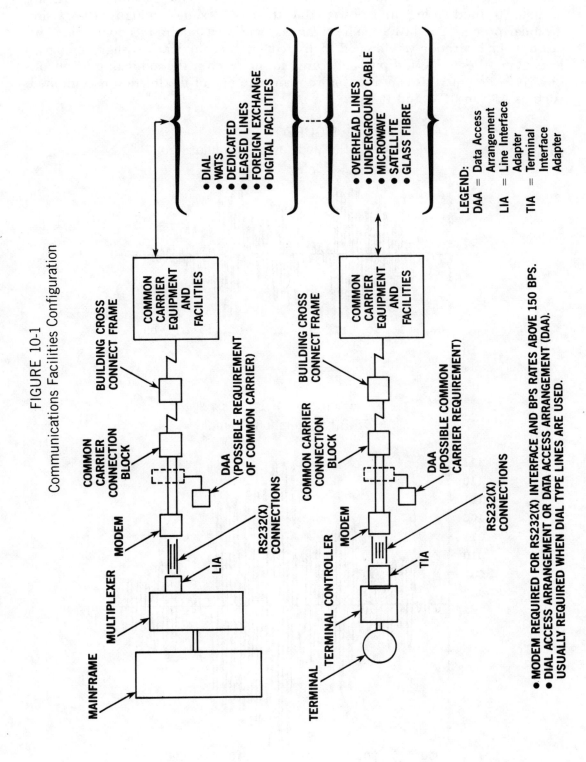

FIGURE 10-1
Communications Facilities Configuration

one level) is used. In a similar manner, MODEM speeds up to 7200 BPS are available by modulating three bits at a time (tri-bits), as shown in Figure 10-3. Using a similar process, 9600 BPS can be obtained by using a quadra-bits operation. This last four-bit operation would need 16 discreet levels of carrier. Any slight change in level along the line would probably result in the receiver demodulating erroneous bits. To overcome this condition more than one type of modulation is combined, such as AM and FM and PM, etc.

FIGURE 10-2
AM Di-Bit Modulation Example

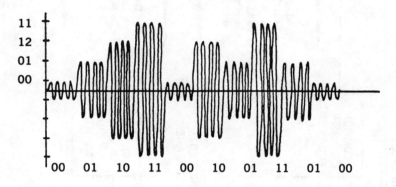

FIGURE 10-3
AM Tri-Bit Modulation Example

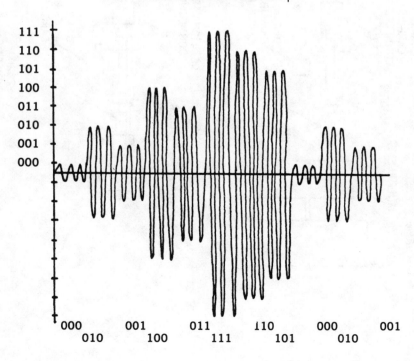

Asynchronous Versus Synchronous MODEM

When the data bits are synchronized or "clocked" by the addition of start and stop bits to the bit grouping, or characters, the MODEM and terminal are operating in an asychronous mode. The stop and start bits are required to synchronize the transmitting and receiving device. If, on the other hand, the terminal and MODEM have some form of automatic bit clocking to lock the two devices and bits together in time, the MODEM and terminal are operating in a synchronous mode. In a synchronous operation the clocking signal may be provided by the terminal or MODEM. Usually it is more efficient to utilize the MODEM timing for both the transmitting and receiving equipment. By using the MODEM clock the receiving MODEM can perform bit timing correction in the local timing clock within the receiving equipment. Bit grouping or character synchronization, as opposed to bit synchronization, is performed by the transmitting and receiving device, and the MODEM is not involved.

Asynchronous MODEMs normally operate up to about 2400 BPS and synchronous MODEMs are used for BPS rates above 2400 BPS. Most low speed MODEMs use Frequency Shift Modulation (FSK), while Amplitude Modulation (AM) is more popular from speeds of 600 BPS to 2400 BPS. Phase Modulation (PM) is used from 2000 BPS to 4800 BPS. Combinations of modulation schemes are used for 4800 BPS to 9600 BPS and above.

The type of line required by a particular MODEM may be either a private line or a dial-up line. Generally, dial-up lines are capable of carrying up to 2400 BPS, while private leased voice grade (conditioned) lines can carry up to 9600 BPS or more. Some MODEMs have the necessary controls to switch from a private line to a dial-up line in the event of line failure on the private line. Also, many of the synchronous MODEMs have controls for either manually or automatically changing speeds due to the type of line being used.

Dial-up lines are usually restricted to half duplex (HDX) operation since the local loops are two-wire connections. Some low-speed (300 BPS) FSK MODEMs can use two different frequency bands within the available voice channel and operate full duplex (FDX). Figure 10-4 shows the 100 series Type F1/F2 full duplex MODEM. The carrier frequencies listed are both the American and European standards. These units must be complements of each other at the terminal and computer rather than identical units as is the general case. The lower frequency band is called the F1 band and is generally used for transmission from the terminal toward the computer.

Echo Suppressors and Turnaround Time

Any MODEM that is to be used for dial-up in the FDX mode must have some arrangement to disable the echo suppressors along the Direct Distance Dial (DDD) network trunks. The echo suppressor is used in all long-length telephone network trunk lines and places 35 decibels (DB) of attenuation in one direction of transmission to suppress voice echoes. This device must be electrically removed for FDX operation and this is done by sending a 200 Hz tone from the answering terminal back to the original terminal before data transmission commences. This frequency disables the echo suppressor.

FIGURE 10-4
Full Duplex Modem Operation
Half Duplex Line

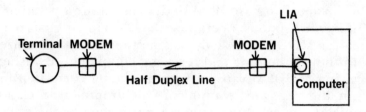

F1/F2 Type Modem Operation

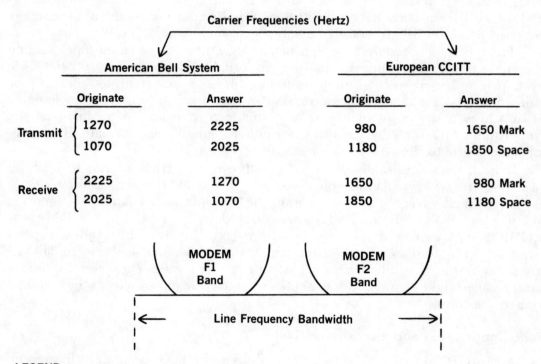

Carrier Frequencies (Hertz)

	American Bell System		European CCITT	
	Originate	Answer	Originate	Answer
Transmit	1270	2225	980	1650 Mark
	1070	2025	1180	1850 Space
Receive	2225	1270	1650	980 Mark
	2025	1070	1850	1180 Space

LEGEND:
LIA   = Line Interface Adapter
CCITT = Communications Consultants
          International Telephone and
          Telegraph

When HDX MODEMs are used on the DDD network, the data transmission efficiency is lessened by the turnaround time of the line. As shown in Figure 10-5, if a feedback error correction technique is used, line turnaround time will reduce operational transmission speeds because of the wait times. To help eliminate this wasted time, the reverse channel is used in some HDX MODEMs. Figure 10-6 shows how the turnaround time is decreased by the addition of the reverse channel. This narrow band channel actually makes the operation full duplex and is sometimes called asymmetric because the speeds of the two channels are different. Reverse channels are in use at speeds as low as 5 BPS compared to the 2400 BPS forward channel speeds.

Originate/Answer MODEMs

Some voice grade line MODEMs have built-in bridge taps for attaching a telephone to the MODEM and providing alternate voice and data over the same line. Other dial-up models have logic for signalling during telephone call placement or answering. Usually, MODEMs manufactured by independents are not required to perform any call placement signalling since these functions are handled in the data access arrangement (DAA). However, the originate/answer capabilities of some 100 series MODEMs are used with data services such as TELEX (TWX). Disconnect on the dial-up network can be performed by the MODEM based on either a long space received or the detection of a code character such as the ANSI end of transmission (EOT) code. These options are sometimes switchable or strappable for the particular situation. Care should be exercised in selecting MODEMs for one-way telephone call placement and "handshaking," and later for FDX data transmission, because the number of unique options is quite large.

FIGURE 10-5
Half Duplex Line Turnaround Time

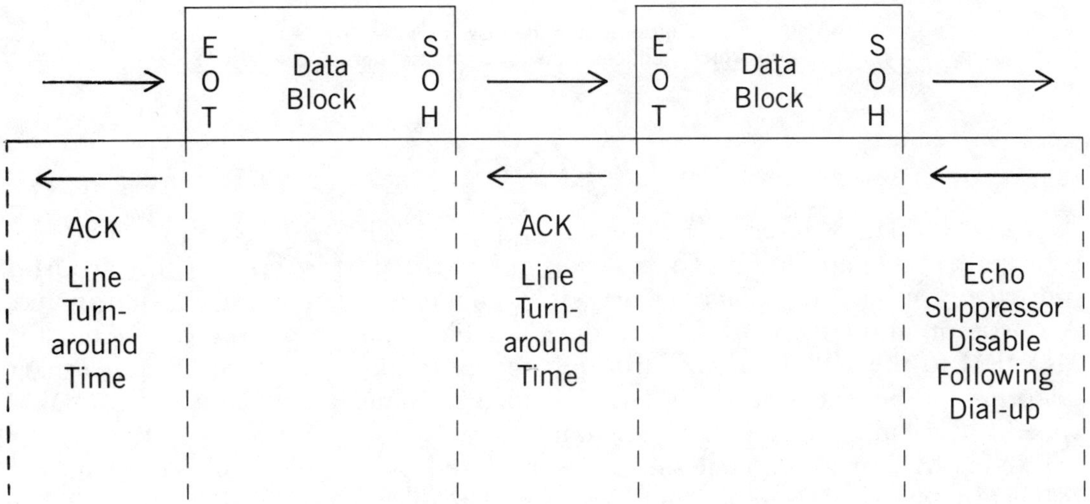

LEGEND: EOT = End of Text, SOH = Start of Header, ACK = Acknowledgment

Figure 10-5 shows how throughput is decreased by the "wait" or wasted time in half duplex transmission when feedback error correction techniques are used in Direct Distance Dialing (DDD) trunk line operations.

FIGURE 10-6
Reverse Channel Modems

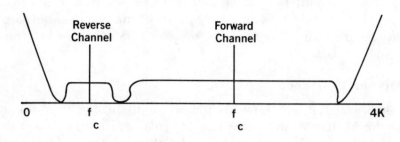

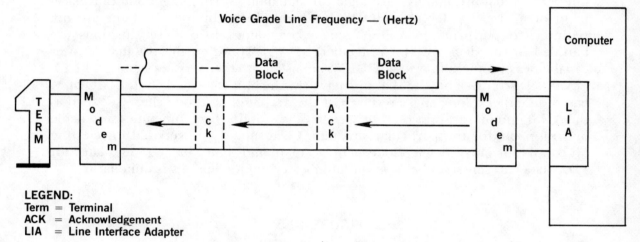

LEGEND:
Term = Terminal
ACK = Acknowledgement
LIA = Line Interface Adapter

ACK Via The Reverse Channel

Line Control Maintained By Terminal
Which Reduces Line Turn Around Time for the ACK

TELEPHONE LINE INTERFACE

The MODEM is usually necessary for interfacing the telephone line and terminal. The telephone line interface is one of three basic types: (1) the acoustic/inductive coupler, (2) dial/data access arrangement (DAA), or (3) hardwired. Acoustic or inductive couplers are devices which can couple the data from the MODEM to the telephone line through the ear and mouthpiece of an ordinary telephone. These acoustic couplers are inherently noisy and limit the MODEM speed but do allow for portable terminals.

The DAA or an equivalent may be required by the telephone companies to protect the network from harm by indiscriminate direct device connecting. Refer to Figure 10-7. However, government rulings have eliminated this requirement in most cases.

The third type of interface to the telephone line is either a two-wire or four-wire private line loop. The usual route of this copper conductor is from the common carrier to the user's building through a connecting frame, over an in-house cable to a connecting block in the immediate vicinity of the terminal or

FIGURE 10-7
Data Access Arrangement Example

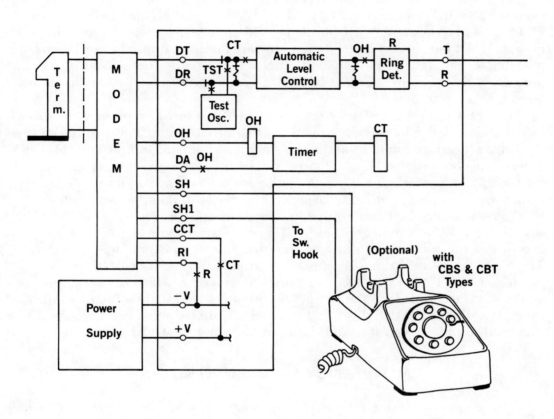

Manual CDT	TYPE Voltage CBS	Contact CBT	DIRECTION	FUNCTION
DT	DT	DT	Both	600-Ohm Transmission Leads.
DR	DR	DR	Both	600-Ohm Transmission Leads.
	OH	OH	To DAA	Control of "Off Hook" Relay.
	DA	DA	To DAA	To Request Data Cut Through.
	RI	RI	To Modem	Ringing Signal Present.
	SG	SG	Both	Signal Ground (CBS only).
	CCT	CCT	To Modem	DAA Data Path Cut Through.
	SH	SH	To Modem	Status of Hook Switch.
		SH1	To Modem	SH Return (CBT only).
		+V	To DAA	Positive DC Power (CBT only).
		−V	Both	Return for DC Power and common for all contacts except SH, SH1 in CBT.

computer port. The data access arrangement is not required on private line circuits since they do not terminate in the switched telephone network. See Figure 10-1.

TERMINAL INTERFACE

The interface between terminal and MODEM may be one of our types: (1) loop current (MODEM not required), (2) EIA RS232-(X), (3) MIL-STD-188-(X), or (4) CCITT V-24 (International Consulative Committee for Telegraphy and Telephony). The loop current interface is a two-wire interface utilized when connecting teletype terminals are used in half duplex operation. These two-wire circuits normally operate with a current of 20 to 65 milliamperes on a make-break basis, and operate up to 300 BPS.

The Electronics Industries Association (EIA) has provided a guideline specification and periodically releases updates of this specification. This is referred to as the RS232 interface standard and is the American standard interface for MODEM to terminal connections. Figure 10-8 provides a list of the circuit letter assignments for the RS232-X interface and a designation for each of the 25 pins of the DB type connector used, along with a description of each circuit. Figure 10-9 illustrates the RS232 remote terminal and host computer connection.

MIL-STD-188-X (military standard) is essentially the same as the EIA interface except that the current levels are reduced to eliminate radiation on secure circuits. This interface is used almost exclusively by the Department of Defense.

The CCITT V-24 interface is a European standard which has about 0.7 volts on the interface leads, and the circuits are numbered as listed on the EIA interface sheet. If a dial-up MODEM is being selected for international use, care should be exercised to obtain both the American standard and the CCITT standard.

AUTOMATIC CALLING UNITS (ACU)

The telephone set provided at a terminal may allow an operator at the terminal to place a call over the dial-up network to a computer port. If calls are to be placed in the opposite direction, an automatic calling unit (ACU) is required. Figure 10-10 is an example of the interface for the Bell System 801 series ACU. This is pretty much a standard in the industry since it is used for calling into a network principally owned by the Bell System Companies. ACUs are further subdivided into two classes: the dial pulse or the push-button multifrequency types. The choice of which to use is determined by the telephone company's serving office to which the dial-up line is connected. If the serving office is one of the older panel or step-by-step offices, it may not be equipped for push-button dialing and the dial pulse ACU must be used.

Some ACUs have the capability to service more than one line or MODEM and computer port. These more elaborate devices make use of some of the interface leads not specifically assigned by the circuit designations shown in Figure 10-10. One spare pin could be assigned to separate a designated fast and slow busy into two interface signals. This would allow for an immediate retry for an urgent call or fast busy, while a wait period could be allowed for the non-urgent call or slow busy.

FIGURE 10-8

Electronics Industries Association
RS # 232 – C
Interface Example

Pin No.	Circuit	CCITT Equiv.	Direction	Description
1	AA	101	Both	Protective Ground
2	BA	103	To MODEM	Transmitted Data
3	BB	104	To Term.	Received Data
4	CA	105	To MODEM	Request to Send
5	CB	106	To Term.	Clear to Send
6	CC	107	To Term.	Data Set Ready
7	AB	102	Both	Signal Ground (Common Return)
8	CF	109	To Term.	Received Line Signal Detector
9	—	—	—	(Reserved for MODEM Testing)
10	—	—	—	(Reserved for MODEM Testing)
11	—	—	—	Unassigned
12	SCF	122	To Term.	Sec. Rec. Line Sig. Det.
13	SCB	121	To Term.	Sec. Clear to Send
14	SBA	118	To MODEM	Sec. Transmitted Data
15	DB	114	To Term.	Transmit Timing (DCE Source)
16	SBB	119	To Term.	Sec. Received Data
17	DD	115	To Term.	Receive Timing (DCE Source)
18				Unassigned
19	SCA	120	To MODEM	Sec. Request to Send
20	CD	108.2	To MODEM	Data Terminal Ready
21	CG	110	Either	Signal Quality Detector
22	CE	125	To Term.	Ring Indicator
23	CH/CI	111	Either	Data Rate Selector (DTE/DCE)
24	DA	113	To MODEM	Transmit Timing (DTE Source)
25	—	—	—	Unassigned

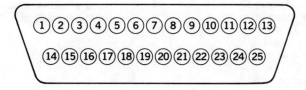

(MALE)

STANDARD CONNECTOR

The connection used in joining terminals to MODEMS and MODEMS to computers. Twenty-five connections are available. On the equipment side (Male) of the RS232 interface there are pins and on the MODEM side (Female) there are receptacles.

FIGURE 10-9

RS232 Remote Terminal and Host Computer Connection
Terminal Facility

TERMINAL FACILITY

REMOTE TERMINAL
Male Connector (Pins)

①②③④⑤⑥⑦⑧⑨⑩⑪⑫⑬
⑭⑮⑯⑰⑱⑲⑳㉑㉒㉓㉔㉕

REMOTE MODEM
Female Connector (Rceptacles)

⑬⑫⑪⑩⑨⑧⑦⑥⑤④③②①
㉕㉔㉓㉒㉑⑳⑲⑱⑰⑯⑮⑭

As long as power is on, the terminal will have the data terminal ready (pin 20). Turned on - when not in test mode.

When a good quality line is available, the terminal's MODEM show an active signal for carrier detect (pin 8), signal quality (pin 21), and data set ready (pin6). It will send the terminal a receive clock signal (pin 17) for matching the terminal's receiving rate with the host sending rate. Also, the transmit clock (pin 15) is active.

HOST FACILITY

HOST MODEM
Male Connector (Receptacles)

①②③④⑤⑥⑦⑧⑨⑩⑪⑫⑬
⑭⑮⑯⑰⑱⑲⑳㉑㉒㉓㉔㉕

HOST CPU
Female Connector (Receptacles)

⑬⑫⑪⑩⑨⑧⑦⑥⑤④③②①
㉕㉔㉓㉒㉑⑳⑲⑱⑰⑯⑮⑭

When the power is on, the host will have the data set ready (pin 6), transmit clock (pin 15), and receive clock (pin 17). The receive clock cycles meaninglessly in the absence of data from the terminal. Clear to send (pin 5) is also always on.

Like the terminal, the host CPU will always have its data terminal ready (pin 20) turned on.

FIGURE 10-10

Automatic Calling Unit Interface Example

PIN NO.	CIRCUIT	DIRECTION	DESCRIPTION
1	FGD	Both	Frame Ground
2	DPR	to ACU	Digit Present
3	ACR	To Term.	Abandon Call & Retry
4	CRQ	To ACU	Call Request
5	PND	To Term.	Present Next Digit
6	PWI	To Term.	Power Indication
7	SGD	Both	Signal Ground
8	—	—	Unassigned
9	—	—	''
10	—	—	''
11	—	—	''
12	—	—	''
13	DSS	To Term.	Data Set Status
14	NB1	To ACU	Digit Lead
15	NB2	To ACU	Digit Lead
16	NB4	To ACU	Digit Lead
17	NB8	To ACU	Digit Lead
18	—	—	Unassigned
19	—	—	''
20	—	—	''
21	—	—	''
22	DLO	To Term.	Data Line Occupied
23	—	—	Unassigned
24	—	—	''
25	—	—	''

(FEMALE)

Figure 10-10 shows the receptacle (female) for the standard connection for the Automatic Calling Unit.

MODEM DIAGNOSTIC

Modern MODEMs usually have diagnostic capability built into the unit. One diagnostic aid that has been on FDX MODEMs for years is the carrier fail sensor and indicator lamp. A loop back (BUST BACK) feature, which allows a data signal to be transmitted to the MODEM and returned via the loop back, is available on the better MODEMs. This loop back feature may be manual or automatic.

Some other diagnostic features found in MODEMs are signal reversals, bit test pattern generators, and error detectors. Some MODEM configurations can automatically send test bit patterns from the remote terminal MODEM when a command from the central site is received. Some users of this technique use expensive monitor equipment at the central site and lower-cost "slave" equipment at the remote terminal locations.

SELECTING A MODEM

Table 10-1 is a checklist which can be helpful in selecting a MODEM. One criterion for selecting a MODEM is that the MODEM used on one end must be completely compatible with the one used on the other end. In the case of a time-share terminal for instance, the MODEM selected must be compatible with the MODEM installed at the system computer port location.

Another criterion in selecting a MODEM is who will maintain the MODEM once it is installed. Usually the vendor will maintain his unit when leasing and many will maintain MODEMs on a service contract when they are bought outright. So called "third party shops" can also be engaged to perform MODEM maintenance. Organizations with large networks may wish to train their own personnel and provide the proper test equipment at the central site, and/or provide portable test equipment that can be moved from terminal to terminal.

TABLE 10-1

Modem Selection Checklist

Transmission Characteristics

Type

Analog
Digital
Combination

Bit Pattern

Parallel
Serial

TABLE 10-1, continued

Mode

    Simplex
    Half Duplex
    Full Duplex
    Reverse Channel

Speed

    Bits Per Second
    Characters Per Second

Modulation Type

    Amplitude Modulation
    Frequency Modulation
    Phase Modulation
    Combination of Above
    Single Side Band

Timing

    Asynchronous
    Synchronous
    Internal
    External
    Optional by Strapping

Interface Characteristics

Line

    Acoustic/Inductive Coupler
    Private Line
    Dial-up
        —CDT Manual DAA
        —CBS Voltage Interface DAA
        —CBT Contact Closure DAA

Terminal

    Loop Current
    EIA RS-232-(X)
    MIL-STD-118-(X)
    CCITT

TABLE 10-1, continued

Operating Characteristics

Mode

Originate Only
Answer Only
Originate/Answer
   —Manual
   —Automatic

Symmetry

Reverse Channel
Fast Turnaround Technique
Adjustable Turnaround Timer
Duplex

Compatibility

Bell Model
Other

Error Rate

Diagnostics

Analog Loopback
Digital Loopback
Remote Loopback
Built-In Test Pattern
Automatic Rate Selection
Error Detection

Options

Voice Adapter
Private Line with Dial-Up Fallback
Data Compression
Forward Error Correction
Bit Pattern Generator
Bit Storage
Data Scrambling

Equalization

Compromise
Prescriptive
Adaptive
Requirements; C-1, C-2, C-4

In order to prevent an entire system from being down, it may be necessary to provide a backup MODEM that can be placed into service when the normal one fails. In addition, on private lines it may be advisable to have a dial-up line terminated into a switchboard, jack panel, or directly into MODEMs so that the dial-up network can be used when the private line fails. In some cases, the speed of operation must be lowered when dial-up lines are used. However, in order to allow higher-speed BPS operation, equalizers may be added to the circuit which can automatically equalize (condition) dial-up lines. Also, to allow two-way high speed operation, two dial-up lines could be used.

Some options available in the more elaborate MODEMs may include such features as:

- The ability to add telephones for voice as well as data,
- Built-in bridges to be used in multipoint networks,
- Forward error correcting firmware,
- Data block storage and feedback error correction on a data block storage,
- Voice data units.

MODEMs are packaged into desk-top models, rack mountable models, card models, and some are being built into the terminals. Built-in MODEMs have the advantage of using the terminal power supply and take up less space. They have the disadvantage of becoming obsolete with the terminal. This is probably one of the reasons for the hesitancy on the part of terminal manufacturers to incorporate MODEMs.

MULTIPLEXER CONSIDERATIONS

The word multiplexing is derived from the words multi (many) and plex (mix). Multiplexing schemes originated because of the cost of communication lines which dictated that several communication channels should be combined on one line.

Two basic methods of multiplexing are used on common carrier facilities: Frequency Division Multiplexing (FDM) and Time Division Multiplexing (TDM). Pulse Code Modulation (PCM) is also a form of time division multiplexing; the difference is that frequency and time division multiplexing are usually performed on alternating current (AC) or analog facilities, where pulse code modulation is utilized on direct current (DC) facilities.

It is not the intent of this section to discuss the internal design of multiplexer units or the common carrier multiplexing procedures, but rather the functional purpose and use of available multiplexer units. Basically, Figure 10-11 shows the difference between FDM and TDM. Frequency division divides up a communications line, such as a voice grade line, by assigning different frequency bands to each service using the line. Speed of service determines the required bandwidth, which in turn determines the number of services that can be placed on the voice grade line. MODEMs are not required for FDM since the signals are generated in AC form. Time division multiplexing divides up the communications line by time-slicing the DC pulses (bits) or bit character streams. The DC is then converted to AC by a required MODEM to utilize the voice grade line. The MODEM may be a part of the multiplexer unit.

FIGURE 10-11
Multiplexing Techniques

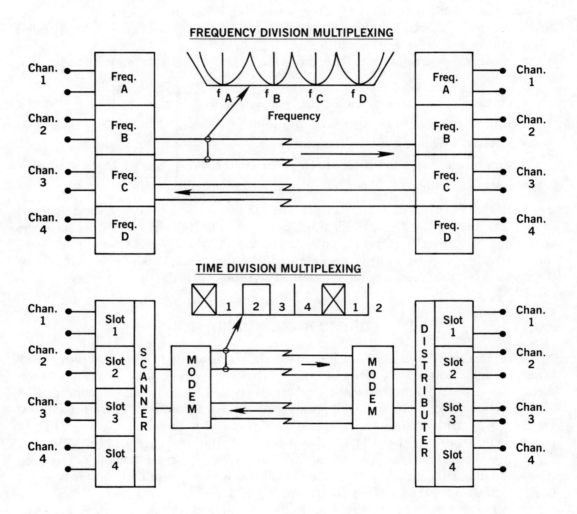

FIGURE 10-11: illustrates the comparison of FDM and TDM and different techniques of handling electrical pulses. FDM splits the circuit into different frequency channels and transmits a continuous stream of analog signals. TDM requires a MODEM which takes the DC signals coming from the terminal or computer and divides them into discreet time slots, converts the slots to AC signals, and transmits the time slots to the MODEM at the distant end of the circuit where the time slots are converted back to DC for distribution to the appropriate channel.

FIGURE 10-12
TDM Applications Example

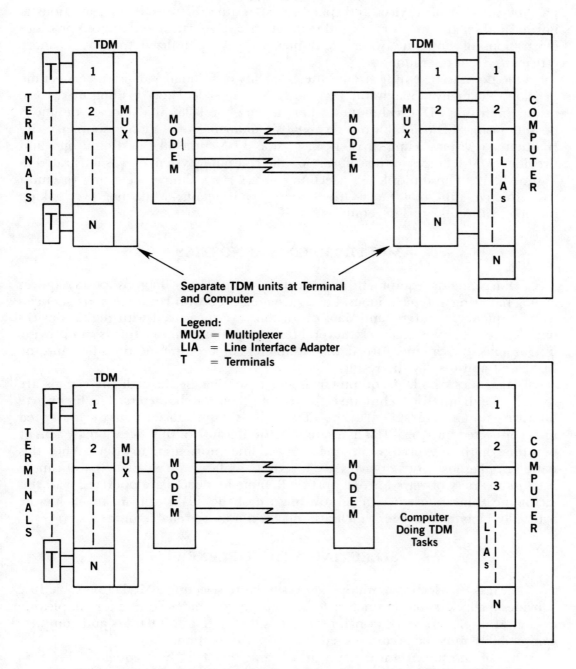

Separate TDM units at Terminal
and Computer

Legend:
MUX = Multiplexer
LIA = Line Interface Adapter
T = Terminals

FIGURE 10-12: illustrates a configuration where the computer (front-end of main-frame) is doing TDM functions. This method eliminates the need for line multiplexer equipment at the counter site (not to be confused with the computer multiplexer equipment).

The multiplexer capability should be specified by the particular vendor under consideration. The prime concerns should be cost, reliability, serviceability, capability (number of services and speed rates), testing features, error conditions at normal and maximum bit rates, and maintenance support. Chapter Seven provides illustrations of how and where multiplexers may be utilized to provide more efficient system operation.

One point to be emphasized is the capability of frequency division versus time division. Normally, a maximum of 1800 BPS is possible when dividing up a voice grade line using FDM techniques, where a full 9600 BPS on a voice grade line is possible using TDM. Multidrop terminal simultaneous operation is simpler using frequency division. Time division may use a TDM unit on the distant end and provide TDM features in the software on the computer system end as illustrated in Figure 10-12. The multiplexer selection process is a matter of selecting the most cost-effective unit that meets the system requirements, while not overlooking possible future expansion requirements.

MULTIPLEXER DIAGNOSTICS

FDM is analog equipment and, in order to perform diagnostics, it requires analog metering and techniques. Levels are measured with DB meters, frequencies with frequency counters, and data distortions are measured with digital devices outside the multiplex channels. Several test equipment manufacturers can provide instruments that can measure all the parameters of a communications line and the FDM unit and display the results digitally.

Diagnostics of TDM equipment is much simpler because all the signals are digital. One diagnostic technique is the use of fill bits or characters. The bit or byte interleave timing rate (speed) of the TDM units is slightly faster than the low-speed lines connected into the TDM as a safety factor. Because of this, occasionally a bit or byte time on the line occurs with no low-speed line information to insert. When this happens, diagnostic bits or bytes are inserted as fill bits or characters and can be used in a variety of ways for diagnostics. Remote loopbacks are operated with this technique. The inherent regenerative nature of the TDM unit makes it operate with a lower bit error rate, which also makes it a more reliable unit.

SELECTING A MULTIPLEXER

The task of selecting a multiplexer is similar to selecting a MODEM. Table 10-2 provides a checklist of parameters to be considered when selecting a multiplexing device. Multiplexers work in pairs over lines the same as MODEMs and complete compatibility must be accomplished for proper operations.

One of the important criteria in selecting FDM is the frequency spectrum layout. CCITT, AT&T, Western Union, and others may all use different frequency assignments and this must be checked carefully in setting up systems.

A problem with TDM is that some line programming is required in the field. Since it is desirable to operate these systems in many locations without trained service personnel standing by, the ease of strapping and programming the units should be taken into account.

TABLE 10-2

Multiplexer Selection Checklist

Type

FDM

    Required Bandwidth
    Number of Channels
        Channel Speeds
        Channel Frequency Assignments
            CCITT
            Bell
            WU
            Others
    Interfaces
    Diagnostics

TDM

    Interleave Technique
        Bit
        Byte
    Scanning Techniques
        Simple
        Complex
        Programmable
    Speed
        High-Speed Lines
        Low-Speed Lines
        Speed Intermix
    Code Sensitivity
    Timing
        Asynchronous
        Synchronous
    Diagnostics
    MODEM Requirements

CONCENTRATORS PERFORMING MULTIPLEXER FUNCTIONS

In simple terms a multiplexer can be called a concentrator. A concentrator could also be a simple device that switches a line from one terminal to another, all sharing the line and transmitting one character or group of characters during each connection time interval. Figure 10-13 illustrates a simple concentrator device which allows a group of terminals to share one line. Where low-speed services are in use, this can be a very economical method of communicating. Also, the concentrator could utilize some form of a minicomputer as the sharing device.

The concentrator could grow from a simple device to a computerized store and forward system. This would allow for simultaneous and continuous send and receive operation for all terminal devices. This is illustrated in Figure 10-14.

FIGURE 10-13
Concentrator Performing Multiplexer Functions

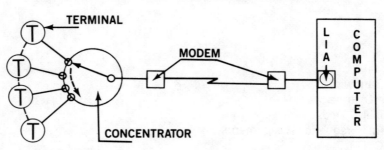

LEGEND: **T** = **Terminal**
         LIA = **Line Interface Adapter**

FIGURE 10-13: illustrates that a concentrator can perform the functions of a multi-plexer. The concentrator usually performs these functions by firmware, while the computer may do multiplexer functions by software or firmware or a combination of both.

FIGURE 10-14
Concentrator Performing Store and Forward Functions

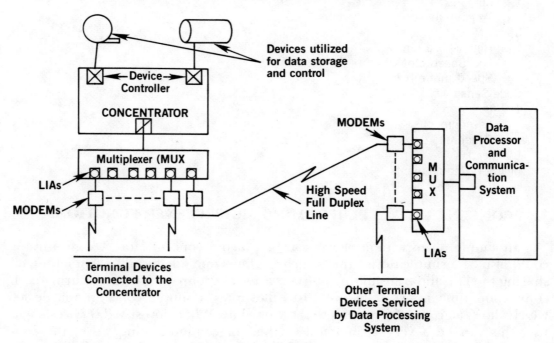

FIGURE 10-14: illustrates the flexibility of the concentrator. A concentrator can perform certain functions that are usually handled by a computer. This diagram depicts a concentrator performing store and forward functions.

CHAPTER ELEVEN

Network Technical Control, Line Consideration And Conditioning

Tech (technical) control facilities are normally incorporated into data communications systems to provide a means of monitoring components and the facilities, e.g., lines, MODEMs, multiplexers, terminals, and associated equipment, to determine quality of lines, status of components, and cause of failures and to allow restoration of failed portions of the system.

Tech control facilities were around long before computers came into existence. Tech control facilities historically are responsible for the physical and electrical integrity of the transmission line or circuit. The primary function of a tech control facility is to bring all the lines from computers, MODEMs, and common carriers to a common interconnect panel. This allows the technicians to monitor the physical and electrical characteristics of the equipment or line terminated in the panel to see if the quality of lines and equipment performance are within accepted levels.

Modern tech control facilities are usually monitored and controlled from a console located within the tech control work area. The console contains manually operated patch panels that terminate equipment and communications lines at the tech control facility, plus test and monitoring equipment, which can be patched into the line or equipment to isolate problems.

Tech control provides control over the equipment terminated at the central data communications site and over equipment connected to the other end of lines that are terminated at the central site. Users who want to monitor and control lines and equipments on a remote portion of a large data communications network, which is not connected to the central computer site where the tech control facility is collocated, must configure the tech control facility to monitor all remote processor nodes of the data communications network.

This chapter treats various aspects of networking, technical control, and network management. The magnitude of the system's technical control facility will be dictated by the data communications system's requirement. This chapter will serve as a primer on tech control and line consideration for data communications systems.

SIMPLIFIED TECHNICAL CONTROL

A simplified technical control facility is illustrated in Figure 11-1. This facility would entail the use of a monitoring and termination jack matrix. Each line would be terminated into a jack or jacks, and then routed to the computer line interface adapter (LIA). The number of jacks required per line would be dictated by the number of RS232 signals to be monitored, controlled, and patched when necessary.

These jacks would allow for quicker restoration of service since a spare line or line interface adapter could be patched in quickly to replace the failed component.

FIGURE 11-1
Simplified Technical Control Facility

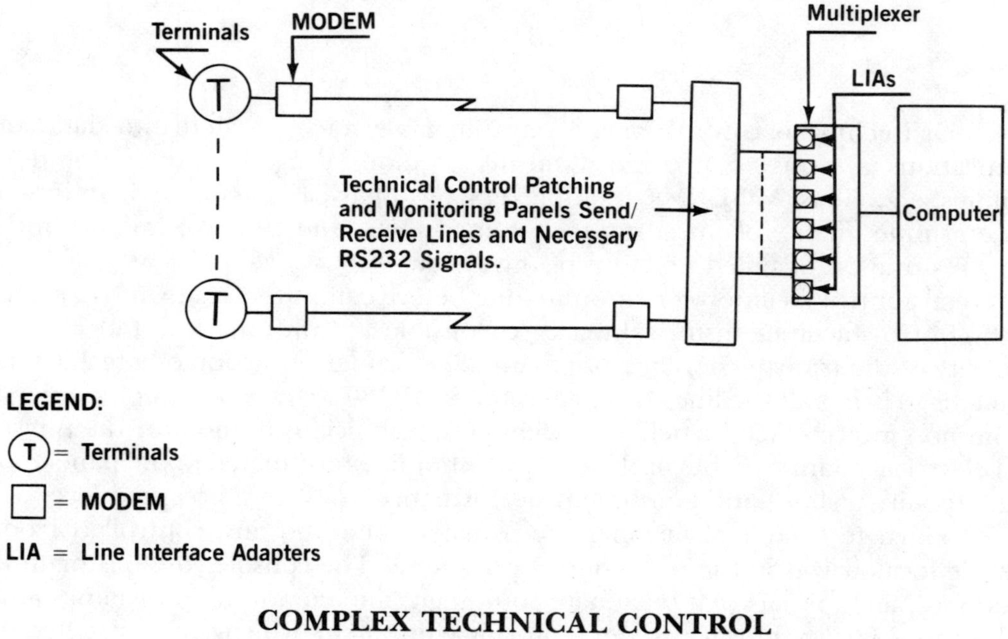

LEGEND:

(T) = Terminals

☐ = MODEM

LIA = Line Interface Adapters

COMPLEX TECHNICAL CONTROL

A very complex technical control facility is illustrated in Figure 11-2. This type of facility could allow for the following automatic or manual capabilities:

FIGURE 11-2
Complex Technical Control Facility

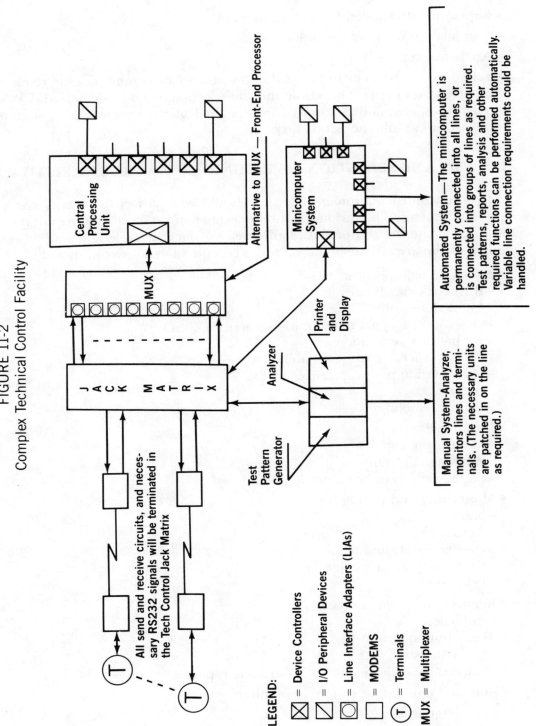

LEGEND:

⊠ = Device Controllers

▨ = I/O Peripheral Devices

◉ = Line Interface Adapters (LIAs)

▢ = MODEMS

Ⓣ = Terminals

MUX = Multiplexer

- Line or equipment failure detection,
- Replacement of failed lines or equipment,
- Compilation of system network statistics,
- Analytical reports,
- Selection of devices or lines to fulfill the immediate communication requirements as they occur. This would include selection of a dial, dedicated, TWX, telex, wats, etc., line as required for the particular connection being accomplished in a multiline network system.

ANALYSIS AND SELECTION OF TECHNICAL CONTROL FACILITIES

Technical control equipment selection should be a part of the overall system design requirements. The various features selected to meet the system requirement will in turn dictate the equipment requirements to meet the need.

Some of the areas that should be reviewed and analyzed would include:

- MODEM features available
  - Bust back capabilities
  - Error detection
  - Detection of signal deterioration (carrier failure)
  - Bit pattern generation
  - Bit rate speed, change capability
  - Line conditioning capability
  - Bit storage
  - Data scrambling

- Jack panels
  - Monitoring capability
  - Patching capability
  - RS232 signals to be controlled/monitored

- Monitoring and testing devices
  - Manual
  - Automatic
  - On-line or off-line features
  - Visual display capability
  - Printouts

- Reports (manual/automatic)
  - Analytical
  - Data flow statistics
  - Error statistics
  - Maintenance alert—immediate trouble report

- Line and equipment swapping requirements

- Line diagnostics
  - Character patterns
  - Bit patterns
  - Fault isolation

 −Test data
 −AC test capability
- Data statistics
 −Transaction sizes
 −Transmission types
 −Transmission times
 −Line type utilized (variable line type system)
- Error statistics
 −Character parity error counts
 −Bit error counts
 −Block retransmission counts
 −Control sequence error counts
 −Handshaking failure counts
 −Erroneous disconnects (dial-up lines)
- Line loopback capability

NETWORK MANAGEMENT

A communication data system normally consists of a network of lines and terminals that provide the means for inputting data into a data processing system. This network requires the same operational management consideration as that given to the main data processing system.

Network Troubleshooting Considerations

A troubleshooting guideline manual for operational or maintenance purposes should be compiled and be readily available to those responsible for network management. The manual should include individual line terminal layout information. This is necessary to determine causes of failures and to accomplish quick line and/or terminal restoration. Some of the questions, comments, or information that could be included in the manual would be as follows:

- What test procedures can be performed in order to isolate the problem?
 −Terminal test capability
 −MODEM test capability
 −Computer site test capability
 −Test equipment availability
- Can the problem be isolated to a major area?
 −Computer site equipment
 −Communication lines
 −MODEM
 −Terminal
- Type of problem
 −Parity errors (intermittent or solid)
 −Carrier failure (MODEM or line equipment)
 −Multiterminal

  −Dial-up
  −Terminal equipment
  −Individual RS232 signals breakdown
  −Computer site equipment failure
- Past history records
  −Lines
  −MODEMs
  −Terminals
  −Computer components

Procedural Checkout Considerations

In addition to the troubleshooting guidelines, a procedural manual may be required to give step-by-step procedures for operations and maintenance personnel to follow. The following are typical procedures examples that could be included in the manual:

- Terminal, input or output failure
- Isolate the terminal and line from the computer equipment
- If automatic loopback features are on the line:
  −Place a loopback at the LIA output in the computer equipment and perform data test patterns from the software and check return pattern for errors (computer equipment confirmation test).
  −Perform a loopback at analog side of computer site MODEM and transmit test pattern; this tests computer site MODEM.
  −Perform a loopback at analog side of terminal MODEM and transmit test pattern; this would test the equipment and lines up to the terminal.
  −Perform a loopback at digital side of terminal MODEM and transmit test pattern from computer and return pattern; this would test the terminal MODEM.
  −Perform a loopback at terminal controller and transmit test pattern from computer and test returned pattern; this would test the terminal connectors, cabling, and jack panels.
  −Send message to terminal for retransmission of original data or test to central site (this test will identify problems in the terminal controller or device(s)).
- If no automatic loopback features are available or the trouble was not clearly isolated by the loopback testing:
  −Measure analog levels at the central site
  −Measure circuit delay and:
  (1) Arrange for a loopback at the terminal MODEM analog side and transmit test data and measure the propagation time delay of data bits returned to the central site.

(2) This test shows if any major reroute of the circuit has occurred in the common carrier facilities, and conditioning may be necessary.

—If equipment is available at the terminal, measure the levels on the analog side of the MODEM.

—If it appears that a facilities problem does exist, call the common carrier facilities maintenance center.

- If the error rate has been increasing and the circuit has been worked on in any capacity, and if error rate measuring equipment is available at either end of the line, it may be advisable to reestablish the error rate of the circuit by retransmitting a minimum of a million bits of information over the circuit with either a Bit Error Rate Tester (BERT) or a Character Error Rate Tester (CERT) and a parity type code set.

TEST AND MONITORING EQUIPMENT

The primary function of test and monitoring equipment is to provide a means of generating various data test patterns and the capability to analyze data patterns. Several types of test and monitoring equipment are available. These units may provide displayed, printed, or graphic output information concerning the data under analysis. Some units test signal distortion, count errors, provide accumulative error counts, give failure alarms, and provide other individual features as required. The equipment may provide the means to generate the necessary bit, character, or analog signals for testing. Signal distortion may be introduced by the unit in order to check equipment operational margins.

It is not necessary to provide individual monitoring or test equipment for each line connected to the computer. With technical control facilities or a simple patching panel, one or two monitoring/test units could be rotated across the network line connections as required. Several equipment arrangements may be configured to generate test pattern data. Figure 11-3 illustrates three possible methods.

The computer hardware and software system can also provide test patterns and data testing features. Software tables can be established to store error counts and those tables could be utilized to produce reports or sound alarms. A test pattern could be produced by software when maintenance testing is required.

FACILITY (LINE) CONSIDERATIONS

Many factors enter into the line selection process. Some significant ones are: cost, data bit rate, on-line time, convenience, and types of associated equipment. There are basically two types of lines available: dedicated (leased) or dial. The dedicated line bit per second (BPS) rate is limited only by the type of line and associated equipment. The dial-up lines place a limitation on the BPS rate because of the common carriers' dial exchange and associated equipment.

FIGURE 11-3
Generating Test Patterns

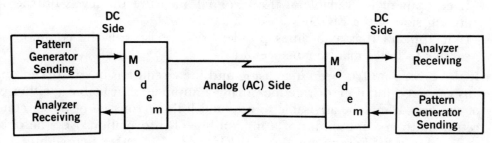

Full Duplex Testing

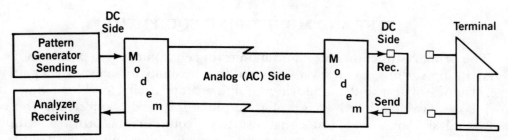

Full Duplex Testing over Digital Loopback

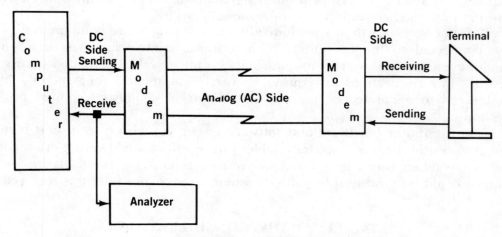

Analyzer Connected to the Receive Circuit

Dedicated Lines

Dedicated lines provide the following features or capabilities:

- Fixed monthly costs
- The availability of BPS rates up to or in excess of 9600 BPS

- Line conditioning available from the common carrier
- Fixed routing, no dial exchange equipment involved
- Absence of common carrier foreign test or control tones
- Echo suppressors not required
- Dial access arrangements are not required
- Full duplex lines (four-wire systems)

Dial Lines

Dial-up lines provide the convenience of dialing connections to many different locations, and possible cost efficiencies where low line usage is a system criterion. Of course, there are some problems when dial lines are utilized. Dial-up lines provide the following features and capabilities:

- Dial connection capability
- Limited BPS rates (up to 4800 BPS and possibly 9600 BPS—but usually below)
- Variable monthly costs
- Conditioning not available from the common carrier
- Variable line routing due to telephone exchange trunk routing during the accomplishment of the dial connection
- Possible foreign tones introduced by the common carrier
- Echo suppressors may be a part of the line equipment
- Possible signal level losses
- Dial access arrangement equipment may be required
- Half duplex lines (two-wire systems)

A typical dial-up connection is illustrated in Figure 11-4.

LINE ROUTING

The proper routing of the connecting lines to a group of terminals or remote computer systems is very important since dedicated (leased) line costs are partly based on a line mileage. Every system configuration is unique and, therefore, requires that a study be performed to determine the best line routing and associated equipment requirements.

A line matrix should be laid out illustrating the required connecting lines and equipment. This illustration should provide a layout of the most efficient line routing and indicate where concentrators or multipler could be utilized to reduce the total line mileage. The end result should be a combination of lines, multiplexer, concentrators, and other necessary equipment that may provide the lowest overall costs, while maintaining efficiency of operation. Chapters Seven and Ten provide an overview of where multiplexing or concentrator equipment may be used to reduce overall line costs. Figure 11-5 provides a simple illustration of several different routings that may be used to connect four terminals together. When line-costs-per-mile are considered, it becomes clear that line routing can be very important.

FIGURE 11-4
Typical Dial-Up Connection

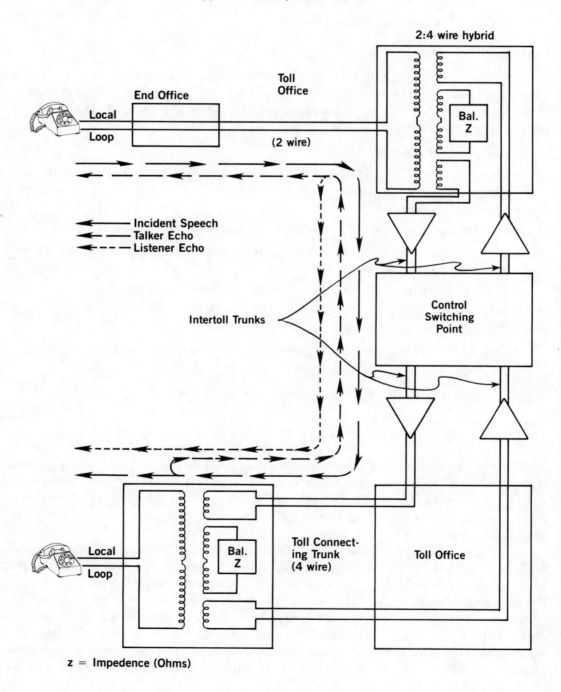

FIGURE 11-5
Routing Considerations

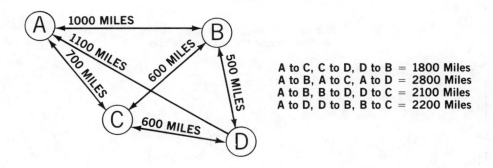

A to C, C to D, D to B = 1800 Miles
A to B, A to C, A to D = 2800 Miles
A to B, B to D, D to C = 2100 Miles
A to D, D to B, B to C = 2200 Miles

LINE CONDITIONING

Several factors determine the ability, or lack of ability, to transmit data over common carrier or user provided lines. These detrimental factors usually cause inefficient operation at the higher BPS operations. Line conditioning or equalizing is used to overcome the line deficiencies that cause problems when operating in the range of 2400 BPS to 9600 BPS or higher.

Three basic types of line conditioners or equalizers are used to condition the lines. The three types are: compromise, prescription, and adaptive. Normally, these conditioners or equalizers are incorporated into the MODEM.

The compromise conditioner is preset to condition the nominal or average line. The inherent deficiency of this conditioner is that it may contribute to the existing line distortion average from one extreme or the other.

The prescription conditioner is manually set up to compensate for the distortion on a particular line. This same type of MODEM conditioner may automatically compensate for line distortion found on dial-up lines.

The third type of conditioner has capabilities similar to the prescription type of conditioner plus a monitor feature which automatically provides continuous fine tuning for correction of line distortion.

Rapid and accurate conditioning of lines can be expensive, but it does provide for increases in frequency bandwidth, which in turn allow higher BPS rates. The amount of line conditioning will be dictated by the operational BPS rate requirements.

CONDITIONER OR EQUALIZER FUNCTIONS

Line conditioners normally correct for amplitude attenuation, signal delay, and phase shifting. Figure 11-6 could represent a typical unconditioned voice grade line. Three curves are used to illustrate the effects of signal attenuation, delay and phase shifting on a possible usable frequency range of 300 to 3300 Hertz.

Figure 11-7 represents the equal and opposite conditions that could be introduced by the line conditioner. The line conditioner would be adjusted to provide approximately equal and opposite signal attenuation, delay, and phase

FIGURE 11-6
Unconditioned Voice Grade Line

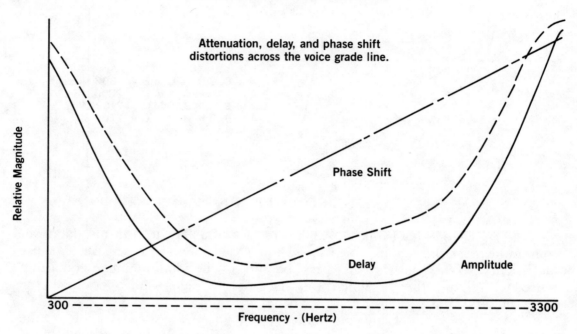

Attenuation, delay, and phase shift distortions across the voice grade line.

FIGURE 11-7

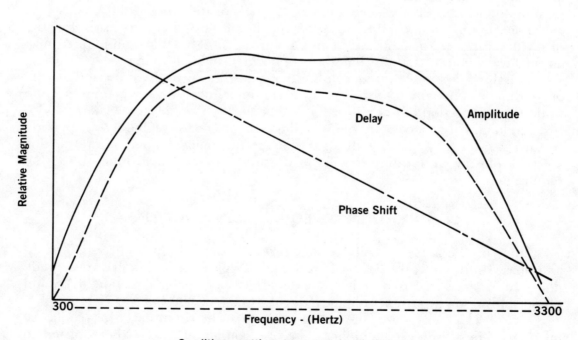

Conditioner settings to correct the distortions

shift. In effect, the conditioner would amplify the received signal, correct for bit pattern delay and correct signal phasing. This would create a constant condition across the total frequency range of 300 to 3300 Hertz and allow the highest possible bit per second range to be utilized.

Figure 11-8 illustrates the affect of several different levels of conditioning on a type 3002 voice grade line. C1, C2, and C4 are conditioning levels offered by a common carrier. The C1 level of conditioning provides the narrowest usable bandwidth and C4 provides the widest usable bandwidth. The wider bandwidth provides the highest BPS capability.

There are other types of problems that occur on the line and within the equipment connected to the lines. These problems include time jitter, phase jitter, line hits, and frequency shifting. Some hardware problems can be corrected by improvements in equipment design. Of course, it may not be possible to correct hits on the line, or other line interference caused by electrical impulses or human error, through equipment design. Compensation for errors caused by these problems may be handled by error detection and correction schemes.

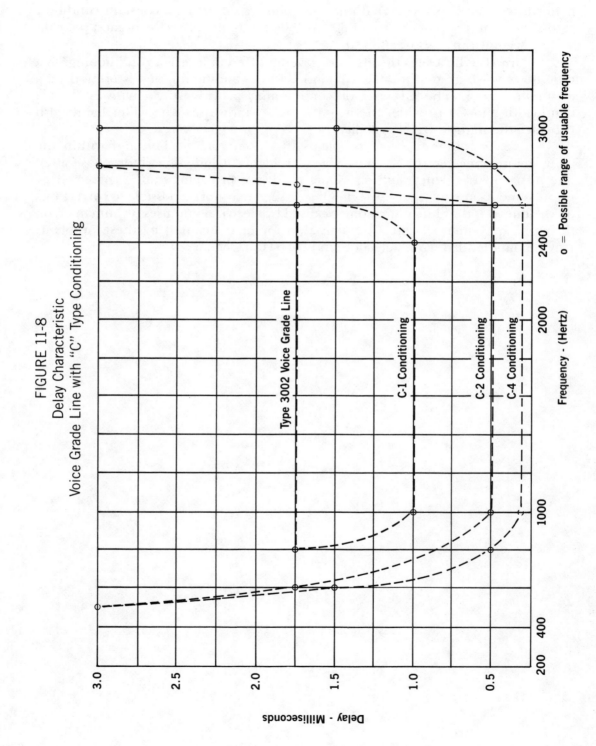

FIGURE 11-8
Delay Characteristic
Voice Grade Line with "C" Type Conditioning

CHAPTER TWELVE

Site Planning, Equipment Installation And System Acceptance

Many times, systems are purchased, installed, operationally accepted and placed in service without a clear, documented definition of all the operational functions. Also, when this happens, an insufficient amount of system acceptance testing is performed. This often results in inadequate system performance, unhappy users, redesign efforts, site modifications and cost overruns.

Many initial system delays and performance failures could be avoided through: (1) Well-defined site planning, (2) A site preparation plan, (3) A series of comprehensive system acceptance tests, and (4) Cutover procedures. With good planning and test (checkout) procedures, most potential problems could be eliminated prior to placing the system on-line. Even with well thought-out plans and a thoroughly tested system, Murphy's Law is likely to prevail—"if anything can go wrong, it will." But the number of failures can be reduced by performing comprehensive acceptance tests.

As data communications networks become more intricate and the operational requirements become more restrictive to unique and complex functional applications, it is increasingly difficult to isolate network problems once a system is accepted for operational use without clearly-defined implementation and test procedures.

It is said that one of the primary reasons for system failure is that the system is not adequately defined at the start and may lack a clear beginning and end.

Without a clear beginning, the project, like the biblical Moses, will wander for months or years without reaching the promised land of a happy "acceptance."

This chapter discusses step-by-step procedures delineating the responsibilities and coordinated efforts of the vendor and user in the installation and acceptance of a system. Procedures for site planning and suggested preinstallation schedules, system layout, environmental requirements, system test criteria and cutover procedures are included to aid the project manager in defining a clear beginning and positive end. The chapter discusses post-acceptance procedures for: (1) evaluating results against system objectives, (2) evaluating integrity of data of the new system, (3) evaluating errors and debugging problems, and (4) determining changes required. Unless careful planning is done in the implementation stages of a system and there is a post-evaluation of its results, the system may be condemned, as Moses was, to wander to the end of its days while being cursed and flogged by its users.

USER/VENDOR RESPONSIBILITY

At the outset of this chapter, Table 12-1 is presented to serve as a checklist or guide that reflects user/vendor responsibilities and things to do in the installation and acceptance of a system. This checklist will vary according to a given system, management procedures used, and the contract stipulations. It generally serves as a "road map," delineating responsibilities and functions required of the user and vendor in the installation and checkout of a system.

TABLE 12-1
Checklist for User Vendor Installation/Acceptance Responsibility

USER	VENDOR

Initiate Scheduling of Site Preparation, Training, Personnel, Facilities, Terminals, etc.
 	
Prepare Budget Material and Control Procedures
 	
Order Terminal and Associated Hardware Required for Test Bed System Testing
	Initiate System Development, Production and Scheduling
	  —Hardware
	  —Software
	  —Documents
	  —Training
	  —Etc.

Schedule and Conduct Review Meeting with all Concerned Departments	Schedule and Conduct Review Meeting with all Concerned Departments Compile Work Plan —Establish Schedules and responsibilities
Review Meeting Possible Schedule/Functional Revisions	Review Meeting Possible Schedule/Functional Revisions

TABLE 12-1, continued

USER	VENDOR
Order Terminal, Facility, etc. Equipment	Prepare Budget Material and Control Procedures
Continuous Coordination	Continuous Coordination
Provide Site/Facility Pertinent Data	Initiate Site/Installation Plan Preparation —Initiate T&A Plan Preparation
Schedule Personnel for Training	Provide Course Material and Instructor Personnel
Review Site/Installation Plan	Present Site/Installation Plan Document
Forward Required Site/Installation Plan Revisions	Revisions to Site/Installation Plan
Initiate/Schedule Site Preparation Activity	Finalize Site/Installation Plan, Forward to User
	Prepare and Forward to User—Operations/Programming/ and Other Pertinent Training Documents
Personnel to Training Courses.	Conduct Training
Possible Participation in Test Bed Activity	System Test Bed Checkout
Review T&A Plan	Forward Initial T&A Plan to User
T&A Plan Revisions	T&A Plan Revisions
Confirm Site Ready for Installation of System	Finalize Necessary System Documentation
Confirm Necessary Test Terminals Will be Available On Site; If not, Make Emergency Arrangements	Perform Test Bed T&A
	Verify Hardware/Software Passes T&A and Confirm It Is Ready for Shipping
Participate in Test Bed T&A	
Handle Personnel Security Access to Site	Provide Names of Individuals Who Will Be On Site
Ensure Site Accessible to Movers and Vendor Personnel	Ship System—Hardware/Software/ Documents/Etc.
Participate In On Site Testing	Install Equipment. Connect Power, Cables, Etc.
Possible Operations Training	Confirm Hardware Status
	Initiate On Site Hardware/Software Checkout

TABLE 12-1, continued

USER	VENDOR
Participate in T&A	System T&A
Confirm T&A Results	Confirm T&A Results
Confirm Correction of Problems	Correct Existing Problems
Cutover System	Support System Cutover
Monitor System Performance	Provide After Cutover Support
Ensure Problems Resolved by Vendor	Hardware Maintenance

SITE PLANNING

A physical site plan should be prepared when a system installation is planned. The site plan may be prepared by the user or by the vendor supplying the equipment, under the guidance and approval of the purchaser. The site plan should include equipment dimensions and weights, floor modification specifications, power requirements, environmental requirements, air conditioning, heating, temperature and humidity, physical security, fire detection, and other required information for equipment installation. The site plan should also provide sufficient information to assist the site or facility engineers and contractors in the preparation of their specifications.

Individual responsibilities should be clearly defined in the site plan. The areas of defined responsibility would include:

- Specification drawings
- Environmental provisions and controls
- Equipment power provisions
- Preparation of the site location for equipment installation
  - Raised floor
  - Floor cutouts
  - Cable and power ductwork
  - Administrative, office, storage and maintenance facilities.
  - Other special requirements
- System hardware and equipment

If it is a turnkey system, the vendor is usually responsible for equipment installation and system shakedown (testing). A turnkey system has some advantages over a user-developed and installed system. If there are any initial maintenance (hardware or software) problems, the vendor is responsible for clearing up these problems prior to user acceptance. However, this advantage may be offset by the cost involved. It is not uncommon for a user to pay as much as 100 percent more for the system components (terminals, MODEMs, multiplexers, and communication lines) when they are purchased in total from one vendor, as opposed to purchasing the various components from different vendors, and assembling and then testing the system themselves. One path followed by many users is the purchasing of the mainframe as a turnkey unit while purchasing the other components from various other vendors. The user, under these circumstances, must ensure adequate site plans and system acceptance tests are prepared.

Commonalities of Installation Planning

Installation planning will always vary with the user's system requirements. Even with this variation in systems there are some commonalities that can apply when installation planning is accomplished. Table 12-2 is a typical pre-installation schedule that will serve as a useful guide in compiling detailed schedules for the installation and testing of a system.

TABLE 12-2
Typical Pre-Installation Schedule

Three Months Before Installation:

• Coordinate installation date with all participating parties
• Identify building space
• Schedule building modification (if any)
  —Floors
  —Partitions
  —Power outlets, etc.
• If user tested, make plans for test data
• Order long distance telecommunication lines
• Order local telecommunication lines
• Specify delivery of mainframe and peripheral equipment
• Specify ancillary equipment
  —MODEMs
  —Cable
  —Multiplexers
  —Rack mounting equipment
  —Other special equipment/services
• Identify expendable supplies
• Prepare benchmark material
• Liaison with vendor
• Identify equipment installation team
• Determine special equipment
  —Air Conditioning
  —Heating
  —Emergency power source (backup)

Two Months Before Installation:
• Monitor building modifications • Order installation of electrical power • Order installation of air conditioning and heating • Develop maintenance plan (if user installed) • Identify team to run test and acceptance for hardware/software (shakedown) • Follow-up on work schedules and equipment previously ordered • Liaison with vendor

TABLE 12-2, continued

One Month Before Installation:

• Check for completion of
  —Building modification
  —Power outlets and cabling
  —Backup power source
  —Air conditioning/heating
  —Special equipment
• Install telecommunications line and facilities.
• Install and check out
  —MODEMs/data sets
  —Remote terminals
  —Local terminals and lines
  —Special equipment
• Prepare test data for test and acceptance (T&A)
• Form T&A team
• Order expendable supplies
• Order the shipment of computer and communications equipment
• Make arrangements for housekeeping (maintenance/cleaning) services
• Obtain/install special test equipment
• Liaison with vendor
• Notify all installation/test participating parties of installation/test schedule

SYSTEM LAYOUT

Included in the site plan should be an equipment layout drawing indicating the exact position of all hardware and equipment. This drawing would indicate the exact position of all computer mainframe hardware, peripherals, operator consoles, MODEM racks, power equipment, administrative equipment, maintenance benches and cabinets, and other equipment to be located at the computer site.

Figure 12-1 provides an illustration of a typical system layout drawing. The equipment's physical dimensions, weight factors, floor support requirements and power could be in the form of a table as illustrated in Figure 12-2.

POWER DISTRIBUTION

All power requirements, type, breaker panels, cable routine and various receptacles should be defined in the site plan document. If fallback power units will be installed, the switching arrangement and other features should be defined. A typical power distribution layout is illustrated in Figure 12-3. Signal cable routing, if necessary, could be illustrated in the same manner as the power distribution.

FIGURE 12-1
System Layout Drawing

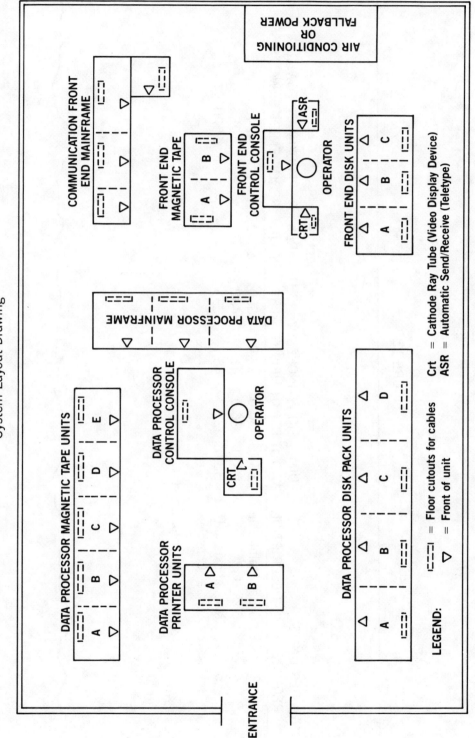
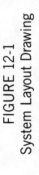

LEGEND: ⊏⊐ = Floor cutouts for cables   Crt = Cathode Ray Tube (Video Display Device)
         ▽ = Front of unit   ASR = Automatic Send/Receive (Teletype)

FIGURE 12-1: is a typical layout for a system equipment configuration. This diagram depicts a mainframe system with a front-end processor (FEP) to handle communications functions for the mainframe processor

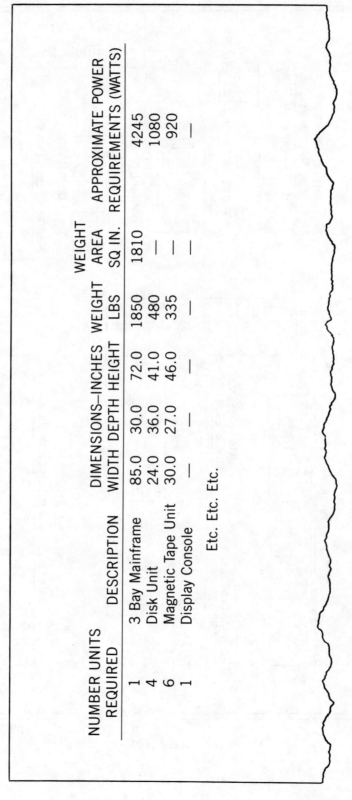

FIGURE 12-2

NUMBER UNITS REQUIRED	DESCRIPTION	DIMENSIONS—INCHES WIDTH	DEPTH	HEIGHT	WEIGHT LBS	WEIGHT AREA SQ IN.	APPROXIMATE POWER REQUIREMENTS (WATTS)
1	3 Bay Mainframe	85.0	30.0	72.0	1850	1810	4245
4	Disk Unit	24.0	36.0	41.0	480	—	1080
6	Magnetic Tape Unit	30.0	27.0	46.0	335	—	920
1	Display Console	—	—	—	—	—	—

Etc. Etc. Etc.

FIGURE 12-3
Power Distribution

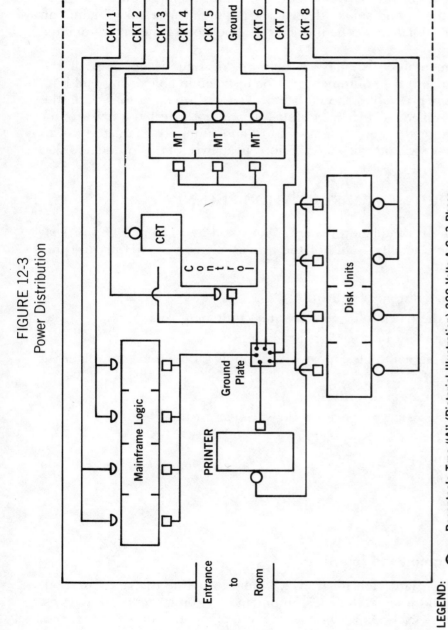

LEGEND:

◖ = Receptacle Type "A" (Pictorial Illustration) 220 Volts A.C. 3 Phase

○ = Receptacle Type "B" (Pictorial Illustration) 110 Volts A.C. 2 Phase

(*) = Amperage should be stipulated

▢ = Ground Connection

MT = Magnetic Tape Unit

CRT = Cathode Ray Tube (Video Display Device)

ENVIRONMENTAL REQUIREMENTS

Normally, two major environmental factors exist in the confines of a computer system site. One is the human comfort factor. The other factor would be the operating requirements of the hardware units. Humidity, temperature, and dust levels must be considered and smoke detection equipment, necessary for human and equipment protection, should be included as a portion of the environmental section.

If the environmental system (air conditioning/heating) is not part of the system's specification, and the equipment is to be installed in an existing building, the existing environmental tables should be checked and updated to include the equipment being installed. The new equipment may not affect the existing air conditioner, but adding the weight, temperature and humidity characteristics to the environmental table will permit a more complete analysis of the installation site.

EQUIPMENT INSTALLATION PLANNING

The objective of an installation plan is to ensure a well-planned and orderly equipment installation activity. Some of the activity areas, with defined responsibilities, would include:

- Equipment unloading procedures
- Routing from the truck into the computer equipment room
- Placing of equipment in preassigned positions
- Connection of signal cables, power, grounding and other miscellaneous cables
- Maintenance testing and verification
- Specifications necessary to perform the various functions
- Checklists as necessary
- Personnel requirements
  - Responsibilities
  - Technical
- Schedules

Equipment Configuration and Interface

An equipment configuration diagram will help to define the configuration, placement, cabling, and interface of the equipment and communications devices. The chart should graphically show where each piece of equipment is to be placed, how the cables are to be connected, and the interface relationship between all the various equipment and communications gear. When preparing the diagram, an important point requiring special attention is the type of interface that each piece of communication equipment requires. The two primary methods of interfacing this equipment are based on voltage and current.

The EIA RS-232 is the industry standard for voltage interfacing. RS-232 dictates, among other things, what the MODEM output signal must be in order to be compatible with the telephone line. With the RS-232 interface, data is bipolar voltage-serial. With current interfacing, the mark and space levels are replaced with current rather than voltage.

Current loop interfacing can be more complex than voltage interfacing. Its principal benefit, depending upon the amount of current and gauge of wire used, is that it can eliminate the use of MODEMs (data sets) or acoustic couplers and is capable of transmitting data at distances up to one mile. If the device has a voltage interface, a cable up to 50 feet in length can be used without a data set or line driver, when connecting the device to another device.

If the distance is greater than 50 feet, the user has several options: (1) The equipment can be rearranged within the 50-foot limit, (2) Make provisions for obtaining a remote connection unit that allows line driving capability up to 300 feet, (3) Obtain a MODEM bypass unit that allows quality data transmission up to 2,500 feet, (4) Use MODEMs, or (5) Consider using equipment with current loop interfacing. Multiplexers, concentrators and terminals can be selected with a current interface option, which permits system configuration without a MODEM, line driver, or couplers, if the terminals and multiplexers are co-located within the distance restraints.

While preparing the configuration diagram showing the type of equipment, components, and communications devices to be installed, the user should supplement the data on the diagram worksheet(s) with the vendor's technical literature.

If a system requirement calls for several MODEMs, multiplexers, and ancillary devices, the use of cabinets, enclosures or rack mounts should be considered. Centralization of this type of equipment will provide these benefits: (1) aid testing and maintenance of the equipment, (2) present an uncluttered appearance, and (3) save space.

SYSTEM TEST AND IMPLEMENTATION

After equipment installation has been completed, some form of system confirmation testing should be performed. These confirmation tests should be scheduled following the normal maintenance hardware validation tests. Systems developed without comprehensive testing and validation of the operational specifications can cause complete chaos during on-line implementation, and for months frustrating problems would occur, both within the software and operational functions. Although programmers may test and debug the individual features or modules of major programs, when these modules are put together to do a particular processing job, it is imperative that they be tested in total against actual "live" conditions as specified in the requirements package.

The measurement of a successful test and implementation of an on-line data communications system depends on many variables that are not present in a stand-alone batch system. Errors can be more easily detected and corrected in a batch system than in an on-line system because of the nature of the two systems. In on-line systems, there are fewer stand-alone programs or subroutines. The majority of the programs/routines must interface, process and "pass on," and, in some cases, alter data and perhaps do this at different core address/locations. This makes the interfacing of numerous interrelated programs extremely difficult and, in turn, makes in-depth testing a logical follow-through in data communications. Various methods of testing are required to ensure that the system is designed and developed-to-specifications. That the system has been developed-to-specifications must be demonstrated by the actual running of programs against test data which have been prepared to simulate a "live" environment.

Levels of Software Testing

Before simulating a live environment, certain levels of test and review inspections of the software should take place while it is being developed. These tests and review methods may require periodic briefings and inspections of diagrams, flowcharts, reports, and program analysis studies and approaches which are to be taken in the development of software. These test review precautions are essential to establish the system integrity prior to the software development efforts. This preliminary verification of various software modular portions as it is being planned and designed will ensure that the system is developed-to-specifications. These reviews will also aid in developing procedures and material for system integration testing and formal system validation.

Formal validation must leave the theoretical and artificial environment of the programmer's office and be demonstrated in the practical aspects of a realistic environment—the computer center. Here, individual as well as collective programs must be run in unison and in parallel operation with the existing system with live input/output data; and the integrated software system must be run on the operationally configured equipment. Procedures should be outlined in the system test and implementation document for preparation of test data and operating procedures necessary to conduct the following levels of testing:

- Individual computer subprogram testing,
- Individual computer program testing,
- System software integration testing,
- System operation acceptance testing.

The first three levels of testing should specify, as applicable, the test formulas, algorithms, techniques, tolerance limits, and procedures to validate programs individually and collectively. The scope and level of testing will depend upon the type of system; but formal testing and validation must ensure that the software meets the specification requirements in a live environment.

Test Material

Testing requirements, specifications, and procedures, along with keypunch instructions, should be developed by the "architectural" designers who developed the functional specifications. Equipment configuration and personnel require-ments necessary for testing should also be specified. Local testing using in-house equipment may be sufficient for some systems. Others may require, in addition to local input/output, that remote terminals be used to simulate actual live conditions. This would be an ideal method for testing. However, with remote testing (unless part or all of the existing terminals can be made available for testing), additional communication lines and equipment will have to be installed to parallel the existing system. This may be an additional cost that management may not want in incur.

The test should be accomplished off-line with a sufficient quantity of predetermined and prepared testing material. Test data should be run through the system in sufficient quantities to test the functionality of the design specifications. To do this, test procedures should specify each step to follow and identify the test material that is necessary to validate each operational feature, and the various categories of messages that may be subject to entering the system. Figure 12-4 provides an example of how each step of the many test procedures could be documented.

Much time may be spent writing the test specifications, procedures, and preparing test material. The time spent may equal that of the functional specifications. But without a comprehensive and in-depth "shakedown," it may take many costly months to render the system reliable.

FIGURE 12-4
System Test Procedure Example

TITLE ___DATA PROCESSOR-FRONT END TEST___ TEST ___#2.0___

DEPARTMENT ___EDP_____ STEP ___#16___

TEST PURPOSE

THE PURPOSE OF THIS TEST IS TO DEMONSTRATE THE OPERATIONAL CHARACTERISTICS OF THE DATA PROCESSOR AND COMMUNICATIONS FRONT END COMPUTER.

1. SINGLE ADDRESS—HI-PRIORITY
   A. ENTER TEST DATA AT FRONT END—TEST DATA #1, STATION B-1
   B. VERIFY TEST DATA IS RECEIVED AND PROPERLY HANDLED BY THE DATA PROCESSOR.

2. BROADCAST DATA OUTPUT FROM THE DATA PROCESSOR
   A. ENTER TEST DATA AT DATA PROCESSOR FOR ROUTING THROUGH THE FRONT END.
   B. VERIFY TEST DATA DELIVERS TO THE APPROPRIATE TERMINALS

CONTENT OF TEST DATA = (USER STIPULATED)
ROUTING OF TEST DATA = (USER STIPULATED)
PROCESSING REQUIREMENTS = (USER STIPULATED)

Test Team

Testing and implementation of the system should be a joint effort comprised of users, programmer(s) analyst, and members of the functional design team. A test coordinator should be appointed to direct the testing and implementation. A lead programmer(s) may be a member of the team for software consultation but he should not head the team.

Saturation Testing

During testing, every condition should be simulated with specially prepared data to specifically test each programming feature. Some features, such as statistical requirements, throughput, and format and control, will be fairly simple to validate. But restart/recovery, data accountability during system failure, and data storage and retrieval during system overload and channel outage, will require more involved test procedures. To adequately test these features, the system should be saturated with sample data of all catagories, and the system purposely stalled and restarted to test all aspects of these features.

It is vital that the overload conditions be tested in an on-line system. This should be done by data saturation. The system should be designed so that overload occurs before the system actually becomes filled to capacity. Given a system of different data priorities, data classifications, and messages with perishable data, overload should be triggered when the storage capacity has reached 80 or 90 percent. This 20 to 10 percent leeway should leave sufficient space to process high priority and other urgent types of data.

To create an overload condition, more data will have to enter the system than the system is capable of handling. This can be accomplished by writing test data to disk, magnetic tape, or some other storage media and then reentering the data into the system simultaneously. If this is not practical, output channels and devices could be shut down, which would create the same effect. When the system reaches this predetermined figure, the overload feature will become activated and low priority data will be written to a "save" area—external storage device. When the system falls below this figure, data should automatically reenter the system and be queued for output processing.

Some errors may occur during the testing of a particular feature, but when repeating the process that seemed to have caused the error, the same error condition may not repeat. For this reason, all errors or error conditions should be fully documented. This will allow future testing to be conducted under the same condition and possibly cause the error to reoccur. Many errors will require thorough researching over a period of time in order to determine the cause. As indicated earlier, errors may be caused by software, hardware or line conditions and may be infrequent because of low data volume or unique conditions.

Another example of errors being difficult, if not impossible, to isolate during testing, is seen when two major programs written by independent programming groups with many interface boundaries are processing the same data and sharing the same computer and I/O devices. Errors may occur in one program that may affect an error-free routine written by the other group. In such an environment special emphasis should be placed on testing these interface points.

SYSTEM CUTOVER AND ACCEPTANCE

There are several general areas that require clear definition and detailed efforts in bringing a system on-line. The following cutover factors must be addressed in detail for smooth cutover and to minimize problems:

- System planning
- Training of personnel
- Delivery of hardware
- Communications line connections
- Installation of user hardware
- Acceptance tests
- Parallel operation

Operator training (terminal and computer) should have been accomplished, and operating manuals and other documentation made available, prior to cutover and acceptance. This is necessary to familiarize operators with the peculiarities of the new system. After cutover, it may be necessary to run the old system in parallel with the new system until sufficient confidence is built up with the new system. At this time, the old system may be disbanded.

The cutover should be handled in the same manner as the testing and implementation phases. Guidelines should be prepared, as necessary, to ensure that each function of the system is implemented in an orderly manner. System analysts and operations personnel should observe the various operations and take immediate action on abnormal conditions as they occur. An abnormal condition, no matter how minor, should not be ignored. Factors that contribute to cutover problems are:

- Inadequate system definition
- Lack of knowledge of the new system
- Unfamiliarity with system operation
- Incomplete checkout of new system
- Lack of alternate or contingency plans
- Duplication of effort

There are two major courses that a system cutover could follow. One would be to completely place all operations, for which the system was installed, into operation and eliminate all previous manual or old system backup operations. The second course would be one of placing all operations on the new system, while maintaining the old system and/or manual operations in an active condition until the new system is proven reliable. In this manner, outputs could be verified and a failed system does not create a total backlog of processed data.

POST-CUTOVER SYSTEM MAINTENANCE

The validity of the system may not be proven until it has been run on-line in a dynamic environment. After the system has been tested, implemented and accepted, it should be under close scrutiny for a period of time by the vendor or vendor-trained user programmers and an operations analyst. These individuals should be readily available to correct any software or operational problems that may arise.

A system may test out successfully when dummy data are used in an off-line environment, but may experience difficulty when run on-line under live conditions. There are certain variables inherent in off-line testing that are not present in an on-line situation. In off-line testing, the input is calculated and controlled, and for the most part, testing is done at favorable times when the processing of live data is low and when the off-line equipment is less likely to be seized for on-line use due to equipment problems with the primary system.

Problems encountered during the testing and observation period, which necessitate software operational changes, should be documented by the vendor, and all the affected software and operational documents updated accordingly. Changes made in the system specifications during testing, and not adequately documented, can cause frustrating problems long after the system is operational. To facilitate debugging of the software features after the system has been declared operational, certain data processing status functions, or check points, should be built-in during architectural design. These status functions should be recorded periodically in preassigned counters and registers, and this should include data or message status indicators for the data being processed. This information may be written to hard copy, disk or some other media.

Post-system maintenance, software or hardware, can be a very critical function and should be performed by responsible software and hardware personnel. Procedures should be implemented for all personnel to follow when system changes or enhancements are to be added to the system. This would include changes placed into the system to correct abnormal conditions.

Many times, system software patches or changes are placed into a system without proper documentation, validation or confirmation testing. The result may be a system failure causing distorted data and/or system downtime. Proper management and documented guidelines would aid in preventing many of the system failures.

CHAPTER THIRTEEN

Establishing Documentation Requirements For the Life Cycle of a Data Communications System*

Modern computers, complex communications facilities and more sophisticated input/output devices have increased the scope and complexity of the manufacturer's software (supervisor and utility) systems. This has made the interface of application programs more difficult and certain aspects of programming, i.e., multiprogramming, multiprocessing, access and linkage, program modularity, file organization, man/machine interactions, and system configuration more exacting. If coordination and controls over the development and life of applicable programs or systems are to be effective, and optimum utilization of man and machine is to be realized, documentation standards and guidelines on all analysis, design, and programming facets must be defined and formulated in the initial stages of data communications analysis and design effort.

This chapter is geared to writing specifications that can be clearly understood for system design and program development, and for preparing program (software) documentation that can be easily understood for (1) training, (2) program maintenance, (3) system operations, or (4) modification for use in similar applica-

* Most of the information in this chapter was written by William L. Harper and was published under the title "Building EDP Success by Standing on Shoulders" in the February 1975 issue of *COMPUTER*, Volume 8, Number 2, pp. 50-56.

tions to eliminate program duplication. Unless documentation standards are developed and enforced, an excess number of programmers will be required to keep the ongoing system patched together. To provide quality documentation and eliminate costly duplication in the life cycle of the system, and to achieve optimum system efficiency, programmers must be able to stand on the shoulders of those who worked before them and build on their success.

STANDARDS—THE KEY TO SUCCESS

Success of a data processing system is directly dependent on the policy and standards established to direct and control the actions of the employees. Documentation standards will vary considerably from system to system. Each data processing system is unique to some degree. They vary in size as well as application, and the overall environment in which they operate can be unusually different. Some factors of documentation may be unique to a particular application but certain aspects of documentation are common to all. However, in many data processing systems, documentation standards are ill-defined or nonexistent.

Documentation principles must be adjusted and tailored to satisfy the particular needs of a given system. Because of the differences in data processing systems, types of applications, and organization philosophy, it would be presumptuous to prescribe a particular documentation policy in this book that would serve as a guide for all systems. Nevertheless, two fundamental guidelines can be expressed. The first is that documentation standards require full and active support from data processing managers. The second lesson is that within data processing organizations, certain definite functions must be assigned as the responsibility of designated individuals in order to achieve quality documentation.

EDP managers have hardware costs documented to the decimal point, and they can quote the dollar cost for their personnel; but they have no way of knowing how much of the personnel cost is spent for program duplication. Duplication can be measured only by documentation policy that requires standards and guidelines for program design, development, storage, and retrieval of this documentation in a form that is immediately usable.

Documentation standards must be established at the outset of a project if EDP managers want to optimize program design and development and minimize program duplication. Standards should be flexible because documentation requirements vary from application to application.

A system's size will determine the volume but not the method of documentation. The size of the programming task should not affect such things as the scope and types of documentation, the need for standards, nor the various controls that are necessary for the design, development, maintenance, and management of a computer system. Without adequate and controlled documentation, the task of updating the software system and converting to newer hardware becomes increasingly difficult and costly. Without rationale and flexible standards, obtaining quality documentation is one of the most difficult jobs in the analysis, design, and development of a system. Quality documentation can be achieved by implementing a four-phase approach in the development of documentation for a given system.

QUALITY DOCUMENTATION BY A FOUR-PHASE DEVELOPMENT

Most systems require three types of documentation before a system becomes operational. These three types are the results of three evolutionary phases in the installation of a given system. Figure 13-1 depicts the evolutionary phases and defines the three types of documentation required. Actually, there are four phases and four types of documentation in the life of a system. The fourth phase is the System Maintenance Period of an ongoing system, and the fourth type of documentation is the User Reference Documentation.

The first three phases are concerned with (1) system conception–the Feasibility/Analysis Study Period, (2) system design–the Program/System Functional Specifications Design Period, and (3) system software development–the Program/System Software Development Period. The documentation which is generated in one phase becomes the interpretive specifications for the development of the next sequential phase. The quality of the documentation, as it leaves one phase and enters the next, will determine the initial success of the system.

SYSTEM CONCEPTION: GENERAL SYSTEM SPECIFICATIONS

This documentation represents the early thinking and planning stages of the system. It is created during Phase I, the Feasibility/Analysis Study Period. This information provides certain analyses and methods of how the system may be accomplished. During this phase of system planning, documentation is provided by a feasibility or analysis study which sets out the General System Specifications. This is shown under Type A documentation on Figure 13-1. These general specifications are concerned with system definition and are based on concept formulation and preliminary design requirements which may later be revised and defined during the Program/System Functional Specifications Design Period which becomes the exact Program/System Specification Requirements.

The purpose of Phase I, the Feasibility/Analysis Study Period, is to identify all general aspects of the system that are to be affected by computer automation, and to identify subsystems and functional areas that will become an integral part of the total system. The scope of system conception is concerned with:

- The effects of performing functions by automated, electrical, and manual means, or a combination thereof, in the installation of a system.
- Identifying functional interfaces and delineating responsibilities between functional areas.
- The cause and effect relationship and trade-offs among equipment, computer programs, and personnel.
- Identifying functional tasks for computer automation.
- The items of equipment (not characteristics or performance criteria) that are required to satisfy automation.
- Identifying human and environmental factors to satisfy the requirements.
- Identifying physical interfaces with which it must be compatible.

FIGURE 13-1
Documentation Requirements in the Evolution of a Computer System

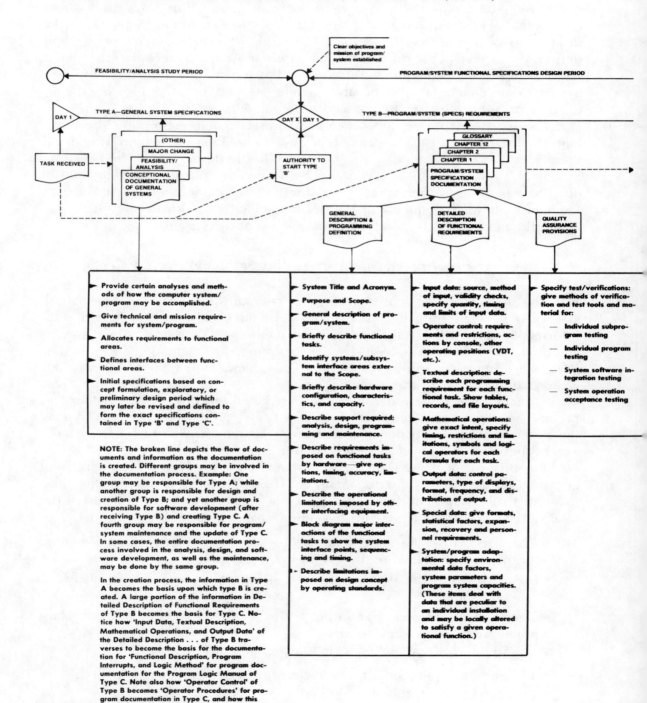

FIGURE 13-1, continued

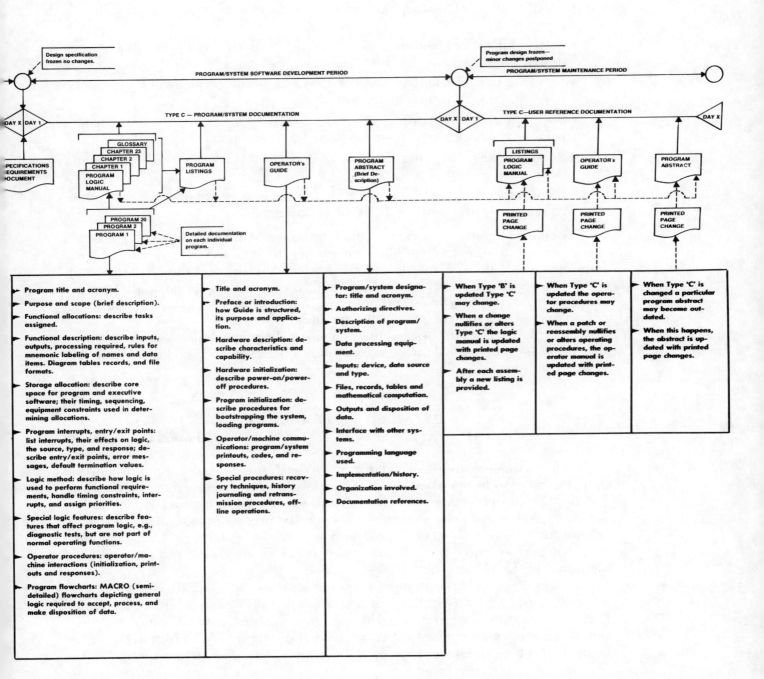

- Creating flowcharts to identify all general system functions, subsystems, and interfaces of functional areas and other ongoing systems.

- Identification of sound and realistic performance criteria and high-risk areas.

- Establishing firm and realistic schedules and cost estimated for system design, development, and installation.

- Identification of standards and test criteria to aid commonality in design, development, and implementation of the system.

- Specifying design constraints and standards necessary to assure compatability with other programs, systems, and equipments.

- Requirements specifying the level of detail necessary to establish limits for design.

- Requirements imposed on system design because of its relationship to other equipments, programs, systems, or functional areas.

The system conception documentation, both narrative and graphic, must be accomplished to the level of detail necessary to establish clearly the general requirements of the system, identify the functional tasks, and the relationship of subsystems and functional areas. Too often, the early conceptual studies fail to recognize that each functional and subfunctional task is a vital element and must be considered as a candidate for a computer program.

Phase I identifies the system and establishes the scope, limitation, and criteria for the Program/System Functional Specification Design Period–Phase II of the system evolution.

DETAILED SYSTEM DESIGN:
PROGRAM/SYSTEM SPECIFICATION REQUIREMENTS

This documentation is created during Phase II. It is a detailed amplification of the General System Specifications and is concerned with specifying the peculiar functional requirements and detailed design specifications for the system before programming starts. The design details specify precise requirements and test criteria for each functional task (program) as it should be developed. Phase II also specifies performance, the allocation and breakout of each functional task as identified in the General System Specifications.

Program/System Specification Requirements documentation should be segmented into three areas: General Description and Programming Definition; Detailed Description of Functional Requirements; and Quality Assurance Provisions. This documentation is shown as Type B on Figure 13-1. Collectively, these three items of documentation become the complete detailed system specifications package, including test procedures. It should be suitable for a team of programmers to start program (not system) analysis, coding, and the preparation of detailed test and verification material to be used for system validation and acceptance.

General Description and Programming Definition

This item of documentation (section or volume) should be considered as an introductory discussion of the software requirements, limitations, and restraints of the system. This information is gleaned and amplified from Phase I documentation. It is a general lead-in identifying the total functional requirements as listed under the above title on Figure 13-1. It should be written to the level of detail suitable for complete system understanding and programming task analysis but not coding. This documentation becomes the basis upon which the Detailed Description of Functional Requirements are derived, as noted under this title on Figure 13-1. The purpose of General Description and Programming Definition documentation is to give a description of the overall system within which the various interactive programs will operate, and identify and describe the various aspects of the system. This description should define and summarize all functional performance requirements by individual programming task by stating the purpose and function of each task. Design constraints and standards necessary to ensure proper development of the system software should be given. This section should also identify the hardware and interface areas of the hardware, software, and operator actions. Descriptive information as well as quantitative requirements should be given. Hardware and interface information should include but not be limited to the following:

- Computer characteristics—language, memory size, word size, access timing, interrupt and I/O servicing capabilities, interfacing relationship of a program with other programs; and interfacing areas specifying I/O requirements of a program so as to show data rate, frequency, message format, bit stream arrangement, etc.
- Hardware/equipment and subsystem interface—peculiar requirements, including environmental factors that may affect the components, peripherals, or system.
- Human interface—machine/human interactions, frequency, response time, type of display, options, etc.

Detailed Description of Functional (Programming) Requirements

This section should contain detailed specifications—narrative, graphic, and mathematical (if required)—for each of the required programs (functional tasks) and subprogram functions. This information should be written to the level of detail that will permit programming analysis and coding. General and detailed coding information may be included in functional block diagrams or equivalent representation. In addition to the information shown under the above title on Figure 13-1, this information must show each operational step to include displays, error detection and recovery procedures, input and output control, diagnostic aids, sequencing control, mode of operation, and other programming requirements as applicable to each program. Operator control requirements should be stated in detail, including names and description of operation action.

Detailed Description of Functional Requirements is a detailed amplification of the General Description and Programming Definition, which is a further amplification and clarification of Phase I documentation, or General System Specifications.

Starting with Phase I documentation, each category of documentation has been moving from general requirements to programming definition to precise details for coding. As it ascends from one phase or category to another, the documentation becomes more specific, and finally it is the exact specifications upon which programs will be written and tested.

Quality Assurance Provisions

This documentation may be a separate document but it is created during Phase II. It becomes part of Program/System Specification Requirements documentation. The purpose of this document is to define plans, methods, procedures, and to specify test/verification requirements as well as the necessary test tools, materials, and facilities to implement and validate the system. Various methods of testing are required to ensure that the system is designed and developed to specifications. These specifications must be demonstrated by the actual running of programs against test data which have been prepared to simulate a live environment.

Before simulating a live environment, certain levels of test and review inspections of the software should take place while it is being developed. These tests and review methods may require periodic briefings and inspections of diagrams, flowcharts, reports, and program analysis studies and approaches which are to be taken in the development of software. These test review precautions are essential to establish the system integrity prior to the software development efforts. This preliminary verification of various software modular portions as it is being planned and designed will ensure that the system is developed to specifications. These reviews will also aid in developing procedures and material for system integration testing and formal system validation.

Formal validation must leave the theoretical and artificial environment of the programmer's office and be demonstrated in the practical aspects of a realistic environment—the computer center. Here, individual as well as collective programs must be run in unison and in parallel operation with the existing system with live input/output data; and the integrated software system must be run on the operationally configured equipment. Procedures should be set out in the Quality Assurance Provisions document for preparation of test data and identification of personnel and operating procedures necessary to conduct the following levels of testing:

- Individual computer subprogram testing.
- Individual computer program testing.
- System software integration testing.
- System operation acceptance testing.
- System hardware acceptance testing.

The first three levels of testing should specify, as applicable, the test formulas, algorithms, techniques, tolerance limits, and procedures to validate programs individually and collectively. The scope and level of testing will depend upon the type of system, but formal testing and validation must ensure that the software and hardware meet the Program/System Specifications Requirements in a live environment.

SYSTEM SOFTWARE DEVELOPMENT: PROGRAM/SYSTEM SOFTWARE DEVELOPMENT

This documentation is created during the Program/System Software Development Period–Phase III of the system evolution. This information may be segmented into several documents, with each document intended for a different user group. It is the documentation which collectively and individually describes the programming techniques used for each program after it is developed. It also defines and establishes associated support documentation required to maintain and operate the system, as identified under Type C–User Reference Documentation on Figure 13-1. Program/System Documentation is the final narrative and graphic write-up—the complete documentation for the system—and it describes the programs as they are produced. Production of a program is complete when the initial coding is finished and the program validated. Program/System Documentation consists of four categories: Program Logic Manual, Program Listing, Operator Guide, and Program Abstracts.

Program Logic Manual

Primarily, this manual serves as the comprehensive document giving complete technical data on the software system. The lead-in section should give an introductory system overview by collectively describing the general software requirements and hardware makeup. Following sections or chapters should be devoted to the documentation of each individual program with the precise symbolic and logic details of the coding techniques used with reference to the flowcharts associated with a given program. Flowcharts should use descriptive symbology and relate to the program listing by mnemonic tags. The documentation for each individual program should contain system printouts and operator responses as appropriate. Figures 13-2A and 13-2B illustrate the breakdown and structure of the Program Logic Manual.

Assuming that a system is composed of 25 program modules, each designed to do a given task(s), and the Program Logic Manual is structured so documentation on each program module is contained in a separate chapter, then each program can be catalogued and an abstract prepared. A copy of each program can now be documented and filed separately, Of course, copies of the bound manual, program listings, and documentation on other aspects (note Figure 13-1) of the system should be available for complete system review at any time during the life of the system.

FIGURE 13-2A

Chapter Ordering	Topic and Subtopic Ordering	Documentation Narrative	Documentation Graphic	Textual Content
Title		X		Title and acronym
Preface		X		Say something about the manual—how it is structured, how the manual is controlled, maintained, updated and distributed.
Table of Contents		X		Chapter, topic titles, paragraph and page numbering.
Record of Changes		X		A "Record of Changes" page to record changes and updates.
CHAPTER ONE (Introduction)	Introduction and Background	X		Devoted to background and general information. Briefly describe historical development.
	Purpose	X		State the general purpose and function of the system.
	Equipment	X	X	Briefly describe the characteristics of the equipment.
	Support	X		Describe the analysis, design, programming, and maintenance responsibility for the system.
CHAPTER TWO (General Requirements)	Software Description (Title)	X		Describe the modular design make-up and the interrelationship of the system software.
	General Description Data Base	X X	X	Describe the software system. Explain its function and purpose. Explain how the programs are modularly structured to handle the various programming tasks. Explain narratively and graphically the data base and buffer control, when appropriate. Include a description of the vendor's supervisor program and its relationship with the modular programs. Then list and generally describe the function allocation and purpose of each program.
	Major Program Module (Title)	X		General description of purpose, function, and task allocation.
	Major Program Module (Title) (ETC)	X		General description of purpose, function, and task allocation.
	System Flowchart		X	First-level system flowchart. An overview of the major processing areas that depicts the hardware configuration and shows the data flow through the system.
CHAPTER THREE (Detailed Requirements)	Major Program Module (Title)	X		Subjective title and acronym.
	Purpose and General Description	X		Give a more detailed functional description of how this program performs the general function listed in Chapter Two. Identify inputs/outputs and rules for mnemonic labeling.
	Logic Method	X	X	Identify and describe timing constraints, other logic aspects of how this program performs its function listed in the general description. Identify storage allocation and describe interrupts and the control logic, and interface points.
	Interrupts, Entry/Exit Parameters	X		List and give effects of interrupts on logic, source, type and response. List entrance and exits, error messages, etc.
	Tables, Records, Files	X	X	Describe tables, records, and files layout associated with this program.
	Special Control Features	X		Special testing required—loop and diagnostic test for on-line debug and maintenance.
	Operator Procedures**	X	X	Step-by-step procedures and diagrams needed for operator and machine communications—system printouts and operator response.
	Macro Flowcharts		X	Second-level semi-detailed flowcharts depicting the system logic. Logic should be machine- and language-independent.
	Micro Flowcharts***		X	Third-level machine logic flowcharts depicting the detailed logic suitable for transcribing to code sheets.
CHAPTER FOUR	Major Program Module (Title)	X	X	Chapter Four and subsequent chapters describing major programs shall be formatted and documented as recommended for Chapter Three. If there are subroutines embedded in or accessed by the major program, they shall be formatted and structured like Chapter Three.

NOTE: **It would not be practical to issue the system logic manual as a computer operator manual. Operator procedures can be lifted from the logic manual and compiled into an operator manual.

***Micro flowcharts may be an option item in a user-developed system. The maintenance and update of these detailed logic flowcharts may make them too unwieldy to become a part of the system logic manual. When a software system is provided by the vendor but maintained by the user, transition from vendor to maintenance programmers is aided by detailed flowcharts, particularly in training and debugging.

FIGURE 13-2B

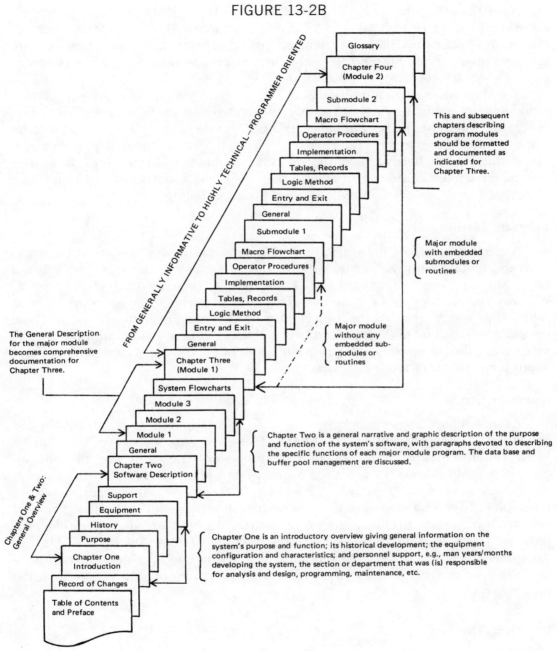

FROM GENERALLY INFORMATIVE TO HIGHLY TECHNICAL—PROGRAMMER ORIENTED

Glossary

Chapter Four
(Module 2)

Submodule 2

Macro Flowchart

Operator Procedures

Implementation

Tables, Records

Logic Method

Entry and Exit

General

Submodule 1

Macro Flowchart

Operator Procedures

Implementation

Tables, Records

Logic Method

Entry and Exit

General

Chapter Three
(Module 1)

System Flowcharts

Module 3

Module 2

Module 1

General

Chapter Two
Software Description

Support

Equipment

History

Purpose

Chapter One
Introduction

Record of Changes

Table of Contents
and Preface

This and subsequent chapters describing program modules should be formatted and documented as indicated for Chapter Three.

Major module with embedded submodules or routines

Major module without any embedded sub-modules or routines

The General Description for the major module becomes comprehensive documentation for Chapter Three.

Chapter Two is a general narrative and graphic description of the purpose and function of the system's software, with paragraphs devoted to describing the specific functions of each major module program. The data base and buffer pool management are discussed.

Chapters One & Two: General Overview

Chapter One is an introductory overview giving general information on the system's purpose and function; its historical development; the equipment configuration and characteristics; and personnel support, e.g., man years/months developing the system, the section or department that was (is) responsible for analysis and design, programming, maintenance, etc.

Note that starting with Chapter Three in Table 1 and Figure 13-2, each program module is documented in detail, including flowcharts and operator procedures (when applicable). As new requirements arise, and as programmers are assigned programming tasks, the catalog of abstracts would refer the programmer to off-the-shelf programs of his interest.

To make documentation available for comparison, library procedures for cataloging, indexing, storing, retrieving, and updating these historical off-the-shelf programs will have to be implemented. Off-the-shelf programs would not be "canned" ready-to-use programs. Minor changes or even major modifications (depending on the hardware configuration and similarity of systems of programs) may be required. Considerable savings, both in programmer spaces and time, can be realized by using previously developed program logic.

Program Listing

A current listing of the software system showing the symbology and instructions used along with the relationship of the flowcharts, completes the Program Logic Manual. The listings and flowcharts should cross-reference each other by statement labels, tags, and comments. Comments at the beginning of a program or subroutine which give a brief description of the purpose and function of the program/subroutine, and maximum use of comments in individual lines of coding to explain the purpose of a program sequence, will aid familiarization and debugging and program maintenance.

Operator Guide

As noted earlier, system printouts and operator response procedures are contained in the Program Logic Manual. However, these procedures should be lifted from the manual and incorporated, along with other operating procedures, into an Operator Guide because the Program Logic Manual would be too unwieldy to be used as an operator guide. The Operator Guide would contain the entire repertoire of system commands and operator responses, to include initialization or bootstrapping, restart/reload, ledgering, journaling, and off-line operating procedures. The type of system will determine the contents of the Operator Guide, but sufficient procedures should be contained in the guide to operate and communicate with the system. Certain required and useful operator information is listed under Type C of Figure 13-1.

Program Abstract

The abstract provides minimal documentation for a computer system or an individual program. It establishes a basis for sharing computer capabilities. The abstract provides key identification and reference information. It gives a brief description of the function and capability as well as the relationship to other computer systems or programs. Suggested information for the Program Abstract is listed under Type C on Figure 13-1 and under Figure 13-3.

FIGURE 13-3A

COMPUTER PROGRAM PRODUCT ABSTRACT		
1. SYSTEM IDENTIFICATION	2. PROGRAM ACRONYM	3. PROGRAM TITLE
4. PROGRAM NUMBER	5. AUTHORIZING DIRECTIVE AND DATE	6. DATE PROGRAM INITIATED
7. DATE PROGRAM COMPLETED	8. ORGANIZATION AND OFFICE SYMBOL	9. PROGRAMMER'S NAME
10. MANHOURS/MONTHS	11. PROGRAMMING LANGUAGE USED	12. COMPUTER MODEL
13. CORE REQUIREMENT	14. SECURITY CLASSIFICATION	15. IMPLEMENTATION/REVISION DATE
16. KEY WORD(S)	17. SYSTEM/PROGRAM INTERFACED	18. USING ORGANIZATION(S)

19. DESCRIPTION: (Provide a concise description of the inputs, files, records, table makeup, and outputs concerning the function, objective or purpose.)

20. DOCUMENTATION REFERENCES: (for Library use only.)

(EXPLANATION ON REVERSE SIDE)

FIGURE 13-3B

1. System Identification: Identify the system to which this information applies.
2. Program Acronym: Provide the symbolic name assigned to the program, e.g. HDRVAL.
3. Program Title: The common language that the above acronym was taken from. (Header Validation).
4. Program Number: (If applicable).
5. Authorizing directive and date: Give the document which directed the development of the program; e.g., contract number.
6. Date Program Initiated: Date the department started working on the program.
7. Date Program Completed: Date program passed Test and Acceptance.
8. Organization and Office Code: Identify the Organization and Department responsible for development of the task/program.
9. Programmer's Name: Name of lead programmer.
10. Manhours/months: State the time required to develop the program.
11. Programming Language Used: State the language used to develop the program; e.g., COBOL.
12. Computer Model: Manufacturer's nomenclature.
13. Core Requirement: Give the core requirement for this program.
14. Security Classification: Classification (if any) assigned to the program.
15. Implementation/revision Date: Date implemented or revised.
16. Key Words: (For documentation library use.)
17. System/Programs Interfaced: List the names of any other Programs/Systems that this program may interface with, i.e. common buffer; routines; code conversion routines, etc.
18. User Department: Identify the using organizations of the program.
19. Description: A brief description of the function, capabilities and organizational make-up of the program.
20. Documentation References: (For library use only.)

USER REFERENCE DOCUMENTATION

The documentation that is developed in the Program/System Software Development Period–Phase III, now becomes the User Reference Documentation for the System Maintenance Period–Phase IV. Once the system is implemented, changes to the ongoing system which affect any of the User Reference Documentation should be updated by issuing printed page changes as suggested under Type C of Figure 13-1.

DUPLICATION–A COSTLY EFFORT

Unless controls are established to specify and monitor the creation of documentation from one phase to the next, certain phases or portions of a phase may go through a costly iterative period of redefinition and rewriting process (not to mention reprogramming and testing) before the system is certified operational. Because the program (software) is an integral and inseparable part of the system, it should be considered as a "manufactured product," and just like any hardware component, it should be given the same production and management control procedures.

Much hidden cost exists in DP systems because of program duplication. This often results from the lack of procedures for compiling complete system documentation which would encourage comparison of previously developed programs having similar functional features. The comparison can be made through the use of the Program Abstract which points to complete documentation of previously developed programs. As noted in Figure 13-3, the abstract may be a single sheet providing pertinent data about any phase of a system or program. When systems are developed to perform the same or similar functions, e.g., digital message switching, inventory control, etc., procedures that require commonality in program design and the identification of the documentation created during the program/system software development period will reduce programming cost when developing subsequent data communications systems or programs.

CHAPTER FOURTEEN

A Guide To Project Management

The techniques and methods used to achieve success (or failure) in project management are a result of (or lack of) training, experience, motivation, and integrity and personality of the project manager.

Chapter One provides an insight into the systems analysis and the selection and supervision of the analysis team. Chapter Two suggests a systems design approach. Chapter Twelve offers suggestions for system installation, testing and acceptance. Chapter Thirteen covers step-by-step procedures for standards and the documentation requirements for the design, development, implementation, and software maintenance for the life cycle of a system. Addendum A covers procedures for specifying and procuring ADP and data communication systems. The other chapters provide data on the characteristics, selection, and configuration of ADP/data communications systems.

This brief chapter will not tell how to manage because there are many variables outside the control of the project manager that will influence his success or failure. Instead, this chapter will discuss various points, pose certain questions, and offer suggestions for the project manager to consider.

PROJECT MANAGEMENT INFORMATION FLOW

Project management can be described as working with and through (and sometimes around) individuals and groups to accomplish a stated objective. Project management may be considered a cyclical information flow process as depicted in Figure 14-1. Project control may take on the information flow as depicted in Figure 14-2.

SCHEDULING AND PROGRESS MONITORING

A well-defined activities and personnel schedule, though it may require subsequent revisions as work progresses, will allow quick analysis of the system progress. A typical schedule could appear as illustrated in Figure 14-3.

The schedule provides a visual means of controlling work loads, expenditures of manpower and money, and a budget control over personnel accounting.

FIGURE 14-1
Project Management Information FLow

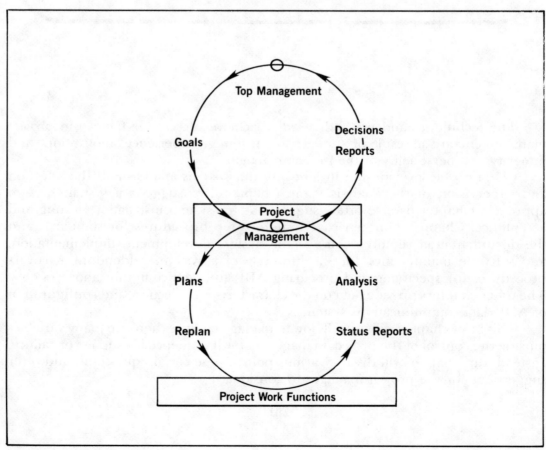

FIGURE 14-2
Project Control

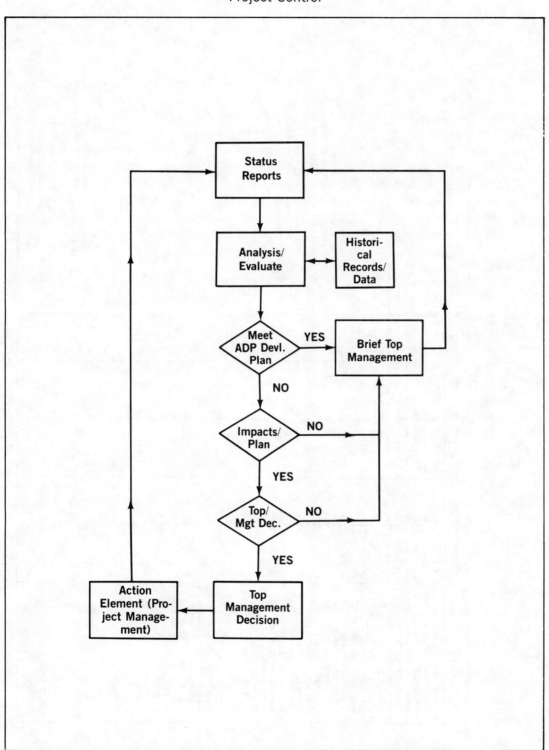

FIGURE 14-3
Activity Schedule

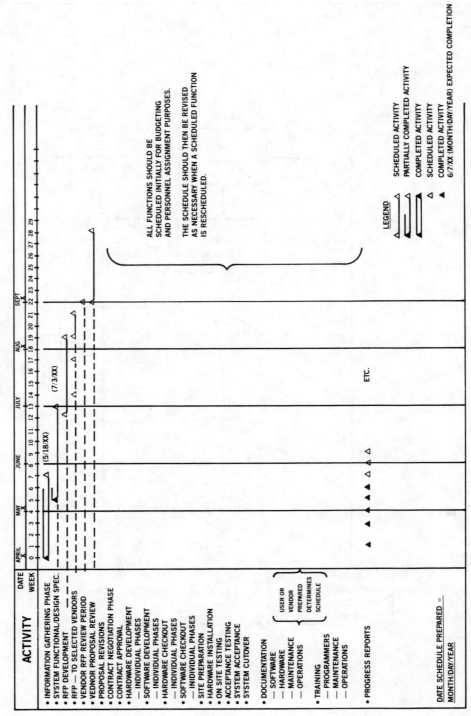

TABLE 14-1
Status Meeting

---

1. Attendees
   (List)

2. Open Items
   A. User Requirements
   B. RFP
   C. Problem Areas
   D. Assignment of Personnel
   E. Technical Information
   F. ETC.

3. Assignment of Responsibility—List Items
   A. Key People

   _____
   _____
   _____

   B. User Items

   _____
   _____
   _____

   C. ETC.

4. Items Discussed During This Meeting
5. Completed Items
6. Open Items
7. Next Meeting Date
8. Possible Organization Chart

REPORTS AND MEETINGS

The activities and personnel schedule should indicate when the progress/status reports are to be generated. These reports should provide a brief but complete analysis of progress and problem areas. The report should be in a format that is suitable for the person(s) reviewing the report. The report should provide information covering the following areas:

- Identify activities that are on schedule.
- Identify activities that are not on schedule—give reasons why they are not.
- Indicate what is being done to correct the problem.

- Rescheduling or replanning requirements; what is the proposed new schedule/plan?
- Discuss scheduled team progress review meetings.
- Discuss scheduled vendor progress review meetings.
- Discuss scheduled management progress review meetings.
- Indicate when a budget overrun is expected.
- Provide in a separate report (if required) results of the project review meeting–Table 14-1 is a suggested format.
- Provide other required information as required by management.

PROJECT MANAGEMENT CONSIDERATION CHECKLIST

- Determine user needs and its relationship to other project requirements. Note Chapters One and Two.
- Begin documenting requirements for the data communications or ADP equipment, software, terminals, personnel, etc. Note Chapter Thirteen.
- Schedule regular review meetings with users and other project managers and lead analyst to review progress and system design requirements. Note Chapters One and Two.
- Establish and coordinate work/responsibility assignments for:
  - Program/activity managers,
  - Systems/analyst personnel,
  - Programming personnel,
  - Operations personnel,
  - Maintenance personnel,
  - Facility personnel (physical floor space, power, environment),
  - Procurement personnel (equipment/communications requirements, etc.),
  - System user personnel.
- Continue meetings to solidify design requirements.
- Construct RFP or Functional Specifications. Note Addendum.
- Present RFP to top management for approval for submission to selected vendors.
- Review proposals returned in response to RFP (Note Appendix A).
- Make requests for additional information from appropriate offerers/individuals/vendors.
- Review answers to requests for information.
- Select the vendor.
- Obtain top management approval of selected vendor.
- Order equipment.
- Install the system (Note Chapter Twelve).
- Prepare the final system documentation (Note Chapter Thirteen).

QUESTIONS FOR PROJECT MANAGEMENT CONSIDERATION

Many, if not all, of the following questions will be answered in the analysis process of the preceding chapters. They are listed here as a reminder to the project manager as consideration factors.

- Why is the system required?
- What are the problems with the existing system?
- Must the design of the new system interface with the existing system?
- What type of system is required?
- From where to where must the data be transferred?
- What is the volume of data to be transferred?
- What is the system throughput requirement?
- At what rate of speed must the data be transferred?
- How fast must the system respond?
- How important are the data; what type of systems design must be considered?
- Can the system tolerate errors and loss of data while achieving throughput?
- Is the equipment available in the marketplace to satisfy system requirements?
- Is the software available to satisfy system requirements?
- Must the system have the ability to grow and expand?
- What system environmental conditions should be considered?
- What type of support will the system require?
- What is the system delivery requirement?
- Is there a dollar limitation for implementing the system?
- Is there an urgent requirement for the system?

ADDENDUM A

System Source Selection

SECTION ONE: PROCEDURES AND PRACTICES OF SELECTION

In order to accomplish effective system component selection and to compete in the data communications/data processing market, there are important procedures and practices that a vendor or buyer should follow in order to remain profitable. Regardless of the status—government or private sector, seller or buyer—the guidelines and checklists provided in this addendum may make a difference in a profitable sell, a profitable buy, or a loss. There are three basic methods of competitive system component procurement: (1) Invitation for Bid (IFB), (2) Request for Quote (RFQ), and (3) Request for Proposal (RFP).

In the government sector, the IFB and RFQ are nonnegotiable procurements, and in some instances may be similarly used in the private sector. Usually, the low dollar wins the contract. The IFB and RFQ are advertised procurements, meaning that the bids and quotes are publicly opened at the announced place, date and time, and any interested person may attend the bid/quote opening.

The IFB or RFQ can be used in the private business sector as a tool to select vendors who may be interested in presenting a cost quote or system proposal. The IFB or RFQ can basically be used for two different purposes: (1) when the system requirement entails minor enhancements such as additional equipment, software or other minor functions, the IFB or RFQ may be used to solicit a direct bid or quote from a group of selected vendors or vendors in general; and (2) when a total system or major enhancement is to be accomplished, the IFB or RFQ may be used to initiate the presentation of the RFP to the interested vendors.

In either case, the IFB or RFQ should include a brief description of the total requirements and functions. This document could be mailed to a selected group of vendors asking for a quote or bidding response, or a bidders' conference could be conducted and the document presented at that time. The advantage of a bidders' conference is that questions can be answered directly and uninterested vendors can be eliminated.

When a major system development is planned, the bidders' conference can be used to lay the groundwork for later presentation of the RFP to the interested vendors. This conference would include a presentation of system requirements and a question and answer session.

The RFP is a descriptive document completely detailing the total system functions and overall requirements. It is a solicitation sent to vendors requesting responses that will satisfy the proposed system's requirements. It is a statement of total requirements which: (1) provides system details, comprehensive technical specifications and support functions, (2) provides for a uniform and orderly response from vendors, (3) is used as the basis for system contractual agreements, and (4) gives general information about the organization submitting the RFP.

The RFP takes the guesswork out of buying a computer system or services. It offers true value in that it forces the vendor to specify in detail precisely what the capabilities of his proposed system are or what the proposed services include.

The RFP is the most frequently used solicitation instrument for buying communications or ADP systems, equipment, and services. The RFP is used because major systems requirements may be too complex and detailed to be procured without some negotiation and dialogue between the prospective contractor and the contracting officer prior to contract award.

Responses to an RFP are normally submitted to an appointed place, date, and time as secretly sealed proposals. After careful examination of all proposals against evaluation criteria, negotiations may be initiated with one or more prospective vendors concerning (1) terms, (2) conditions, (3) pricing, (4) maintenance, (5) delivery schedules, (6) options, and (7) a host of other things that may affect the life cycle of the contract.

Government Contract Termination Problems–Vendors

If your firm gets into contracting trouble, seek out a good procurement and contracting attorney who has extensive experience in handling such cases. This is important when your firm is doing business with the government because the government can buy against your contract from another vendor, then charge your firm the difference in price for equipment, products, or services that your firm failed to deliver/perform.

If your firm is ultimately faced with a default, prepare your defense well. If it is a government contract, you may beat the government's case because the government sometimes keeps inadequate records. This makes it difficult, if not impossible, for the government to convincingly present its case. In such situations, the case is dropped and the default is charged to a "termination for convenience." When this happens, or if it is ruled that the default was not warranted, the firm may countersue and collect damages for the firm's costs and expected profits that the contract would have brought to the firm.

There are certain things that a firm can do to avoid contractual problems or cancellation. The following points may be useful when dealing with government agencies or the private business sector:

- Live up to the conditions of the contract–perform well.
- Keep good records–document all modifications and other instructions for contract changes.
- Don't deal with anyone except the contracting officer or person in authority.
- Don't make engineering, production, or delivery changes based on verbal orders–changes/instructions must be in writing.
- Be alert to and react fast to potential problem areas.
- Know your subcontracting help–hire competent firms.
- Don't hesitate to hire consultants where the firm is short in expertise.
- Maintain a good interface with the business or government technical and procurement staffs.
- Know the rules and regulations (government):
  - Federal Property Management Regulations (FPMRs).
  - Code of Federal Regulations (CFRs).
  - Armed Services Procurement Regulations (ASPRs).

- Be very familiar with terms and conditions of the contract including the:
  - Statement of Work (SOW).
  - Technical Specifications.
  - Mandatory items.
  - Support requirements, i.e., maintenance, training, documentation, etc.

- If you are confronted with default:
  - Hire an experienced attorney.
  - Fight back.

SECTION TWO: GUIDE FOR PREPARATION OF THE RFP

The following is a suggested guideline for identifying system requirements and conditions contained in the RFP. The requirements should not be so rigid that the vendor has no leeway to offer alternate approaches to a particular system design, or propose different hardware/software in order to take advantage of system technology or advances in hardware/software architecture.

Introduction–(Buyer Prepared Section of RFP)

Provide a brief description of your organization and the overall system to be provided.

General Requirements Section
(Basic Descriptions and Vendor Response Requirements)

- Bidding (responses) requirements
- System description
  - Brief overview of CPU and devices
  - Include pictorial diagrams
  - Brief overview of terminal types
  - Type of data/message volume
  - Overview of expected system operation

- CPU/system requirements
  - Necessary throughput, response time
  - Intermediate storage–volume
  - Data base requirements–volume, management
  - Expandability–modularity
  - Reliability–uptime requirements
  - Manual or automatic recovery requirements
  - Redundancy requirements–hardware and software
  - Recovery–power or air conditioning loss
  - Message or data type/priorities to be utilized
  - Error detection/control requirements
  - Code sets, protocols, standards
  - Line terminal requirements

- Terminal requirements
  - List types or functions required

- Summary of overall requirements

Detailed System Requirements–(Buyer Prepared Section of RFP)
(This section should provide detailed descriptive requirements for the listed areas. The vendor should respond accordingly)

- Hardware
  - Reliability
  - Availability
  - Flexibility
  - Compatibility
  - Expandability
  - Modularity
  - Maintainability
  - Type of system
  - Operator interface
  - Type of processing
  - Message or data handling capability
  - Interfaces–peripherals and terminals
  - Peripherals
  - Line types
  - Performance criteria
  - Terminals
  - Technical control equipment
  - Failure recovery

- Software
  - Types of languages desired
  - Executive/operating system
  - Routing capabilities
  - Format editing
  - Poll/call/dial
  - Queuing requirements
  - Code conversion
  - Priority
  - Retrieval
  - History
  - Validation routines
  - Line/terminal handlers
  - Error recovery
  - Operator interface (supervisory control)
  - Report generator
  - Load leveling–overload alarms

- Data management routines
- Alarms–type desk, CPU, etc.
- Failure recovery/restart controls
- Modularlity–maintainability–ease of operation

- Support software
  - Assembler
  - Utilities
  - Diagnostics (software and hardware)

- Network layout description (pictorial and narrative).

Implementation Criteria–(Buyer Prepared Section of RFP)
(Specified areas for vendor descriptive responses)

- Schedules
- Test plans
- Site/installation specifications for:
  - System layout
  - Power distribution specifications
  - Grounding requirements
  - Signal cable routing
  - Environmental requirements
  - System support space and equipment requirements
  - Equipment physical characteristics
  - Equipment ship preparation/packing
  - Shipping method
  - Unloading and routing clearances through building to computer floor
  - System assembly
  - Cabling
  - Testing

Support–(Buyer Prepared Section of RFP)
(Specify areas where vendor support is expected or necessary)

- Support concept
- Level of maintenance (hours)
- Preventive maintenance requirements
- Maintenance diagnostic routines
- Software/hardware maintenance
- Identification of items that wear out and their expected life cycle
- Support personnel
- Training
- Documentation
  - Operations

　　　–Maintenance
　　　–Hardware
　　　–Programming/software

Cost Analysis*–(Buyer Prepared Section of RFP)

- Cost limitation (if appropriate)
- R&D allowances (if any)
- Disclaimers (if any)

　　　*Usually all the cost information is available in the RFP to enable the vendor to size and price the proposed system. The vendor may be asked to submit his costs in a separate document. The reason for this is that the organization that submitted the RFP does not want the technical individuals who will evaluate the vendor's proposal to be initially influenced by the price of the proposed system. After the technical evaluation is completed on all vendors proposals, and a decision is made as to which vendors are "qualified," evaluation and cost-weighted factors can be applied to pick the winning vendor.

SECTION THREE: GUIDE FOR PREPARATION OF VENDOR'S RESPONSE TO THE RFP

　　This guide should be forwarded along with the RFP to all vendors, and should be used as a guide by the responding vendors, to provide a uniform proposal format. This uniform proposal format will ease the review burden and allow for easy comparisons of the proposals. The vendors should be instructed to follow this outline and instructions where possible.

Introduction–(Vendor's Response to RFP Guide)

　　Provide a brief description of your approach to the RFP, problems in meeting any conditions of the RFP, alternate recommendations, or proposals, and other general information that will aid the buyer in evaluating your firm's proposal. It may be acceptable to submit, as attachments to the technical proposal, standard corporate brochures that provide supplemental data indicating your capability to provide the system described in the RFP.

Suggested Format of the Proposal–(Vendor's Response to RFP Guide)

　　The following format should be used as a guide for preparation of the technical proposal in response to the RFP:

- Foreword
- Table of Contents
- Part I–Technical Proposal
  –Technical approach

　　　　–System description
　　　　–Operational diagram
　　　　–Block diagram
　　　　–Performance
　　　　–Compatibility
　　　　–Degree of risk
　　　　–Quality assurance, quality control, and reliability
　　　　–Reliability and maintainability plans
　　　　–Installation and maintenance support
　　　　–Delivery and scheduling
　　　　–Project direction and management

- Part II–Technical Capabilities
- Part III–Corporate General Information
　　　–Corporate background
　　　–Corporate organization structure
　　　–Corporate facilities
　　　–Biographical sketches of key personnel (if required)

PART I–Technical Proposal–(Vendor's Response to RFP Guide)

The technical approach section should present an analysis of the problem, a discussion of the operational environment, and an accurate and clear technical description of the proposed system software and hardware, including drawings and sketches of the proposed configuration.

Description

This section should include a concise presentation of how the proposed system functions operationally, and what its capabilities and limitations may be. To clarify the explanations, reference may be made to the operational diagram and block diagram that should follow. This should be a fairly short section, since detailed performance and compatibility considerations will be covered in later sections.

Operational Diagram

The operational diagram should be a simple drawing of the main elements of the system and associated systems as used in the working environment. It should be carefully conceived and clearly rendered to orient the reader quickly to the usefulness of the proposed system.

Block Diagram

The block diagram should provide a graphic representation of the essential "building blocks" —subsystems, equipments, and components–that constitute the system to be provided. It should show the functional relationships of the blocks to each other and to other associated systems.

Performance

The performance subsection should provide data on the ability of the proposed system to meet the requirements established by the RFP. The basic data should be presented in a simple form that lists the requirements characteristics and capabilities of the proposed system.

Compatibility

The interfaces between the proposed system and other associated equipments must be clearly defined. Where it is impossible to define an interface concisely, the program planned to resolve the problem areas should be described.

Degree of Risk

The requirements of the RFP should call for use of state of the art items to build the proposed system. Thus, no appreciable degree of risk is entailed with equipment development.

Quality Assurance, Quality Control, and Reliability

The term "Quality Assurance" covers all the actions necessary to determine adequately that product requirements are met. "Quality Control" is the system and management function by which the vendor controls and insures that the quality of the product, equipment, supplies or services meet the requirements of the RFP specifications. "Reliability" is the ability of an item to function without failure over a given time period.

Reliability and Maintainability Plans

This section should outline plans for assuring that the system to be supplied is capable of meeting the stated reliability and maintainability objectives. The objectives should be examined carefully with respect to feasibility.

This section should be afforded as much attention as any other section in the proposal, since reliability and maintainability are performance parameters of the system. Since every element of the system contributes to overall system reliability and maintainability, it is necessary to delineate programs of definition, prediction, monitoring, and evaluation that will assure that the system to be provided is operationally acceptable.

Installation and Maintenance Support

The installation and maintenance support that will be provided to place the system in service and maintain it in operation should be fully described. The discussion should include details of maintenance, engineering, technical training, technical data and publications, installation procedures to be followed, the vendor's facilities for maintenance and support, spare part provisions, etc.

Delivery and Scheduling

The delivery requirements established by the RFP are as important as the technical requirements. In this section the vendor should make clear his intended compliance with, or exceptions to, these requirements and show in detail by scheduling charts, inventories, etc., exactly how he will comply.

Project Direction and Management

This section should show the vendor's method of management. It should elaborate on organization, personnel, and manpower controls, and must outline the overall management concepts employed by the company and the specific type of concepts employed by the company and the specific type of management that will be provided for the proposed system. It must demonstrate that the vendor has an understanding of the external organizational relationships that are needed between the vendor and the system users and between the vendor and subcontractors for the successful accomplishment of the requirements of the RFP.

PART II–Technical Capabilities–(Vendor's Response to RFP Guide)

Part II of the proposal must provide sufficient information to permit evaluation of the vendor's technical ability to comply with the requirements of the RFP. Information that would be useful in this regard includes the following:

- Specific examples of similar projects successfully completed,
- Specific applicable experience of personnel to be associated with the project,
- Availability of specific personnel,
- Details on technical strengths and weaknesses, and methods to be used to combat weaknesses (subcontract, consultants, etc.),
- Availability of technical space and facilities, and production facilities,
- Availability of special technical facilities,
- Availability of subcontractors and consultants, if required.

PART III–Corporate General Information

This section should provide general information contained in the body of the technical proposal, or attached to it. Corporate brochures that provide supplemental data on the vendor's capabilities and background may be requested in the RFP.

SECTION FOUR: BUYER'S GUIDE FOR EVALUATION OF VENDOR'S PROPOSAL

Cost and technical proposals submitted in response to the RFP should be evaluated in accordance with the following general guidelines:

- The technical proposals should be evaluated first, independently of the cost proposal.
- The cost proposal should then be evaluated.
- The evaluations should then be combined so that an overall evaluation can be made and the successful vendor selected.

Primary Factors

The technical proposal should be evaluated on the basis of the following three primary factors, listed in their order of importance:

- Technical approach
- General quality and responsiveness of the proposal
- Organization, personnel, and facilities

Technical Approach

- Performance
- Modularity
- Reliability
- Delivery time
- Installation and maintenance
- Compatibility
- Support
- Training
- Maintenance (software/hardware)

General Quality and Responsiveness of the Proposal

- Grasp of the problem
- Responsiveness to terms, conditions, and time of performance
- Completeness and thoroughness

Organization, Facilities, and Personnel

- Record of past experience
- Adequacy of facilities
- Experience in similar or related fields
- Evidence of good organizational and maintenance practices
- Qualification of personnel

Cost Proposals

- Apply weighted factor approach
- Look for hidden costs
- Weigh support (maintenance, training, etc.) cost
- Unique pricing
- Discounts
- Disclaimers
- Etc.

ADDENDUM B

Glossary of Common Data Communications Terms And Abbreviations

ACCESS LINE (WATS—A telephone line connected to the customer's premises to either establish or receive calls to or from a particular WATS Service Area.

ACCESS TIME—(1) The time between the instant at which information is requested from storage and the time at which it is delivered. (2) The time between the instant at which information is ready for storage and the instant at which it is stored.

ACK (Acknowledge)—A communications control character transmitted by a receiver as an affirmative response to a sender.

ACM—An Alterable Control Memory system. A form of high-speed memory controlling the interpretation of higher level machine instructions.

ACOUSTIC COUPLER—A form of modem that sends and receives data as tones over a telephone line using a standard telephone handset.

ACU—Automatic Calling Unit. Equipment used to generate dial pulses and touch-tone signals for computer-controller dialing of terminals on a switched network. See Automatic Calling Unit.

ADDRESS—Where something is stored in the memory or routing information when used as part of a message. Part of a message header.

ALLOCATION—The allotment or apportionment of available main memory and file storage to accommodate programs and data.

ALPHANUMERIC--A contraction of alphabetic-numeric. A character set consisting of alphabet and numbers.

ALTERNATE FREQUENCY—Frequency assigned for use at a certain time, or for a certain purpose, to replace or supplement the frequency normally used.

ALTERNATE ROUTE—A secondary communications path used to reach a destination if the primary path is unavailable.

ALTERNATE USE—The provision of facilities which may be used by the customer alternately for separate purposes (e.g., voice and data).

AMA—(Automatic Message Accounting)—Equipment that automatically records all data concerning customer-dialed long distance calls necessary for billing purposes.

AMPLITUDE DISTORTION—Distortion in the amplitude of a wave form particularly due to attenuation.

AMPLITUDE MODULATION (AM)—Modulation in which the amplitude of a wave is the characteristic varied. Method of modulating a carrier wave to cause it to vary in amplitude corresponding to the amplitude of the original signal.

ANALOG—The representation of numerical quantities by means of physical variables; e.g., translation, rotation, voltage, or resistance.

ANALOG COMPUTER—A computer based on the principle of measured angles.

ANALOG TRANSMISSION—A method of information transfer in which the variable received information bears an exact relationship to the original or transmitted information.

ANSCII—American National Standard Code for Information Interchange. A later version of the ASCII Code. See ASCII.

ANSI—American Standards Institute. See ASCII

ANSWERBACK (Data)—A signal or tone sent by the receiving business machine or data set to the sending station for identification or to indicate it is ready to receive transmission.

AREA CODE—The three-digit code used when dialing long distance calls from one Number-Plan Area (NPA) to another.

ARITHMETIC/LOGIC UNIT—Performs the various arithmetic operations within the computer. The accumulator section performs no arithmetic functions but holds the result of the arithmetic operation.

ARQ—Automatic Repeat Request. An error control technique in which the receiving station responds with a "NAK" character if a message is received in error. The NAK is interpreted by the sending station as an Automatic Repeat Request.

ASCII—American Standard Code for Information Interchange. This is the code established as an American standard by the American National Standard Institute. New version is the ANSCII Code.

ASR—Automatic send-receive. A teletypewriter equipped with a paper tape reader and a paper tape punch.

ASSEMBLE—(1) To convert a program written in nonmachine language into actual machine instructions and to assign memory storage for those instructions. (2) To accumulate in main or auxiliary memory portions of an incoming long message.

ASYNCHRONOUS TRANSMISSION—A mode of transmission using start and stop bits to frame a character (hence, frequently call "Start/Stop transmission"). Requires that timing information be included in each character, i.e., start and stop bits. Character occurrence is not predictable.

ATTENUATION—A general term used to denote a decrease in signal magnitude during transmission from one point to another. It may be expressed as a ratio, or by extension of the term, in decibels.

AUDIO—Frequencies which can be heard by the human ear (usually between 15 cycles and 20,000 cycles per second).

AUDIO RESPONSE UNIT—Used in "voice answer back" applications, an Audio Response Unit is digitally controlled to produce syllable and word responses to persons entering keyboard data.

AUTOPOLLING—Performing the polling function automatically to reduce the data communication tasks of the host computer. Autopolling can be performed by communication preprocessors, multiplexors, data concentrators, etc.

AUTO-RESTART—The capability of a computer to perform automatically the initialization functions necessary to resume operation following an equipment or power failure.

AUTOMATIC CALLING UNIT (ACU)—A dialing device supplied by the communication common carriers which permits a business machine to automatically dial calls over the communications network. See ACU.

AUTOMATIC ELECTRONIC DATA—Switching Center- Communications center designed specifically for the transmission, relay, switching, and reception of digitized data by automatic electronic methods.

AUTOMATIC ERROR CORRECTION—A technique, usually requiring the use of special codes and/or automatic retransmission, which detects and corrects errors occuring in transmission. The degree of correction depends upon coding and equipment configuration.

AUTOMATIC FEED PUNCH—A card punch having a hopper, a card tract and a stacker. The movement of cards through the punch is automatic.

AUTOMATION—(1) The implementation of processes by automatic means; (2) the theory, art, or technique of making a process more automatic; (3) the investigation, design, development, and application of methods of rendering processes automatic, self-moving, or self-controlling.

AUTOMONITOR—To make an electronic computer prepare a record of its own data processing operations, or a program or routine for this purpose.

AUXILIARY STORAGE—Device which is normally capable of holding a larger amount of information than the main memory of the computer but with slower access.

BACKGROUND PROCESSING—Low-priority processing permitted to take place when no higher-priority real-time entries are being handled by a system. A batch processing job, such as payroll, might be treated as background processing, subject to interruption on receipt of an inquiry from a terminal.

BADGE READER–A device used to read an employee identification code contained in a preset form.

BANDPASS FILTER–A filter which permits free passage to frequencies within a specific range and which bars passage to frequencies outside of that range.

BANDWIDTH–The difference, expressed in hertz, between the highest and lowest frequencies of a band group of frequencies. A measure of the ability of equipment or transmission links to pass a range of electromagnetic frequencies.

BASEBAND–In the process of modulation, the baseband is the frequency band occupied by the aggregate of the transmitted signals when first used to modulate a carrier.

BATCH PROCESSING–A method of processing in which a number of similar input items are accumulated and processed together.

BAUD–The shortest signal element which is transmitted by the communications medium. The speed of a given device in bauds is equal to the number of signalling elements per second.

BAUDOT CODE–A five-unit code in which each bit is of equal length. By using different combinations of the five bits it is possible to form 32 symbols.

BCD Binary Coded Decimal–A six-bit code. Uses three levels to provide 96 characters of information. A card, if used, is also a different size than the Hollerith (IBM) Card.

BEL (Bell)–A character for use when there is a need to call for human attention. It may control terminal alarm or attention device.

BINARY–A numbering system based on 2. 0 = absence of a bit or 1 = bit present. A binary bit has two possible states, 1 or 0, marking or spacing, current or not current, etc.

BINARY CODED DECIMAL–A system of binary numbering where each decimal digit is represented by 4 bits.

BINARY DIGIT–A numeral in the binary scale of notation. This digit may be zero (0) or one (1). It may be equivalent to an on or off condition, a yes, or a no. Often abbreviated as (bit).

BINARY SIGNALLING–A communications mode in which information is passed by the presence and absence, or plus and minus variation of one parameter of the signalling medium only.

BINARY STREAM–Serial flow of binary digits (bits).

BI-STABLE–The capability of assuming either of two stables states, method of storing one bit of information.

BIT (Binary Digit)–The smallest amount of information possible. Two possible states. A hole punched in a card or tape represents a one (1) bit. Absence of a hole represents a zero (0) bit. See Binary.

BIT RATE–The speed at which bits are transmitted, usually expressed in bits per second.

BL–Blank Character.

BLOCK–A group of characters, bytes, or words communicated as a unit.

BLOCK-BY-BLOCK TRANSMISSION MODE—A transmission mode in which a line block is not transmitted until proper acknowledgement is received for the preceding line block.

BLOCK DIAGRAM—A diagram of a system, instrument, computer or program in which selected portions are represented by annotated boxes and interconnecting lines.

BLOCKING—A condition where connections cannot be made due to "all lines busy."

BOOLEAN ALGEBRA—A process of reasoning, or a deductive system of theorems using a symbolic logic, and dealing with classes, propositions, or on-off circuit elements. It employs symbols to represent operators such as AND, OR, NOT, EXCEPT, IF ... THEN, etc. to permit mathematical calculations. Named after George Boole.

BP—Block Parity.

BPI (Bits Per Inch)—Used to specify packing density of magnetic tape devices. Synonymous with characters per inch.

BPS—Bits Per Second.

BREAK—In machine telegraphy, a prolonged spacing impulse, exceeding the duration of one character. This may be introduced deliberately or may be caused by a line fault. A break is frequently used by the receiving terminal to interrupt the transmitting terminal.

BROADBAND—See Wideband

BROADCAST—The transmission of a single message to a group or all terminals on a communication circuit(s).

BROM—Bipolar Read-Only Memory. A read-only memory module.

BS (Backspace)—A format effector which controls the movement of the printing position one printing space backward on the same printing line (applicable also to CRT display devices).

BSC—Binary Synchronous Communication. Refers to a specific communications procedure using synchronous data transmission.

BTAM—Basic Telecommunications Access Method. Refers to the use of macro instructions to achieve data communications with specific terminals.

BUFFER; STORAGE—A synchronizing element between two different forms of storage, usually between internal and external. An input device in which information is assembled from external or secondary storage and stored ready for transfer to internal storage. An output device into which information is copied from internal storage and held for transfer to secondary or external storage. Computation continues while transfers between buffer storage and secondary or internal storage or vice versa take place. Any device which stores information temporarily during data transfers.

BUS—A circuit over which data or power is transmitted. Often one which acts as a common connection among a number of locations.

BUSINESS MACHINE CLOCKING—The derivation of synchronous clocking signals from the terminal or computer, rather than from the modem.

BUSY CONDITION—A condition in which communications lines or trunks are unavailable for use.

BUSY HOUR—The peak 60-minute period during a business day when the largest volume of communications traffic is handled.

BYTE—Same as a character, usually eight bits.

CABLE, COAXIAL—Consists of a conductor suspended in the center of, and insulated from, another tubular conductor. One or more may be used within a single cable.

CALLED STATION—Station to which a message is routed or a transmission is directed.

CALLING DEVICE—An apparatus which generates the pulses required for establishing connections in an automatic telephone switching system.

CALLING STATION—(1) Station initiating a transmission. (2) Station preparing a tape for transmission.

CAMP-ON—Holding a call for a line that is in use and signalling when it becomes free.

CAN (Cancel)—A control character used to indicate the data with which it is sent is in error or is to be disregarded.

CARD—See EAM and IBM card.

CARD COLUMN—One of the single digit columns on a tabulating card. When punched, a column contains only one digit, one letter, or one special code.

CARD DIALER—Automatic dialer and regular telephone combined in one desk-top unit. Phone numbers coded on plastic cards are inserted in the dialer slot for fast, accurate dialing or TOUCH TONE entry of fixed data into a data processing system.

CARD FIELD—A set of card columns, established as to number and position, into which the same information item is regularly punched.

CARD PUNCH—A machine which punches cards in designated locations to store data which can be conveyed to other machines or devices by reading or sensing the holes. Synonymous with card punched unit.

CARRIAGE RETURN—In a character-to-character printing mechanism, the operation that causes the next character to be printed at the left margin.

CARRIER, COMMON—A company regulated by the Federal Communications Commission or a public utilities commission, and required to supply communication service to all users at published rates.

CARRIER, DATA—A single frequency or tone which is modulated by voice or data to communicate information.

CARRIER SYSTEM—A means of obtaining a number of channels over a single path by modulating each channel upon a different "carrier" frequency and demodulating at the receiving point to restore the signals to their original form.

CARRIER WAVE—The basic frequency or pulse repetition rate of a signal, bearing no intrinsic intelligence until it is modulated by another signal which does bear intelligence. A carrier may be amplitude, phase, frequency modulated, or a combination of these modulation schemes.

CATHODE RAY TUBE (CRT)—A television-like picture tube used in visual display terminals.

CCSA (Common Control Switching Arrangements)—Designed for customers having extensive private line communications requirements.

CDC (Call Directing Code)—Used for terminal selection (calling). A character or sequence of characters.

CENTRAL OFFICE—The place where communications common carriers terminate customer lines and locate the equipment which interconnects those lines.

CENTRAL PROCESSING UNIT (CPU)—Made up by the Control Unit, Storage (memory) and arithmetic/logic unit of the computer.

CENTREX—A type of private branch exchange in which incoming calls can be dialed direct to any extension without an operator's assistance. Outgoing and intercom calls are dialed direct by the extension users.

CHAD—A small piece of paper tape or punch card removed when punching a hole to represent information.

CHADLESS—A way of punching paper tape in which each chad is left fastened by about a quarter of the circumference of the hole, at the leading edge. This mode of punching is useful where it is undesirable to produce chad. Chadless punched paper tape must be sensed by mechanical fingers, for the presence of chad in the tape would interfere with reliable electrical or photoelectric reading of the paper tape.

CHANNEL—A path for electrical transmission between two or more points. Also called a circuit, facility, line, link or path.

CHANNEL COORDINATION—Interaction between terminals of a transmission line to effect synchronism, exchange of message responsibility, etc.

CHARACTER—The actual or coded representation of a digit, letter, or special symbol. May be referred to as a byte.

CHARACTER DENSITY—The number of characters that can be stored per unit of length; e.g., on different makes of magnetic tape drives, 200, 556, 800 or 1600 bits can be stored linearly per inch.

CHARACTER INTERVAL—The total number of unit intervals (including synchronizing, intelligence, error checking, or control bits) required to transmit any given character in any given communication system. Extra bits which are not associated with individual characters are not included.

CHARACTER READER—A specialized device which can convert data represented by one of the typing formats or handwritten script directly into the machine language. Such a reader may operate optically; or if the characters are printed in magnetic ink, the device may operate magnetically or optically.

CHARACTER RECOGNITION—The technology of using a machine to sense and encode into a machine language characters which are written or printed to be read by human beings.

CHECK CHARACTER (OR DIGIT)—One or more characters (or digits) carried in a symbol, work or block; coded, depending on the remaining elements, in such a way that if an error occurs it will be detected (excluding compensating errors).

CHECK NUMBER—A number composed of one or more digits used to detect equipment malfunctions in data transfer operations. If a check number consists of only one digit, it is synonymous with check digit.

CIRCUIT—Communications line or electrical transmission facility. Connection between terminals or terminals and computer. A communications link between two or more points.

CIRCUIT, FOUR-WIRE—A communication circuit with two separate paths for passing information simultaneously in opposite directions.

CIRCUIT CAPACITY—The number of communications channels which can be handled by a given circuit at the same time.

CLEAR TEXT—Text or language which conveys an intelliglble meaning in the language in which it is written, with no hidden meaning.

CLEAR TO SEND—An EIA RS-232-C designation. Used by a terminal or computer to detect that its modem is ready to send data.

CLOCK—A device for timing events. In data communications, a clock is required to control the timing of bits sent in a data stream, and to control the timing of the sampling of bits received in a data stream.

CLOCK RATE—The time rate at which pulses are emitted from the clock.

COBOL—(Common Business-Oriented Language)—Developed to aid commercial data processors. Cobol allows the programmer to express a problem in near English and permits editing of the output.

CODE—A system of symbols and rules for use in representing information. It is a defined number of bits (1's or 0's) within a column or group. Each column is then a byte (character). The code determines the pattern (1's and 0's) of the byte.

CODE CONVERSION—The process by which a code of some predetermined bit structure (for example, 5, 7, 14 bits per character interval) is converted to a second code with more or less bits per character interval. No alphabetical significance is assumed in this process. In certain cases, such as the conversion from start/stop telegraph equipment to synchronous equipment, a code conversion process may only consist of discarding the stop and start elements and adding a sixth element to indicate the stop and start condition. In other cases, it may consist of addition or deletion or control and/or parity bits.

CODE LEVEL—The number of bits used to represent a character (e.g., the five-bit Baudot code is a "five level code").

CODE SET—A pattern of bits in groups used to represent characters. A different pattern is used to represent each individual character of a particular Code Set.

COMMUNICATION—The transmission of information from one point to another by means of electromagnetic waves. Means of conveying information of any kind from one person or place to another person or place.

COMMUNICATION CENTER—Agency responsible for the receipt, transmission, and delivery of messages.

COMMUNICATIONS CHANNEL—A path for flow of information, particularly digits or characters.

COMMUNICATIONS COMMON CARRIER—A company which dedicates its facilities to a public offering of universal communication services, and which is subject to public utility regulations.

COMMUNICATIONS NETWORK—Interconnection of specific organizations or geographical locations by communications means, and for functional purposes. Two or more networks interconnected make up a communications system.

COMMUNICATIONS PREPROCESSOR—A computer connected between a general-purpose processor and communication channels to perform communication functions more efficiently than would be possible if the general-purpose processor performed both communications functions and general-purpose functions.

COMMUNICATIONS PROCESSOR—A computer dedicated to the performance of a complete communications function such as message switching.

COMMUNICATIONS SYSTEM—Series of interconnected communications networks, circuits, stations, and facilities for fulfilling communications needs on a broad scale. An interdependent assemblage of communications media providing efficient communication service consistent with the requirement.

COMPILE—To produce a sequentially ordered machine language program from a series of symbolic operation codes or statements. A special compiling program is used to perform this transformation from a nonmachine to machine language.

COMPILER—A program that translates high level language statements into more than one machine language instruction.

COMPUTER CODE CHECKING—There are three types: character parity check, block parity check, and cyclic parity check. A means of determing if errors have occurred.

COMPUTER/COMPUTER SYSTEM—A high-speed data processor, communications, or general-purpose problem solver composed of input, processor and output units.

COMPUTER UTILITY—A service which provides computational ability. A "time-shared" computer system. Programs as well as data may be made available to the user. The user also may have his own programs immediately available in the central processor, may have them on call at the computer utility or he may load them by transmitting them to the computer prior to using them. Certain data and programs are shared by all users of the service; other data and programs because of proprietary nature have restricted access. Computer utilities are generally accessed by means of data communications subsystems.

CONTENTION—A condition on a multipoint communication channel when two or more locations try to transmit at the same time.

CONTINUOUS TRANSMISSION MODE—A transmission mode in which line blocks are sent without any pause between them as long as no more than one completely transmitted block is unacknowledged. Receipt of acknowledgment for a line block is expected during the transmission of the succeeding line block.

CONTROL CARD—Informs the operating (Program) system in a computer what its next task will be.

CONTROL CHARACTER—A character inserted into a data stream with the intent of signalling the receiving station to perform some function.

CONTROL PROGRAM—The program responsible for handling input/output for both terminals and file storage, establishing processing priorities, maintaining waiting lists of work in process, activating operational programs, and performing other supervisory functions in a real-time system. Words sometimes used synonymously to designate such a program include driver, executive, monitor, supervisor.

CONTROL UNIT—A computer internal unit (assembly) responsible for directing and coordinating the entire computer system and is comparable to a telephone exchange. It will access/fetch the instruction and then execute it.

CONTROLLERS—Controllers convert bits or bytes into words, convert (translate) data code, match the speed of the device to the speed of the memory and control the device. e.g., Communication's Controller, Card Reader/Punch Controller, Line Printer Controller, Console Controller, Drum Controllers, Disk Controller, Magnetic Tape Controller.

CONSOLE—A portion of the computer which may be used to control the machine manually, correct errors, determine the status of storage, and manually revise the contents of storage.

CONSTANT—A fixed value that many programmers will reference rather than each having his own.

CONVERSATIONAL MODE—A procedural mode for communication between a terminal and the computer in which each entry from the terminal requires a response from the computer and vice versa.

CONVERT—To change numerical information from one number base to another. To transfer information from one recorded medium to another.

CORE (Memory)—Does no work. It stores program instructions, addresses, modifiers, device addresses, tables, data and constants.

COUPLING—The connecting of two or more devices in such a manner that information or energy is transferred from one to the other.

CPM—Characters Per Minute or Cards Per Minute.

CPS—Characters Per Second.

CPU—Central Processing Unit. Contains the control unit, arithmetic unit normal registers, and storage (memory).

CR—Carriage Return Character. A format control which causes the printing mechanism to return to the first printer position on the same printing line (also applicable to CRT display devices).

CRC—Cyclic Redundancy Check character(s). A CRC character generated at the transmitting terminal based on the contents of the message transmitted. A similar CRC generation is performed at the receiving terminal. If the two characters match, the message was probably received correctly.

CRJE—Conversational Remote Job Entry. An IBM designation referring to conversational language employed by a terminal user in submitting jobs and controlling their processing.

CROSS-BAR—An automatic telephone switching system using movable switches mounted on bars. Dialed information is received and stored by common circuits which select and test the switching paths and control the operation of the switching mechanisms.

CROSS TALK—The unwanted signals in a channel which originate from one or more other channels in the same communication system. Signals electrically coupled from another circuit, usually undesirably, but sometimes for useful purposes.

CRT—Cathode Ray Tube used to display information.

CURSOR—A position indicator employed in a video terminal (CRT) to indicate a character to be corrected or a position where data will be entered.

CUSTOMER—Denotes the person, firm, or corporation which orders service and is responsible for the payment of charges.

CUSTOMER-PROVIDED EQUIPMENT—Term applies to equipment owned by the customer or leased from vendors other than the Telephone Company.

CYCLE—A term applied to alternating current. Specifically, the time required for an electric current to start at zero, go through some positive value, through zero, then through some negative value and return to zero. Expressed in hertz which means cycles per second.

CYCLIC CHECK CHARACTER—See CRC.

CYCLIC REDUNDANCY CHECK—See CRC.

DATA—Any representations such as characters or analog quantities to which meaning might be assigned.

DATA ACCESS ARRANGEMENT—An electronic unit used to connect interface customer-owned equipment to the telephone type facilities.

DATA BLOCK—The accumulation of a specific number of characters into a group or block of information.

DATA CIRCUIT—Communication facility permitting transmission of information in digital form. See Circuit.

DATA COLLECTION—The act of bringing data from one or more points to a central point.

DATA COMMUNICATION—The transmission of data messages.

DATA FILE—A collection of records. It should be well-organized, updated periodically, easily accessed, and should contain only required information.

DATA LINE OCCUPIED—A designation applied to a sense circuit in an Automatic Calling Unit. When ON, the circuit indicates to the computer that the ACU found the telephone circuit to be in use and unavailable.

DATA MESSAGE—Information in a form and format which is to be machine processed. See Message.

DATA MODEM—A MODulation/DEModulation device that enables computers and terminals to communicate over telephone circuits. See Modem or Data Set.

DATA MODEM CLOCKING—The derivation of synchronous clocking signals from the modem, rather than from the terminal or computer.

DATA ORIGINATION—The earliest stage at which the source material is first put into machine readable form or directly into electrical signals.

DATAPHONE–An AT&T designation for a service which provides data communication over telephone facilities.

DATA-PHONE DATA SET–A registered trademark of AT&T Company to identify the data sets manufactured and supplied by the Bell System for use in the transmission of data over the regular telephone network.

DATA PHONE SERVICE–A registered service mark of the AT&T Company which identifies the transmission of data over the Bell System telephone network.

DATA PROCESSING–Any operation or combination of operations on data.

DATA SET–Interconnection device. Converts terminal/computer digital signals to common carrier signals. Also provides for other control signals.

DATA SET ADAPTER–An interconnection device located in terminal or computer equipment. It provides various controls and features, and interfaces the Data Set. May, in some cases, replace the Data Set.

DATA SET READY–An EIA RS-232-C designation applied to a sense circuit used by a terminal or computer to detect that power is applied to its modem, and that the modem is connected to a communication circuit.

DATASPEED SERVICE–Transmission of data from teletypewriters or other business machines which produce punched paper tape; carried over the regular telephone network at 750, 1050, or 1200 words per minute. A registered trademark of the AT&T Company.

DATA TERMINAL–Equipment employed at the end of a transmission circuit for the transmission and reception of data. See Terminal.

DATA TERMINAL READ–An EIA RS-232-C designation applied to a control circuit used by a terminal or computer to tell its modem that the terminal or computer is ready for operation. In some applications this circuit is used to enable the modem to answer or terminate calls.

DATA TERMINAL SUBSET–Another term for Data Set or Data Set Adapter.

DATA STREAM–Binary bits not necessarily representing characters. May be continuous for long periods of time.

DC1, DC2, DC3, DC4, (Device Controls)–Characters for the control of ancillary devices associated with data processing or telecommunication systems, more especially switching devices "on" or "off." (If a single "stop" control is required to interrupt or turn off ancillary devices, DC4 is the preferred assignment.)

DDD–Direct Distance Dialing. A facility used for making long-distance telephone calls without the assistance of a telephone operator. DDD is frequently used to mean the switched telephone network.

DEBUGGING–The process of determining the correctness of a computer routine and taking action to correct any errors. Also the detection and correction of malfunctions in the computer itself.

DECIBEL (DB)–Measure of the ratio of two power values $= \text{LOG}_{10}(P_1/P_2)$.

DECK–A collection of punched cards, commonly a complete set of punched cards which have been punched for a definite service or purpose.

DECODE–To apply a code so as to reverse some previous encoding. To determine the meaning of individual characters or groups of characters in a message. To determine the meaning of an instruction from the set of pulses which describes the instruction, command, or operation to be performed.

DEGRADATION–A condition in which the system continues to operate, but at a reduced level of service. Unavailability of major equipment subsystems, or components is the usual case.

DELAY DISTORTION–Distortion resulting from nonuniform speed of transmission of the various frequency components of a signal through a transmission medium.

DEL (Delete)–This character is used primarily to "erase" or "obliterate" erroneous or unwanted characters in perforated tape. (In the strict sense, DEL is not a control character).

DEMODULATION–The process of retrieving an original signal from a modulated carrier wave. This technique is used in data sets to make communication signals compatible with business machine signals.

DEVICE ADDRESS–Required for input/output instructions. Required by a computer in order to access the devices connected to the associated device channels.

DI-BIT–A pair of bits occurring sequentially in a bit stream.

DIAGNOSTIC ROUTINE–A routine used to locate a malfunction in a computer, or to aid in locating mistakes in a computer program. Thus, in general, any routine specifically designed to aid in debugging or troubleshooting.

DIAL SWITCHING EQUIPMENT–An automatic telephone system whereby one user can establish, through electro-mechanical or electronic equipment, a connection to another telephone user without the assistance of the attendant.

DIAL-UP–The use of a dial or push-button telephone to initiate a station-to-station telephone call.

DIGIT–One of the symbols 0, 1 to 9. Also used in telephone to describe the impulse sequence produced by the telephone dial.

DIGITAL–As opposed to analog. Signals made up of pulses of discrete duration, amplitude, etc.

DIGITAL COMPUTER–Based on the principles of numerics (counts), usually binary.

DIGITIZE–To convert an analog measurement of a physical variable into a numerical value, thereby expressing the quantity in digital form. Synonymous with (quantize).

DIODE–A device used to permit current flow in one direction in a circuit and to inhibit current flow in the other. In computers, these are primarily germanium or silicon crystals.

DIRECT DISTANCE DIALING (DDD)–A telephone service which enables a user to dial directly telephones outside the user's local area without the aid of an operator.

DISK STORAGE–The storage of data on the surface of magnetic disks. Sometimes called secondary storage.

DISPLAY UNIT–A device which provides a visual representation of data.

DISTORTION—Usually an undesired change in a waveform. The principal sources of distortion are: (a) a nonlinear relation between input and output at a given frequency; (b) nonuniform transmission at different frequencies; and (c) phase shift not proportional to frequency. Facsimile condition which may cause the recorded copy to be other than a perfect reproduction of the transmitted copy.

DLE (Data Link Escape)—A communication control character which will change the meaning of a limited number of contiguously following characters. It is used exclusively to provide supplementary controls in data communication networks.

DOUBLE PARITY—A system using both vertical and horizontal parity schemes.

DOWNTIME—The period during which a computer or communication channel is malfunctioning or not operating correctly due to mechanical or electronic failure, as opposed to available time, idle time, or standby time, during which the computer is functional. Contrasted with uptime.

DRAIN MESSAGE—A means of removing (routing) accumulated messages in a store-and-forward message switching system. May inhibit acceptance of any input message to the system during the drain process.

DROP—The wire that leads to the customer's premises—as from a pole to the building.

DRUM STORAGE—A storage device that uses magnetic recording on a rotating cylinder.

DUPLEX—In communications, pertaining to a simultaneous two-way and independent transmission in both directions (sometimes referred to as "full duplex"). Contrast with half duplex.

DUPLEX CHANNEL—A communication channel with the capability of simultaneous two-way communication, equivalent to full duplex.

EAM CARD—Electronic Accounting Machine. More commonly referred to as an IBM card. See IBM CARD.

EBCDIC CODE—Extended Binary Coded Decimal Interchange Code. A specific code using eight bits to represent a character.

ECHO—A portion of the transmitted signal returned from a distant point to the transmitting source with sufficient time delay to be received as interference.

ECHO CHECK—An error control technique wherein the receiving terminal or computer returns the original message to the sender to verify that the message was received correctly.

ECHO-PLEX—A communication procedure where the characters keyboarded by the operator do not print directly on his printer, but are sent to a computer which echoes the characters back for printing. This procedure, requiring full duplex communication facilities, provides a form of error control by displaying to the operator an indication of the character received by the computer.

ECHO SUPPRESSOR—An electrical device that blocks the echo path through use of directional gated amplifiers. In telephone long-distance lines, it prevents reverberation, a form of echo.

EDGE PUNCHED CARD—A card of fixed size into which information may be recorded by punching holes along one edge of the card.

EIA–Electronic Industries Association.

ELECTRONIC SWITCH–A circuit element causing a start and stop action or a switching action electronically, usually at high speeds.

ELECTRICALLY CONNECTED–Connected by means of a conducting path or through a capacitor, as distinguished from connection merely through electromagnetic induction.

EM (End of Medium)–A control character associated with the data which may be used to identify the physical end of the wanted portion of the information. (The position of this character does not necessarily correspond to the physical end of the data.)

ENCODE–To apply a code, frequently one consisting of binary numbers, to represent individual characters or groups of characters in a message.

END OF ADDRESS (EOA)–One or more specific sequential characters that are used to identify the end of address section of a message. This character(s) may be present in other sections of a message but only the first detection will be used as the EOA indicator.

END OF MESSAGE (EOM)–One or more specific sequential characters that indicate the end of message.

END OF TRANSMISSION (EOT)–The end of transmission field is one or more specific sequential characters used on a controlled input circuit to indicate that no more messages will be sent from that station until it is repolled.

ENQ (Enquiry)–A communication control character used in data communication systems as a request for a response from a remote station. It may be used as a "Who Are You" (WRU) to obtain identification, or may be used to obtain station status, or both. May be used during polling/calling.

ENTRANCE FACILITY–The facility between the customer's premises and the Telephone Company Central Office or the customer-provided interexchange facilities.

ENVELOPE DELAY–Characteristics of a circuit which result in some frequencies arriving ahead of others, even though they were transmitted together.

EOA–End of Address

EOB–End of Block. Not necessarily the End of Message.

EOF–End of File. End of a group of data characters.

EOM–End of Message. A unique group of characters used to designate the end of a message transmission.

EOT (End of Transmission)–A communication control character used to indicate the conclusion of a transmission, which may have contained one or more blocks of text and any associated headings. See End of Transmission.

EQUALIZER DELAY–A corrective network which is designed to make the phase delay or envelope delay of a circuit or system substantially constant over a desired frequency range.

ERROR–Any discrepancy between a computed, observed, or measured quantity and the true, specified, or theoretically correct value or condition.

ERROR CODE–A specific character which may be punched into a card or tape to indicate that a known error was made in the associated block of data, and which is read for action by the receiving device.

ERROR CONTROL–A plan, implemented by hardware, software, procedures, etc., to detect and/or correct errors introduced into a data communications system.

ERROR CORRECTION–System which detects and inherently provides correction for errors occasioned by transmission equipment or facilities.

ERROR DETECTION–System which detects errors occasioned by transmission equipment or facilities.

ERROR TRANSMISSION–A change in data resulting from the transmission process. The change in data may be the result of outside interference with the normal transmission process.

ESC (Escape)–A control character intended to provide code extention (supplementary characters) in general information interchange. The Escape character itself is a prefix affecting the interpretation of a limited number of contiguously following characters.

ESS (Electronic Switching System)–A communications switching system which uses solid state devices and other computer-type equipment and principles. It operates in millionths of a second and gives customers many new services.

ETB (End of Transmission Block)–A communication control character used to indicate the end of a block of data for communication purposes. ETB is used for blocking data where the block structure is not necessarily related to the processing format. Punched cards may require this character during transmission.

ETX (End of Text)–A communication control character used to terminate a sequence of characters started with STX and transmitted as an entity. At times may be used as an End of Message.

EXCHANGE–A defined area, served by a communications common carrier, within which the carrier furnishes service at the exchange rate and under the regulations applicable in that area as prescribed in the carrier's filed tariffs.

EXECUTIVE ROUTINE–A routine which controls loading and reloading of routines and in some cases makes use of instructions which are unknown to the general programmer. Effectively, an executive routine is part of the machine itself.

EXTERNAL CLOCKING–In synchronous communication, a terminal or computer is Externally Clocked when the bit-timing signal is provided by the modem.

EXTERNAL STORAGE–(1) The storage of data on a device which is not an integral part of a computer, but in a form prescribed for use by the computer. (2) A facility or device, not an intergral part of a computer, on which data usable by a computer is stored, such as magnetic tape or disk units.

FACILITY–See Channel, Line or Circuit.

FACSIMILE (FAX)–A form of document communication where the original image is scanned and converted to an electrical signal, and the electrical signal is subsequently converted to a replica of the original image at the receiving terminal.

FAIL SOFT–A system method designed to prevent the irretrievable loss of facilities or data in the event of a temporary outage of some portion of the system.

FCC–Federal Communications Commission.

FDM–Frequency Division Multiplexing.

FDX–Full Duplex (Communication Circuit)

FEEDBACK CONTROL–A type of system control obtained when a portion of the output signal is operated upon and is fed back to the input in order to obtain a desired effect.

FEED HOLES–A series of holes in paper tape which engage with a sprocket and permit transport of the tape.

FF (Form Feed)–A format effector which controls the movement of the printing position to the first predetermined printing line on the next form or page (applicable also to CRT display devices).

FIGS–Figure Shift Character.

FILE–An organized collection of information directed twoard some purpose; for example, a file of savings accounts or airline passenger names.

FILE GAP–An interval of space or time associated with a file to indicate or signal the end of the file.

FIELDATA CODE–The U.S. Military code used in data processing as a compromise between conflicting commercial codes.

FIELD (Fields of Data)–Specific information assigned to certain sections of a card.

FILE MAINTENANCE–The processing of a file to effect changes in the file; for example, updating a master file. Cycling of a file is a form of file maintenance.

FILTER–Device used to either suppress unwanted frequencies or noise, or to separate channels in communication circuits.

FINAL ROUTE–The last choice route in the automatic routing of DDD calls.

FIRMWARE–That portion of control-memory hardware which can be tailored to create microprograms for a user-oriented instruction set.

FLAG–A bit of information attached to a character or word to indicate the boundary of a field. An indicator used frequently to tell some later part of a program that some condition occurred earlier. An indicator used to identify the members of several sets which are intermixed.

FLIP-FLOP–(1) A bi-stable device; i.e., a device capable of assuming two stable states.

FLOWCHART (Flowcharting)–A method of diagrammatically representing the steps involved in solving a problem. The special symbols used in flowcharting correspond to the standards of the International Organization for Standardization. Flowcharts are used to guide the writing of program instruction sequences.

FOREGROUND PROCESSING–High-priority processing, usually resulting from real-time entries, given precedence by means of interrupts over lower priority "background" processing.

FOREIGN EXCHANGE SERVICE (FX)–A service which connects a customer's telephone to a remote exchange. This service provides the equivalent of local service from the distant exchange.

FORM FEED–Device to permit correct positioning of documents or business forms on a teletypewriter or business machine to ensure that the form is in the correct position on the machine to receive data.

FORM FEEDOUT–The rapid, accurate positioning of document forms on a teleprinter or business machine.

FORMAT–A contraction meaning the FORM of MATERIAL, designating the way in which information is organized.

FORTRAN (Formula Translation)–High-level programming language originally developed to aid mathematicians and engineers in problem solving. The highly developed arithmetic statements resemble algebraic statements.

FOUR-OUT-OF-EIGHT CODE–A communication code which facilitates error detection because four of the eight bits representing a character are always marking.

FORWARD ERROR CORRECTION–Error correction without retransmission.

FRAME–A time period encompassing a character, a character group, or a bit-group cycle in a multiplexing process.

FREQUENCY–The rate of recurrence of some cyclic or repetitive event, such as the rate of repetition of a sine-wave electrical current, usually expressed in cycles per second, or hertz.

FREQUENCY DIVISION MULTIPLEXING–The merging of several signals of lesser bandwidth into a composite signal for transmission over a communication channel of greater bandwidth. Example: five signals with a bandwidth of 100 Hz each might be accommodated on a channel having a bandwidth of 500 Hz.

FREQUENCY MODULATION–A method of transmission whereby the frequency of the carrier wave is changed to correspond to similar changes in the signal wave.

FS (File Separator), GS (Group Separator), RS (Record Separator) and US (Unit Separator)–These information separators may be used within data in optional fashion, except that their hierarchial relationship shall be: FS is the most inclusive, then GS, then RS, and US is least inclusive. (The content and length of a File, Group, Record or Unit are not specified.)

FSK–A form of frequency modulation called Frequency Shift Keying, typically with marking signals represented by one frequency, and spacing signals represented by another frequency.

FULL DUPLEX (FDX)–A communication facility providing simultaneous transmission and reception. See Circuit, Four-Wire.

FULL PERIOD–Circuit comprised of leased or owned lines which are in continuous use.

FUNCTION CODES–Codes inserted in tape or cards to effect specific machine functions (e.g., tabulate).

FUNCTION SWITCH–A circuit having a fixed number of inputs and outputs designed such that the output information is a function of the input information, each expressed in a certain code, signal configuration, or pattern.

GANG PUNCHING–High-speed parallel method of reproducing fixed information from a master card into a whole series of detail cards.

GATE–A circuit which yields an output signal that is dependent on some function of its present or past input signals.

GATE PULSE–A pulse which enables a gate circuit to pass a signal.

GIGACYCLE–A kilomegacycle per second, 10^9 cycles per second.

GROUP ADDRESS–An address assigned to a group of terminals, which may or may not share a single communication channel.

HALF DUPLEX–Pertaining to an alternate, one-way-at-a-time, independent transmission (sometimes referred to as "single"). Contrast with Duplex. See HDX.

HAMMING CODE–One of the forward error correction code systems named after the inventor.

HANDSHAKING–A preliminary procedure performed by modems and/or terminals and computers to verify that communication has been established and it is OK to proceed.

HARDWARE–The electrical and mechanical capabilities built into the computer. This varies with the design.

HARD COPY–A printed copy of machine output in readable form for human beings; for example, reports, listings, documents, summaries.

HARDENED–(1) A term for blast-resistant construction. (2) A hardened transcontinental cable system to protect against atomic blasts was recently completed by the Bell System.

HDX–Half Duplex (Communication Circuit).

HEAD–The assembly which reads, records, or erases information on a storage device.

HEAD GAP–The space between the reading or recording head and the recording surface, such as tape, drum or disk. The space or gap intentionally inserted into the magnetic circuit of the head in order to force or direct the recording medium.

HEADER–The part of a message preceding the text, normally specifying message destination, source, priority, etc.

HERTZ (Hz)–Named after discoverer of alternating current and is used to express cycles per second.

HEXADECIMAL–A numbering system with 16 combinations represented by the symbols 0 through 9 and A through F.

HIGH-SPEED PRINTER–A printer which operates at a speed more compatible with the speed of computation and data processing so that it may operate on-line.

HIGH-SPEED READER–A reading device capable of being connected to a computer so as to operate on-line without seriously holding up the computer.

HIT–An isolated electrical noise impulse of sufficient strength to mutilate data.

HOLDING TIME–The length of time a communication channel is in use for each transmission. Includes both message time and operating time.

HOLLERITH CODE–The most common coding structure used for punched cards. Uses four types of symbols: alpha, numerical, special, and control. A 12-unit code.

HOLOVISION–Transmission of a three-dimensional image.

HOUSEKEEPING–Operations within a computer that do not contribute directly to the solution of problems but are necessary to the operation of the system.

HOME LOOP–A short, local transmission path.

HT (Horizontal Tabulation)–A format effector which controls the movement of the printing position to the next in a series of predetermined positions along the printing line (applicable also to CRT display devices and the skip function on punched cards).

HUBBING POINT–Similar to a concentrator. Method of connecting several circuits to one shared circuit.

IBM CARD–Holds all the information about a certain subject, item or thing. Top edge of card is known as the 12 EDGE, whereas the bottom edge is known as the 9 EDGE. The front of the card is known as its FACE. The card contains 80 vertical columns and 12 horizontal rows. ROWS 0, 11 and 12 are considered ZONES. Cards measure 7¼ inches long, 3¾ inches wide are are .007 inches thick, Cards may be sectioned off into different fields, some of which may be fixed or variable. See EAM CARD.

IDENTIFICATION, TERMINAL–A character or sequence of characters used to identify a transmitting or originating terminal.

IMA–Input Message Acknowledgment. An acknowledgment message returned to the sender from the receiving station.

IMPULSES–The making and breaking of a circuit by pulsing contacts to sympathetically operate remote devices.

IMPULSE NOISE–A form of noise characterized by high amplitude and short duration, sometimes occurring as a group of impulses, or burst. Heard on the line as sharp clicks, impulse noise is a common source of error, originating from switching equipment, electrical storms, etc.

INFORMATION–The meaning assigned to data by known conventions.

INFORMATION RETRIEVAL–That branch of computer technology concerned with techniques for storing and searching large quantities of information and making selected information available. An information retrieval system may or may not be a real-time system.

IN-LINE PROCESSING–A method of processing in which each individual input action is completely processed and all pertinent records updated without previously having been batched or grouped. In this sense, a real-time system may or may not be an in-line system.

IN-PLANT SYSTEM–A data handling system confined to one building or a number of buildings in one locality.

INPUT–(1) The data to be processed. (2) The state or sequence of states occurring on a specified input channel. (3) The device or collective set of devices used for bringing data into another device. (4) A channel for impressing a state on a device or logic element. (5) The process of transferring data from an external storage to an internal storage.

INPUT CIRCUIT–The communications link between the computer and the input station for transmission of characters to the computer.

INPUT DEVICES–The devices used to get information into the computer. Example: Card Reader, Magnetic Tape, Paper Tape Reader, Optical Character Reader and keyboard.

INPUT/OUTPUT DEVICES–These devices can be used to get information into the computer or receive information from the computer. They may also serve as secondary storage. Communications terminals are not referred to as input/output devices.

INPUT-OUTPUT LIMITED–Pertaining to a system or condition in which the time for input and output operation exceeds other operations.

INQUIRY–A request for information from storage; for example, a request for a display of the number of available airline seats or for the initiation of a search of library records.

INQUIRY STATION–The remote terminal device from which an inquiry into computing or data processing equipment is made.

INSIDE PLANT–That part of the plant within a central office, intermediate station, subscriber's premises which is on the office or station side of the point of connection with the outside plant.

INSTRUCTION–Set of characters which, as a unit, causes a device to perform one of its operations.

INSTRUCTION ADDRESS REGISTER–Stores the address of the next instruction to be executed. Instructions are stored in memory.

INSTRUCTION REGISTER–See Control Unit.

INTEGRATED COMMUNICATIONS SYSTEM–Communications system on either a unilateral or joint basis, in which a message can be filed at any communication center in that system and be delivered to the addressee(s) by any other appropriate communication center in that system without reprocessing en route. Such a system requires uniformity of procedures, through linking between the various communications systems and established arrangements for necessary relay.

INTEGRATED DATA PROCESSING–Information processing organized, directed, and carried out according to a system approach that gives recognition to the interrelated aspects of various applications.

INTELLIGENT TERMINAL–A terminal with some level of programmable "intelligence" for performing preprocessing or post-processing operations.

INTERACTIVE–See Conversational.

INTERCEPT–A communication device assigned to accept undeliverable messages within a switching system. Routing of otherwise undeliverable messages.

INTERCOM–Communications between locations on a customer's premises. A feature of modern communications for homes and businesses.

INTERFACE–A well-defined boundary, such as the interface between a modem and a terminal, or the interface between a communications controller and a computer's I/O bus.

INTERFERENCE–Presence of undesirable energy in a circuit.

INTERNAL CLOCKING–In synchronous communication, a terminal or computer is Internally Clocked when the bit-timing signal is provided from within the terminal or computer, rather than from a modem.

INTERNAL STORAGE–Storage facilities forming an integral physical part of the device, from which instructions may be executed.

INTERRUPT–A break in the normal flow of a system or routine such, that the flow can be resumed from that point at a later time. An interrupt is usually caused by a signal from an external source.

INTER-RECORD GAP–An interval of space or time, deliberately left between recording portions of data or records. Such spacing is used to prevent errors through loss of data or overwriting, and permits tape stop-start operations.

I/O–Input/Output.

IPS (Inches Per Second)–Normally used to indicate the speed of tape across the Read/Write head of magnetic tape devices.

JOB STREAM–A series of jobs (application programs) that are processed one after the other.

JOINT USER–The term denotes a person, firm, or corporation who is designated by the customer as a user of a private line service of the customer and to whom a portion of the charge for the service will be billed under a joint user agreement.

KEYBOARD–An arrangement of keys for manual operation. Similar to a typewriter keyboard.

KEYBOARD DEVICES–Teleprinters and other devices that use a keyboard for manual entry of information.

KEYBOARD INQUIRY–The interrogation of the contents of a computer's storage initiated at a keyboard.

KEYBOARD-PERFORATOR–Mechanism which consists essentially of a keyboard, similar to a typewriter keyboard, and a punch, by which paper tape is perforated with code symbols that correspond to depressed character-keys of the keyboard. Messages may be transmitted automatically from the tape by a transmitter-distributor.

KEY PUNCH–A key-operated perforator, usually for cards.

KEY SET–Another name for push-button telephones, wherein the buttons are used for intercom, holding, signalling and/or pick-up of additional telephone lines.

KILO–A prefix meaning thousand. A kilocharacter (KCh) equals one thousand characters.

KSR–Keyboard send and receive. A teletype machine which has only a keyboard and page printer.

LANDLINE–A telegraph or telephone line passing over land as opposed to submarine cables.

LASER–A maser which operates at optical frequencies.

LDX (Long Distance Xerography)–A name used by the Xerox Company to identify its high-speed facsimile system. The system uses Xerox terminal equipment and a wide band data communication channel.

LEASED LINE–A communication channel leased for exclusive use from a common carrier, and frequently referred to as a Private Line.

LEADED LINE NETWORK–Generally a telephone network leased from the telephone company; may also refer to a teletypewriter network leased from the telephone company.

LEVELS–The rows of recorded information on paper or magnetic tape. Also used to designate the storage devices of various speeds within a computer.

LF (Line Feed Character)–A format control which caused the printing mechanism to move to the next printing line (also applicable to CRT display devices).

LINE–Communication channel or telephone circuit. Sometimes called a facility.

LINE ADAPTER–A communications interface between the bit-parallel I/O format of a computer and the bit-serial format of a communication channel.

LINE ADDRESS–A character or set of characters designating a specific communication channel.

LINE DROPOUT–A large, momentary change in the transmission characteristics of a telephone circuit.

LINE FEED–Teletypewriter function code which rotates the platen of a page machine to a position to accept the next printed line. See LF.

LINE LOADING–The use of resistors, capacitors, and inductors to compensate for the frequency distortion and delay distortion characteristics of telephone lines.

LINE PRINTER–A device capable of printing one line of characters across a page; i.e., 100 or more characters simultaneously as continuous paper advances line by line in one direction.

LINE SWITCHING–The connection of lines through the switching center prior to the start of a communication and the disconnecting of the lines at the end of the communication. The switching technique of temporarily connecting two lines together so that the stations directly exchange information.

LINE TURNAROUND–In half duplex communication, the switching of modems and communication channel from transmission in one direction to transmission in the opposite direction.

LINK–See Channel, Circuit or Line.

LOADING–The addition of an inductive element to a circuit to counteract capacitive characteristics which distort the signal.

LOCAL CHANNEL–A channel connecting a communications subscriber to a central office.

LOCAL LOOP–A line connecting a terminal to a nearby telephone company's central office equipment.

LOCATION–A place in the main memory or auxiliary storage where a unit of data may be stored or retrieved.

LOGICAL DIAGRAM–In logical design, a diagram representing the logical elements and their interconnections without necessarily expressing construction or engineering details.

LONGITUDINAL REDUNDANCY CHECK–A method of error detection using a parity bit for each level in the code being transmitted. Following a block of characters, an

LRC character is inserted to make the number of bits transmitted on each of the code levels either odd or even. To check the accuracy of the received data, an LRC character is generated by the receiving terminal and compared with the LRC character received from the transmitting terminal.

LONG-SPACE DISCONNECT–A feature of some modems which causes the modem to terminate a telephone call in response to the receipt of a space signal for an extended period of time.

LOOP–(1) In computers, a coding technique whereby the same group of instructions is reused with modification of the data being manipulated. (2) In communications, it signifies a type of facility; normally the circuit between the subscriber and central office. See Local Loop.

LOST MESSAGE–Message not received at the destination directed by the instructions in the message header. Message not delivered within the normal delivery period.

LRC–Logitudinal Redundancy Check.

LSI–Large Scale Integration. A method of packaging related to logic density.

LTRS–Letters Shift Character (lower case).

MACHINE LANGUAGE–The only language a computer understands. All programs are either written in or converted to machine language prior to operation in the computer.

MACRO INSTRUCTION–A symbolic program language statement that produces several machine instructions.

MAGNETIC CORE–A magnetic substance capable of assuming and remaining in one or two or more conditions of magnetization.

MAGNETIC CORE STORAGE–A storage device in which binary data is represented by the direction of magnetization in each unit of an array of magnetic material, usually in the shape of toroidal rings, but also in other forms such as wraps on bobbins.

MAGNETIC DISK STORAGE–A storage device or system consisting of magnetically coated disks, on the surface of which information is stored in the form of magnetic spots arranged in a manner to represent binary data. These data are arranged in circular tracks around the disks and are accessible to reading and writing heads on an arm which can be moved mechanically to the desired disk and then to the desired track; are read or written sequentially as the disk rotates.

MAGNETIC DRUM–A cylinder having a surface coating of magnetic material, which stores binary information by the orientation of magnetic dipoles near or on its surface. Since the drum is rotated at a uniform rate, the information stored is available periodically as a given portion of the surface moves past one or more flux detecting devices called heads located near the surface of the drum.

MAGNETIC HEAD–A transducer for converting electric variations into magnetic variations for storage on magnetic media, or for reconverting energy so stored into electric energy. It may be used for erasing such stored energy. See Head.

MAGNETIC STORAGE–A device or devices which utilize the magnetic properties of materials to store information. e.g., disk, drum, magnetic tape, etc.

MAGNETIC TAPE STORAGE–A storage device in which data are stored in the form of magnetic spots on metal or coated plastic tape. Binary data are stored as small magnetized spots arranged in column form across the width of the tape. A read-write head is usually associated with each row of magnetized spots so that one column can be read or written at a time as the tape traverses the head.

MCS–Main Core Storage; or microseconds. Depending on application.

MAINFRAME–The central processor of the computer system. It contains the main storage, arithmetic unit and special register groups. All that portion of a computer exclusive of the input, output, peripheral and in some instances, storage units.

MAIN STORAGE–Usually the fastest storage device of a computer and the one from which instructions are executed, (contrasted with storage, auxiliary).

MANUAL CONTROL–The direction of a computer by means of manually operated switches.

MANUAL SYSTEM–A system whereby telephone or other connections are established with the assistance of an attendant.

MARK (Marking)–The state of a communication channel corresponding to a binary one. The Marking condition exists when current flows (hole in paper tape) on a current-loop channel, or when the voltage is more negative than -3 volts on an EIA RS-232-C channel.

MARK SENSE–Process of using pencil to mark preprinted cards with information. In EDP, a machine responds to the graphite penciled marks as though they were punched holes in the cards.

MASER–A device capable of amplifying or generating radiation. Maser amplifiers are used in satellite communication ground stations to amplify the extremely weak signals received from communications satellites.

MASKING–A technique for sensing specific binary conditions and ignoring others. Typically accomplished by placing zeros in bit positions of no interest, and ones in bit positions to be sensed.

MASTER FILE–A main reference file; for example, a set of flight/date seat inventory records.

MASTER STATION–The main station in a group of stations, that controls the transmission of all the stations.

MATRIX–An array of quantities in a prescribed form; in mathematics, usually capable of being subject to a mathematical operation by means of an operator or another matrix according to prescribed rules. An array of coupled circuit elements; e.g., diodes, wires, magnetic cores, and relays, that are capable of performing a specific function; such as, the conversion from one numerical system to another. The elements are usually arranged in rows and columns. Thus, a matrix is a particular type of encoder or decoder.

MCS–Microseconds.

MEGA–A prefix meaning million. A mega bit equals one million bits.

MEMORY–(1) An organization of storage elements, primarily for the retrieval of information; examples are: magnetic core memory, semiconductor memory. (2) The rapid-access storage elements from which instructions are executed and data operated on are referred to as main memory; and the less rapidly accessed, but high-capacity elements used for storing large quantities of data are called auxiliary memory.

MEMORY DATA REGISTER–The interface between the input, output, memory and Central Processing Unit. Normally, information can only get out of or into the memory via the memory data register.

MEMORY DUMP–A listing of the contents of storage devices.

MEMORY PROTECTION–A means of assuring, with special hardware, that the contents of main memory within certain specified, but variable bounds, will not be destroyed or altered. Memory protection devices help guard a real-time system against the effects or equipment malfunctions and program bugs.

MESSAGE–A communication, prepared for information interchange, in a form suitable for passage through the interchange medium. It includes: (1) All portions of the communication, such as machine sensible controls; (2) An indication of the start of the message and the end of the message.

MESSAGE CENTER–Agency charged with the responsibility for acceptance, preparation for transmission, receipt, and delivery of messages.

MESSAGE FORMAT–Rules for the placement of such portions of a message as message heading, address, text, and end of message.

MESSAGE HEADING–Part of a message containing all components preceding the text.

MESSAGE, MULTIPLE ADDRESS–A message destined for more than one terminal.

MESSAGE NUMBERING–The identification of each message within a communications system by the assignment of a sequential number.

MESSAGE RETRIEVAL–The capability to retrieve a message some time after it has entered an information system.

MESSAGE ROUTING–The function performed at a central message processor of selecting the route, or alternate route if required, by which a message will proceed to the next point in reaching its destination.

MESSAGE SWITCHING–The switching technique of receiving a message, storing it until the proper outgoing circuit and station are available, and then retransmitting it toward its destination.

METALLIC CIRCUIT–A telephone circuit providing a direct-current connection between terminating points, without intervening transformers, amplifiers, etc.

MICROCOMMAND–A command specifying an elementary machine operation to be performed within a basic machine cycle.

MICROPROGRAM–A series of microcommands assembled to perform a specific function.

MICROSECOND–One millionth of a second, 10^{-6} seconds.

MICROWAVE–All electromagnetic waves in the radio frequency spectrum above 890 megacycles per seconds.

MICR (Magnetic Ink Character Recognition)–Machine recognition of characters printed with magnetic ink. Contract with OCR.

MILLISECOND—One-thousandth of a second.

MNEMONIC—As used in data communications: A symbolic routing designator consisting of alphabetic characters, or numeric characters, or combinations of alphabetic and numeric characters.

MODE—A style or method of operation characterized by the use of specific facilities in a specific way.

MODEL, MATHEMATICAL—A collection of equations that represent mathematically what goes on in a process. A mathematical description of the process.

MODEM—A MODulation/DEModulation device. Same as Data Set.

MODIFIER—Is a value added to a direct memory address to obtain a new memory address.

MODULATION—The process by which some characteristic of one wave is varied in accordance with another wave. This technique is used in data sets to make business-machine signals compatible with communications facilities.

MODULATION, AMPLITUDE—A method of transmission whereby the signal wave voltage is impressed upon a higher frequency carrier wave, which is varied in accordance with amplitude variations of the signal wave.

MODULE—An interchangeable plug-in item containing components. An incremental block of storage or other building block for expanding the computer capacity.

MONITOR—The supervision of system activities. A program that supervises, controls, and schedules system activities.

MOS—Metal Oxide on Silicon.

MSI—Medium Scale Integration. See LSI.

MULTIDROP CIRCUIT—A communication system configuration using a single channel or line to serve multiple terminals.

MULTIPLE ADDRESS CODE—An instruction code in which an instruction word can specify more than one address to be used during the operation.

MULTIPLE ADDRESS MESSAGE—A message to be delivered to more than one destination. A message containing more than one address.

MULTIPLEX—The process of transferring data from several storage devices operating at relatively low transfer rates to one storage device operating at a high transfer rate in such a manner that the high-speed device is not obliged to wait for the low-speed devices.

MULTIPLEXING—The division of a transmission facility into two or more channels.

MULTIPOINT CIRCUIT—A circuit interconnecting several stations. See Multidrop.

MULTIPROGRAMMING—The concurrent execution of more than one program on a single computer.

MULTIPROCESSOR—A computer with multiple arithmetic and logic units for simultaneous use.

MULTISTATION—Any network of stations capable of communication with each other, whether on one circuit or through a switching center.

MUX–Contraction of the word multiplex.

NAK (Negative Acknowledge)–A communication control character transmitted by a receiver as a negative response to the sender.

NANOSECOND–One thousandth of a millionth of a second, 10^{-9} seconds.

NARROWBAND–A communications channel with a bandwidth less than that of a voice grade channel.

NCSU–Network Control Signalling Unit.

NETWORK–(1) A series of points interconnected by communications channels. (2) The switched telephone network is the network of telephone lines normally used for dialed telephone calls. (3) A private line network is a network of communications channels confined to the use of one customer.

NOISE–Any extraneous signal not deliberately generated by the transmitting device in a data link. Noise tends to degrade signal quality.

NONSYNCHRONOUS–See Asynchronous.

NUL (Null)–The all zeros character which is used as a fill character, nonprintable, and may serve to accomplish time.

OBJECT PROGRAM–The machine language version of a high level or assembly language program, which the computer can understand.

OCTAL–A numbering system of 8 admissible combinations represented by the symbols 0 through 7.

OCR (Optical Character Recognition)–The machine recognition of printed or written characters based on inputs from photoelectric transducers. Contrast with MICR.

OFF-LINE–An operating mode characterized by a terminal or peripheral accomplishing tasks when it is not connected to a communication channel or computer.

ON-LINE–An operating mode in which a terminal or peripheral accomplishes tasks when connected to a communication channel or computer.

ONE-WAY CHANNEL (SIMPLEX)–A channel which permits transmission in one direction only. See Simplex.

OPEN-ENDED–The quality by which the addition of new terms, subject headings, or classifications does not disturb the preexisting system.

OPEN-WIRE–Overhead telephone or telegraph line having each physical wire separately supported by insulators.

OPERAND REGISTER–Holds the addresses of the memory location being serviced.

OPERATING SYSTEM–Is a set of control programs that guide the overall functioning of the computer.

OPERATING TIME–The time required for seizing the line, dialing the call, waiting for the connection to be established, and coordinating the forthcoming transaction with the personnel or equipment at the receiving end.

ORIGINATING STATION–The telecommunications station from which the message is first transmitted.

ORIGINATOR–The composer of the message.

OUTPUT–(1) Data that has been processed. (2) The state of sequence of states occurring on a specified output channel. (3) The device or collective set of devices used for taking data out of a device. (4) A channel for expressing a state of a device or logic element. (5) The process of transferring data from an internal storage to an external storage device.

OUTPUT BLOCK–A block of computer words considered as a unit and intended or destined to be transferred from an internal storage medium to an external destination. A section of internal storage reserved for storing data which are to be transferred out of the computer. A block used as an output buffer.

OUTPUT DEVICES–Devices that are used to receive the information from the computer. Example: Card Punch, Paper Tape Punch and Line Printer.

OUTPUT STATION–The telecommunications station to which the computer transmits characters, also known as "receive station."

OUTPUT CIRCUIT–The communications link between the computer and the output station for transmission of characters by the computer to the output station.

OVERLAY–A technique for bringing routines into high-speed storage from some other form of storage during processing, so that several routines will occupy the same storage locations at different times. Overlay is used when the total storage requirements for instructions exceed the available main storage.

PACKING DENSITY–The number of characters or units of useful information contained within a given linear dimension.

PAD CHARACTER–A character inserted to fill a blank time slot in synchronous transmission, or inserted to fulfill a character-count requirement in transmissions of fixed block lengths.

PADDING–A technique used to fill out a block of information with dummy records.

PAGE COPY–Message, in page form, which is the result of a transmission.

PAPER TAPE READER–A device capable of sensing information punched on a paper tape in the form of a series of holes.

PARALLEL ACCESS–The process of obtaining information from or placing information into storage where the time required for such access is dependent on the simultaneous transfer of all elements of a word from a given storage location.

PARALLEL COMPUTER–A computer in which the digits or data lines are handled concurrently by separate units of the computer. The units may be interconnected in different ways as determined by the computation to operate in parallel or serially. Mixed serial and parallel machines are frequently called serial or parallel according to the way arithmetic processes are performed. An example of a parallel computer is one which handles decimal digits in parallel although it might handle the bits which comprise a digit either serially or in parallel. Contrast with a serial computer.

PARALLEL OPERATION–The performance of several actions, usually of a similar nature, simultaneously through provision of individual similar or identical devices for each such action. Particularly flow or processing of information. Parallel operation is performed to save time over serial operation. Parallel operation requires more equipment.

PARALLEL TRANSMISSION–Method of information transfer in which all bits of a character are sent simultaneously. Contrast with serial transmission.

PARITY (Parity Bit)–A method of error detection using an extra bit to make the total number of marking bits in a character either odd or even. If a character is sent with odd parity, it should be received with odd parity if no errors are introduced by the communication process.

PARITY CHECK–The examination of a character and its parity bit to determine if the character has been received correctly.

PASS BAND–Range of frequency spectrum which can be passed with low attenuation.

PATH–See Channel, Circuit or Line.

PATCH–Connecting circuits temporarily by means of a cord, known as a patch cord.

PAX–Private Automatic Exchange.

PBX–A Private Branch Exchange connected to the public telephone network.

PERFORATOR–A term sometimes applied to a paper tape punch.

PDM–Possible Duplicate Message.

PHASE MODULATION–A method of modulation using a change of phase of the carrier to convey information.

PICTUREPHONE–A registered service mark of the AT&T Company to identify a telephone service that permits the user to see as well as talk with the person at the distant end.

PLANT–Equipment and line facilities installed and operated to serve the purpose of providing communications by electronic means. Physical property of the telephone or telegraph company used for communication.

PL/1 (Programming Language 1)–Developed by IBM as a general purpose language. Has some capabilities of both Fortran and Cobol.

POINT-TO-POINT–Communication between two terminal points only, as opposed to Multipoint and Multidrop.

POLAR OPERATION–Circuit and operation in which mark and space transitions are represented by a current reversal.

POLL–A flexible systematic method, centrally controlled, for permitting stations on a multipoint circuit to transmit without contending for the line.

POLLING–The regular and systematic interrogation of terminals to determine if a terminal has messages awaiting transmission, and to determine the state of readiness of a terminal to accept messages.

PONY–Local circuit not having direct entry into a relay network.

PRECEDENCE (Priority)–Designation assigned to a message to indicate the relative order of handling.

PREVENTIVE MAINTENANCE–The maintenance of a computer system, which is necessary in order to keep equipment in top operating condition and to preclude failures during production runs.

PRIMARY STORAGE–The memory of the computer. Example: Delay Line, thin film, core, crystal, MOS, etc.

PRINTER PERFORATOR–In telegraph practice, a perforator which automatically prints the intelligence on the tape as it is being punched. When printing is done over the area in which the punching occurs, the printer character usually appears six punched codes after the associated punched code.

PRINTOUT–See Hard Copy.

PRIORITY OR PRECEDENCE–Controlled transmission of messages in order of their designated importance, e.g., urgent or routine.

PRIVATE LINE OR PRIVATE WIRE–A channel or circuit furnished a subscriber for his exclusive use.

PROGRAM–A collection (series) of instructions. These instruct the computer to perform certain tasks. A logical sequence of events (instructions) which the computer must follow and execute to solve a problem.

PROGRAM FLOWCHARTING–A series of detailed pictorial instructions defining a logical solution to a problem. The flowchart is used to guide the actual coding of the computer language. See Flowcharting.

PUNCH CARD–A heavy stiff paper of constant size and shape, suitable for punching in a pattern that has meaning, and for being handled mechanically. The punched holes are sensed electrically by wire brushes, mechanically by metal fingers, or photoelectrically by photocells.

PUNCHED TAPE OR PERFORATED TAPE–A narrow paper strip containing holes placed in rows perpendicular to its length. Characters are represented by the arrangement of the holes within a given row.

PROM–Programmable Read-Only Memory. A semiconductor diode array which is programmed by fusing or burning out diode junctions.

PROTOCOL–A set of procedures or conventions used routinely between equipment such as terminals and computers, to permit communication and the exchange of data between them.

PUC–Public Utilities Commission.

PULSE–A unit of energy characterized by its duration and amplitude. When representing information, it can be regarded as a bit; when not representing information, it can be regarded as noise.

PULSE CODE–Pulse train modulated so as to represent information. Loosely, a code consisting of pulses, such as Morse Code, Baudot code, binary code.

PULSE GROUP–A group of pulses of similar characteristics.

PULSE REPETITION RATE–The number of electric pulses per unit of time experienced by a point in a computer, usually the maximum, normal or standard pulse rate.

QTA–A communications term indicating that a message has been interrupted, but that it will be repeated in its entirety without further action on the part of the station receiving the QTA notice.

QTAM–Queued Telecommunication Access Method (IBM designation)–Refers to the use of macro instructions to achieve data communications with specific terminals.

QTB–A communications term indicating that a message has been interrupted while being relayed, and cannot be automatically furnished in complete form. It is the responsibility of the station receiving a QTB notice to contact the station that originally prepared the message and request that it be repeated.

QUERY MESSAGE–A message directed back to the originator in order to check correctness of the text received by the addressee.

QUEUE–Waiting line resulting from temporary delays in providing service. Term used for communication computers when messages are stored for delivery.

QUEUING–A method of controlling the sequence in which information is processed.

RAM–Random Access Memory.

RANDOM ACCESS (Storage)–Access to a storage such that each position from which information is to be obtained is in no way dependent on the previous one.

READ-WRITE HEAD–A small electromagnet used for reading, recording, or erasing polarized spots, which represent information, on magnetic tape, disk or drum. See Head or Magnetic Head.

READ–To transfer information from any input device to main memory or auxiliary storage.

READER (TAPE)–A device associated with a Teletypewriter or other business machines that has the function of a transmitter.

REAL-TIME–(1) Pertaining to the actual time during which a physical process takes place. (2) Pertaining to the performance of a computation during a period short in comparison with the actual time that the related physical process takes place in order that results of the computations can be used in guiding the physical process.

REAL-TIME CLOCK–A clock which indicates the passage of actual time, in contrast to a fictitious time set up by the computer program.

REAL-TIME COMMUNICATION–Information transmitted, received, and processed concerning a current event currently taking place. Action may be taken that influences the event either by the person or the CPU.

RECORD–A group of related facts or fields of information treated as a unit.

REDUNDANCY–A repetition of information; or the insertion of information which is not new, and therefore redundant. Example: the use of check bits and check characters in data communication is a form of redundancy, hence the terms: cyclic redundancy, longitudinal redundancy, vertical redundancy.

REDUNDANCY CHECK–The use of redundancy to check errors. See CRC, LRC, VRC.

RELAY–Transmission forwarded through an intermediate station. Electrically operated switch, usually comprised of an electromagnet, and armature, and a number of contact springs. Device in which a small current or power flow can be made to control a larger current or power flow in a secondary circuit by opening or closing contacts. Usually contains an electromagnet and armature.

RELIABILITY–A measure of the ability to function without failure. The amount of credence placed in a result.

REMEDIAL MAINTENANCE–The maintenance performed by the contractor following equipment failure; therefore, it is performed as required, on an unscheduled basis.

REMOTE–Physically distant from a local computer, terminal, multiplexer, etc.

REMOTE ACCESS–An arrangement whereby distant terminals have access to a central computer via communications channels.

REPEATER STATION–An intermediate point in a transmission system where line signals are received, amplified or reshaped, and retransmitted.

REPEATER–A combination of apparatus for receiving either one-way or two-way communications signals and delivering corresponding signals which are either amplified or reshaped or both. A repeater for one-way communications signals is termed as "one-way repeater" and one for two-way communication signals a "two-way repeater." Device which receives telegraph signals from one circuit and retransmits them to another. Switch by which originating central-office calling-telephone dialed pulses are repeated to switches at a distant office.

REPERFORATOR–A device that automatically punches a paper tape from received signals.

REPERFORATOR SWITCHING CENTER–Message relaying center at which incoming messages are received on a reperforator which punches a storage tape from which the message is retransmitted into the proper outgoing circuit. The reperforator may be of the type which also prints the message on the same tape, and the selection of the outgoing circuit may be manual or under control of selection characters at the head of the message.

REPORT GENERATOR–A technique for producing complete data processing reports giving only a description of the desired content and format of the output reports, and certain information concerning the input file.

REQUEST TO SEND–An EIA RS-232-C designation applied to a control curcuit used by a terminal or computer to cause its modem to go into the "send" mode of operation.

RESPONSE TIME–The amount of time elapsed between generation of an inquiry at a data communications terminal and receipt of a response at that same terminal. Response time, thus defined, includes: (a) transmission time to the computer, (b) processing time at the computer, including access time to obtain any file records needed to answer the inquiry, and (c) transmission time back to the terminal. Comparisons of response time assume program execution time is zero.

REVERSE CHANNEL–A capability for signalling in a direction opposite to the main flow of data, usually only a fraction of the bandwidth or bit rate of the main channel. Sometimes called a supervisory channel, the reverse channel is frequently applied to acknowledging the correct receipt of data.

RFP or RFQ (Request for Proposal/Quote)–This document is produced from the system study and design phases. It is sent to the appropriate vendors who respond with a proposed system and/or cost quote to meet the requirements defined in the RFP or RFQ.

RING INDICATOR–An EIA RS-232-C designation applied to a sense circuit used by a terminal or computer to detect the presence of ringing voltage on the communication circuit, and hence predict an incoming call.

RJE–Remote Job Entry (IBM designation)–Refers to the programs used to submit processing jobs from terminals.

RO–A designation used to indicate the Receive Only capabilities to Teletypes and other equipment lacking keyboards and paper tape equipment.

ROM–Read Only Memory system. The stored bit patterns cannot be rewritten or otherwise altered.

ROTARY DIAL–A telephone that sends dial pulses to the telephone switching equipment to establish a connection.

ROTR–Receive Only Teletype Reperforator.

ROUTINE–A sequence of machine instructions that carry out a well-defined function; a program or part of a program.

ROUTING–The selection of a path or channel for sending data.

RPG (Report Program Generator)–This program provides the computer with ability to produce reports very easily.

RSC–Receiver Select Code (Terminal receive selection).

RS-232–A technical specification published by the Electronic Industries Association establishing the interface requirements between modems and terminals and computers.

RT–Reperforator-Transmitter.

SATELLITE COMPUTER–A processor connected locally or remotely to a larger central processor, and performing certain processing tasks–sometimes independent of the central processor, sometimes subordinate to the central processor.

SAMPLING–(1) A technique of systems analysis whereby traffic volumes, file activity, and so forth, are estimated, based on a representative sample. (2) A method of communication line control whereby messages on a circuit are sampled by a computer that selects only those for which computer processing is required.

SCAN–(1) To examine stored information for a specific purpose–for content, for arrangement. (2) To examine the status of communication lines or other input/output channels, in order to determine whether data is being received or transmitted.

SECONDARY STORAGE–Storage outside of the computer. Example: Magnetic Tape, Drum, Disk.

SELECTIVE CALLING–A capability of communication with a specific terminal within a group of terminals connected to a single communication channel.

SELF-CHECKING CODE–A self-checking, or error-detecting code, uses expressions such that one or more errors in a code expression produces a forbidden combination. A parity check makes use of a self-checking code employing binary digits in which the total number of 1s (or 0s) in each permissible code expression is always even or always odd. A check may be made for either even parity or odd parity. A redundancy check employs a self-checking code which makes use of redundant digits called check digits.

SEMIAUTOMATIC TAPE–Method of communication whereby messages are received and retransmitted in teletypewriter tape form, involving manual intervention in transfer of the tape from the receiving reperforator to transmitter.

SEMICONDUCTOR–A solid with an electrical conductivity that lies between the high conductivity of metals and the low conductivity of insulators. Semiconductor circuit elements include crystal diodes and transistors.

SENSE–To examine, particularly relative to a criterion. To determine the present arrangement of some element of hardware, especially a manually-set switch. To read punched holes or other marks.

SEQUENTIAL/SERIAL ACCESS–Pertaining to the process of obtaining information from or placing information into storage where the time required for such access is dependent on the necessity for waiting while nondesired storage locations are processed in turn.

SERIAL OPERATION–The flow of information through a computer in time sequence using only one digit, word, line or channel at a time.

SERIAL TRANSMISSION–The transmission of the bits of a character in sequence, one at a time. Contrast with Parallel Transmission.

SERVICE (By Carriers)–The function performed by the common carriers in supplying the needs of the subscribers.

SERVICE BUREAU–An installation where the user can lease processing time on a central processor and peripheral equipment. The user supplies the programs, and the center will load both program and data to be processed, process the data and deliver the results to the user. The program and data for processing may be delivered or sent between user and center in any of several forms: cards, punched tape, magnetic tape, etc. Data communications may be used between the user and the center to move the information electrically. The service bureau may also provide such services as keypunching the data and preparing it for processing.

SERVICE MESSAGE–A message originated between relevant switching centers and/or communications stations concerning such matters as the transmission of previous messages; reports of garbling, nondelivery or misdirection; communications count discrepancies, and incidents of equipment or circuit difficulties.

SERVICE ROUTINE–A broad class of routines which are standardized at a particular installation for the purpose of assisting in maintenance and operation of the computer as well as the solution of production problems. This class includes monitoring or supervisory routines, assemblers, compilers, diagnostics for computer malfunctions, simulation of peripheral equipment, general diagnostics and input data. The distinguishing quality of service routines is that they are generally standardized so as to meet the servicing needs at a particular installation, independent of any specific production type routines requiring such services.

SI (Shift In)–A control character indicating that the code combinations which follow shall be interpreted according to the standard code table.

SIDEBAND–A band of frequencies containing components of either the sum (upper sideband) or difference (lower sideband) of the carrier and modulating frequencies.

SIGNAL ATTENUATION–The reduction in the strength of electrical signals.

SIGNAL ELEMENT–A signal element is that part of a signal which occupies the shortest interval of the signalling code. It is considered to be of unit duration in building up signal combinations.

SIGNAL TO NOISE RATIO–The ratio of the power of the signal to that of the noise.

SIGNALLING–A procedure of informing the distant end on a communication circuit that intelligence is to be transmitted to it.

SIMPLEX–Communication in only one direction.

SIMULATOR–(1) A program, or routine, corresponding to a mathematical model or a physical model. (2) A routine that runs on a computer to imitate the operations of some other system or subsystem.

SINGLE SIDEBAND–Carrier system in which one sideband is transmitted and the other is suppressed. The carrier may or may not be transmitted.

SINGLE-ADDRESS MESSAGE–A message to be delivered to only one destination.

SKIP CODE–A function code which directs a machine to omit certain fields of information.

SO (Shift Out)–A control character indicating that the code combinations which follow shall be interpreted as outside of the character set of the standard code table (nonprintable) until a Shift In character is reached.

SOFTWARE–A set of codes, instructions, or group of programs that cause the computer to perform its functions.

SOM–Start of Message.

SOURCE DATA AUTOMATION–The many methods of recording information in coded forms on paper tapes, punched cards, or tags that can be used over and over again to produce many other records without rewriting.

SOURCE PROGRAMS–Programs written by the programmer and requiring translation to operate the computer.

SPACE–A term which originated with telegraph to indicate an open key condition. Present usage implies the absence of current or carrier on a circuit. It also indicates the binary digit "0" in computer language.

SP (Space)–A normally nonprinting graphic character used to separate words. It is also a format effector which controls the movement of the printing position One *SP* is equal to one print position. (Applicable also to display CRT devices.)

SPACING–A term used to indicate an open circuit (no current flow).

SPIRAL PARITY–A system whereby the check character is developed by making diagonal rows, either odd or even.

SPROCKET FEED–Term applied to documents in continuous form having holes in both sides of the document to provide accurate positioning on a platen; the term is also used to describe a machine whose platen is equipped with sprockets for this purpose.

SPX–Simplex circuit.

SS (Start of Special Sequence)–A control character used to indicate the start of a variable length sequence of characters which have special significance or which are to receive special handling.

SSI–Small Scale Integration. See LSI.

STAND-ALONE CAPABILITY–A multiplexor designed to function independent of a host computer, either all of the time or some of the time.

STANDBY COMPUTER–The computer in a dual system that is waiting to take over the real-time processing burden whenever the need arises.

START BIT–A bit used in asynchronous transmission to precede the first bit of a character transmitted serially, signalling the start of the character.

START OF ADDRESS (SOA)–Synonymous with the Start of Message in some code sets.

START OF HEADER (SOH)–Synonymous with the Start of Message.

START OF MESSAGE (SOM)–One or more specific sequential characters that are used to identify the start of message. This character or sequence of characters is optionally permitted depending on the type of code, in any other sections of a message and thus has the meaning of SOM only the first time that it appears in a given message (i.e., after the previous EOM).

STATION–One of the input or output points on a communications system.

STATUS REPORTS–A term used to describe the automatic reports generated by a message switching system generally covering service conditions such as circuits and stations out of service and back in service.

STEP-BY-STEP–Automatic dial system in which calls go through the central office by a succession of switches which move a step at a time, each step being made in response to the dialing of a number or letter.

STOP BIT–A bit (or bits) used in asynchronous transmission to signal the end of a character transmitted serially, and representing the quiescent state in which the line will remain until the next character begins.

STOP CODE–A control character which, in the case of a Teletype, turns off the paper tape reader.

STORAGE–A general term for any device capable of retaining information.

STORE-AND-FORWARD MESSAGE SWITCHING–A facility for accepting messages as rapidly as they are received from originating terminals, storing the messages, and sending the messages to destination terminals when communication channels are available.

STUNT BOX–A designation applied to Teletype equipment which performs allied communication functions such as response to selective calling, parity checking, etc.

STX (Start of Text)–Synonymous with the End of Address.

SUPERVISORY CONTROL–A control system which furnishes intelligence, usually to a centralized location, to be used by an operator to supervise the control of a process or operation. May be used to prepare and transmit supervisory control messages to the Switching Center computer.

SWITCHING CENTER–A telecommunications facility (exchange) which handles the local collection and distribution of messages and/or their transfer from one circuit to another by automatic means.

SWITCHED LINE–Typically a telephone line that is connected to the switched telephone network.

SWITCHED-MESSAGE NETWORK–A common carrier network service providing selective calling compatible terminals by one another, as in the case of the TELEX network service.

SYN (Synchronous Idle)–A communication control character used by a synchronous transmission system in the absence of any other character to provide a signal from which synchronism may be achieved or retained. Start and stop bits are not required when this mode of operation is used.

SYNC CHARACTER–A character transmitted to establish character synchronization in synchronous communication. When the receiving station recognizes the Sync Character, the receiving station is said to by synchronized with the transmitting station, and communication can begin. See SYN.

SYNCHRONIZATION–The process of achieving synchronous operation of a transmitting and receiving station. The process of first transmitting a series of synchronizing characters prior to the characters being transmitted. This synchronizes the transmitter and receiver. Synchronizing characters may be interspersed among the data characters to maintain synchronization. The start and stop bits are not required. See SYN or SYNC Character.

SYNCHRONOUS–Events occurring at the same time. In Synchronous data communication, the bit sampling rate at the receiving station must be precisely the same as the bit transmission rate at the transmitting station, and the point at which one character ends and the next character begins must be recognized by the receiving station by means of a Sync Character. See SYN or SYNC Character.

SYNCHRONOUS COMPUTER–A computer in which all operations and events are controlled by equally spaced pulses from a clock.

SYNCHRONOUS TRANSMISSION–A mode of transmission using a precisely timed bit stream and character stream. See SYN or SYNC Character.

SYSTEM–A switching center and its associated network. A computer (data processing) and its associated devices.

SYSTEMS FLOWCHARTING–Represents a series of events in a logical order. Not as detailed as program flowcharting.

SYSTEM OPERATION–Operation of communication equipment in such a manner as to enable the individual components to function at the degree of efficiency and reliability for which the system was designed.

SYSTEM PLANNING–Establishment of the general requirement and the general form of a communication system.

TABLE LOOK UP–To obtain a function value corresponding to an argument, stated or implied, from a table of function values stored in the compuuer. Also, the operation of obtaining a value from a table.

TABLE OF LABELS–The actual storage location in the computer where certain instructions or locational values can be found.

TABLE OF STRUCTURE–List or matrix where you put something in to get something back. Example: Code converting one code to another code.

TAPE TRANSPORT–Term generally used to describe a magnetic-tape handler. The device is usually equipped as follows: (a) reels to wind and unwind the tape in either direction; (b) heads designed to read and/or write in magnetic pulses; (c) power units to operate the wind and rewind reels and to pass the tape through the read-write heads; and (d) electronic circuits to provide read-write capability. This term may, by extension, be used to describe a paper-tape handler unit containing the above features.

TARIFF–Services, including rates and definitions filed by the common carriers with state and federal agencies.

TCAM–Telecommunications Access Method (IBM designation)–refers to the use of macro instructions to create message control programs and application programs.

TD–Transmitter-Distributor (Teletype Equipment).

TDM–Time Division Multiplexing.

TECHNICAL CONTROL–In systems or networks, particularly those employing cryptographic equipment, it is customary to provide signal quality monitoring facilities on each side of the red/black interface. The monitoring devices may be manual, semiautomatic, or fully automated. Technical control facilities monitor and control such things as signal amplitudes, wave shapes, frequencies, and timing by using test equipment designed for that purpose.

TELECOMMUNICATIONS–The reception and/or transmission of information of any nature by telephone, telegraph, radio or other electro-magnetic system.

TELEGRAPH CONCENTRATOR–An automatic or manual switching arrangement where a number of branch, subscriber lines or station sets may be connected to a lesser number of trunk lines, operating positions, or instruments.

TELEGRAPHY–A system of communication for the transmission of graphic symbols.

TELEGRAPHY, PRINTING–A method of telegraph operation in which the received signals are automatically recorded in printed characters.

TELEPRINTER/TELETYPEWRITER–A unit which generates electrical signals in response to a keyboard entry or tape reading, and a receiver which converts received electrical signals into typed copy or punched tape.

TELEPROCESSING–A form of information handling in which a data processing system utilizes communications facilities.

TELETYPE–Any of several configurations of keyboards, printers, and paper tape equipment manufactured by the Teletype Corporation.

TELETYPEWRITER EXCHANGE SERVICE (TWX)–Commercial service in the U.S. permitting telegraph communication on the same basis as telephone service, operating through central switchboards to stations within the same city or in other cities. This service is limited to subscribers, as in telephone service.

TELETYPEWRITER SYSTEM–Assemblage of printing telegraph stations, lines, channels and switching arrangements with all the accessories for providing printing telegraph communications.

TELEX–An Automatic Teletype Exchange Service provided by Western Union.

TELPAK–A type of communication link provided by common carriers. It represents a band of frequencies which can be subdivided into voice and data channels of various bandwidths.

TERMINAL–An end point in a communications link, with the term frequently applied to both computer and operator-oriented equipment comprising keyboard, printer, card reader, punches, CRT, etc.

TERMINAL ADDRESS–An identifying character (or group of characters) used to direct a message to a specific terminal within a group of terminals connected to a multidrop or multipoint communication circuit.

TEST–That part of a message which contains the thought or idea which the originator desires to be communicated. In a data message it is that part of the message that contains the information that is to be machine processed.

TEST BOARD–Switchboard equipment with testing apparatus, so arranged that connections can be made from it to telephone lines or central office equipment for testing purposes. Commercial switchboard equipped with apparatus for making tests and for temporary circuits, usually toll circuits.

TEXT–The information portion of a message, as contrasted with the header, check characters, and end-of-text characters.

THROUGHPUT–A measured volume of data or messages a computer (or mechanized) switching system can handle in a given period of time.

THROUGHPUT TIME–The total length of time needed to complete an entire operation. May be referred to as Response Time.

TIE LINE–A line leased from a common carrier to link two or more points.

TIME DIVISION–Interleaving several message channels which are separated from each other in time on a single transmission medium.

TIME DIVISION MULTIPLEXING–The merging of several bit streams of lower bit rates into a composite signal for transmission over a communication channel of high bit-rate capacity. Example: five bit streams operating at 100 bps might be accommodated on a channel having a capacity of 500 bps. Combining the data streams is accomplished by assigning a "time-slice" of the high-speed channel to each of the low-speed channels.

TIME-OUT–A system action based upon the absence of an expected event during a prescribed time interval.

TIME SHARING–A method of operation in which a computer facility is shared by several users for different purposes at (apparently) the same time. Although the computer actually services each user in sequence, the high speed of the computer makes it appear that the users are all handled simultaneously.

TORN-TAPE MESSAGE SWITCHING SYSTEM–Incoming messages are punched into paper tape and the paper tapes are transmitted to the destination specified in the heading of the message. Storage, routing, and priority procedures are essentially manual, rather than automatic.

TOUCH TONE–An AT&T designation for dialing or data entry system using a 12-key pad that generates multiple tones.

TRACKS–The longitudinal channels on a magnetic tape of a magnetic drum where information bits are recorded.

TRANSCEIVER–A device which is capable of transmitting and receiving.

TRAFFIC–Another term used to identify messages being switched, transmitted or received.

TRAFFIC ANALYSIS–Obtaining information from a study of communications traffic. It includes statistical study of message headings, receipts, acknowledgments, relays, routings, and services; tabulation of the volume, types, and directional flow at each point, noting departure from established instructions (operating routine).

TRAIL, AUDIT–A system of providing a means for tracing items of data from processing step to step, particularly from a machine produced report or other machine output back to the original source data.

TRANSLATION–In data communication, the conversion of one code to a second code on a character-by-character basis.

TRANSLATOR PROGRAM–A computer program capable of analyzing high-level and assembly language instructions and substituting the machine language version. (Assembly program) Used for assembling programs and preparation of programming systems.

TRANSMISSION SPEED–The number of information elements sent per unit time, usually expressed as bits, characters, word groups, or records per second or per minute.

TRANSMITTER-DISTRIBUTOR–Motor-driven device which translates teletypewriter code combinations from chad or chadless paper tape into electrical impulses, and transmits these impulses to the circuit.

TRANSPARENCY–A data communication mode which enables the equipment to send and receive bit patterns of any form, without regard to their possible interpretation as control characters.

TROUBLESHOOT–To search for the cause of malfunction or erroneous program behavior, in order to correct the malfunction.

TRUNK–A major link in a communication system, usually between two telephone switching centers.

TSC–Transmitter Start Code.

TTY–Abbreviation for teletypewriter equipment.

TURNAROUND–See Line Turnaround.

TURNAROUND TIME–The time required for line turnaround in half duplex communication systems.

TWR–Transmitter/Receiver.

TWX–An abbreviation for Teletypewriter Exchange Serve. Formerly provided by AT&T, and now provided by Western Union.

UART–Universal asynchronous receiver transmitter.

UNATTENDED OPERATION–An automatic feature that allows transmission and/or reception of information without the presence of an operator.

UNDERGROUND CABLE–A cable installed below the surface of the ground.

USAGE COUNT–Count indicating the number of times a circuit or piece of equipment is used during a certain period.

USASCII–An abbreviation for United States of America Standard Code for Information Interchange, a specific code using seven bits to represent a character. See ASCII.

USART–Universal synchronous/asynchronous receiver/transmitter.

USRT–Universal synchronous receiver/transmitter.

VAB–Voice Answer Back. Provides a spoken response to the entry of data or inquiries. See Audio Response Unit.

VARIABLE NAME–A table within the computer whose contents may vary with each program.

VOICE CONNECTING ARRANGEMENT–Permits direct electrical connection of customer-provided voice transmitting and receiving equipment to the telephone network.

VOICE COUPLER–See Voice Connecting Arrangement.

VOICE GRADE CHANNEL–A channel suitable for transmission of speech, digital data, analog data, or facsimile, generally with a usable frequency range of about 300 to 3000 cycles per second (HZ).

VOLATILE DISPLAY–The nonpermanent image appearing on the screen of a visual display terminal.

VRC–Vertical Redundancy Check. See Parity.

VT (Vertical Tabulation)–A format effector which controls the movement of the printing position to the next in a series of predetermined printing lines (applicable also to CRT display devices).

WATS–Wide Area Telecommunications Service. An AT&T service which provides lower rates for high-volume users of the switched network.

WAY STATION–Teletypewriter connected to a line between, and in series with, other teletypewriter stations.

WHITE NOISE–Noise (electrical or acoustical) whose energy spectrum is uniformly distributed across all frequencies within a band of interest.

WIDEBAND CHANNEL–A communication channel having a bandwidth greater than that of a voice-grade line, and usually some multiple of the bandwidth of a voice-grade line.

WORD–(1) In telegraphy, six characters (five characters plus one space). (2) In computing, an ordered set of characters which is the normal unit in which information may be stored, transmitted, or operated upon within a computer.

WORD LENGTH–The number of characters in a machine (computer) word. In a given computer, the number may be constant or variable.

WPM–Words Per Minute. A measure of transmission speed computer on the basis of six characters (five plus a space) per word.

WRAP DATA–The transmission of data through a communications system and the return of the data to its source to test the accurancy of the system.

Index